THE FANTASTIC 4

INTO THE BREACH

MARVEL COMICS

COVER
CARLOS PACHECO
JESUS MERINO
AND LIQUID

BOOK DESIGN
JOHN 'JG' ROSHELL
OF COMICRAFT

PRODUCTION
ASSISTANT
JESSICA SCHWARTZ

ASSISTANT EDITOR
MATTY RYAN

COLLECTIONS EDITOR
BEN ABERNATHY

MANUFACTURING
REPRESENTATIVE
STEFANO
PERRONE, JR.

DIRECTOR:
EDITORIAL
OPERATIONS
BOB GREENBERGER

EDITOR IN CHIEF
JOE QUESADA

PRESIDENT
BILL JEMAS

SPECIAL THANKS TO
KWANZA JOHNSON

"INTO THE BREACH"
FANTASTIC FOUR VOLUME 3, NUMBER 40

"MAROONED"
FANTASTIC FOUR VOLUME 3, NUMBER 41

"A CLEAR AND
PRESENT DANGER"
FANTASTIC FOUR VOLUME 3, NUMBER 42

"AND THE WALLS CAME
TUMBLING DOWN"
FANTASTIC FOUR VOLUME 3, NUMBER 43

"ANNIHILATION"
FANTASTIC FOUR VOLUME 3, NUMBER 44

"YOU CAN'T GET
THERE FROM HERE"
FANTASTIC FOUR VOLUME 3, NUMBER 45

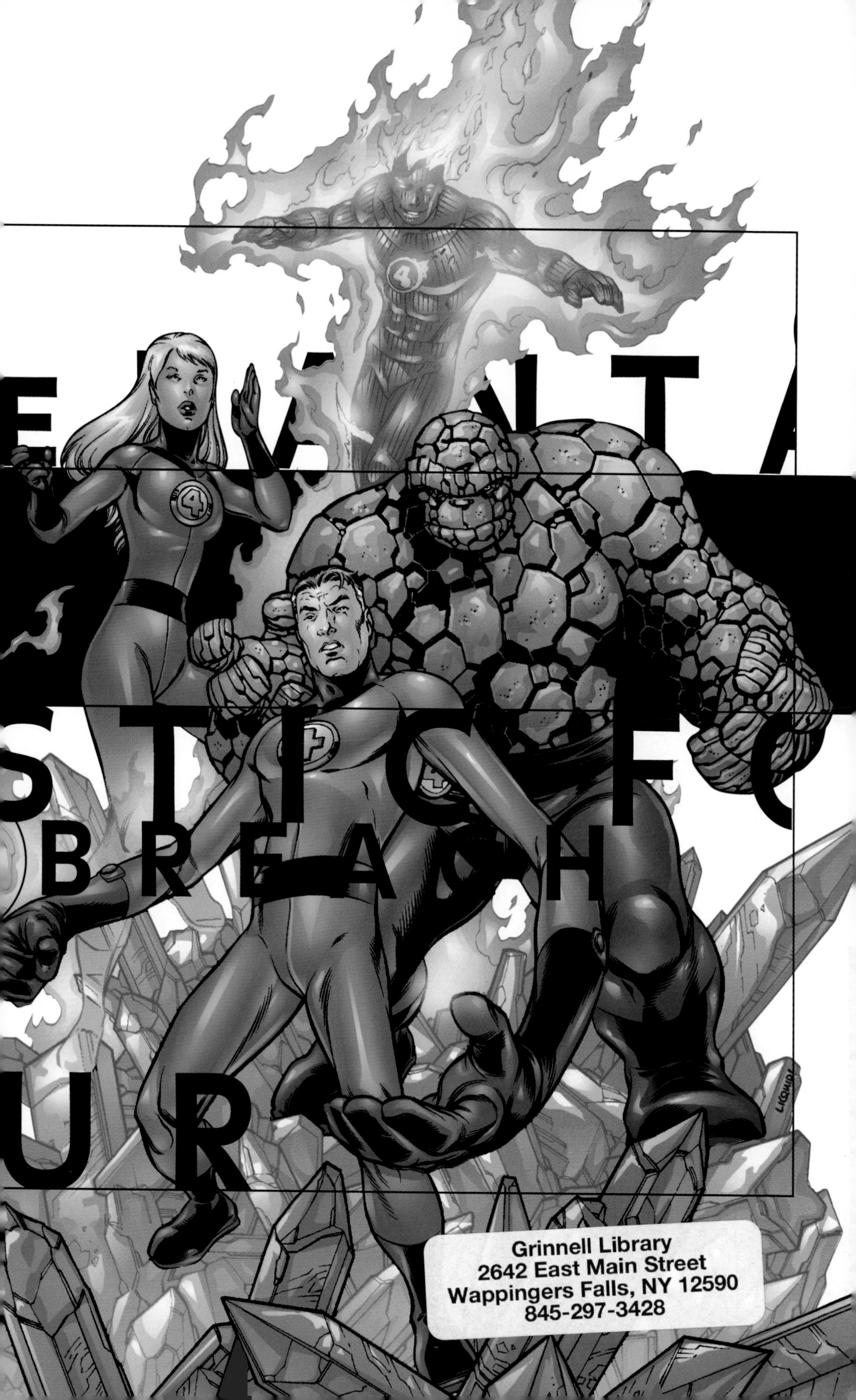
BREACH

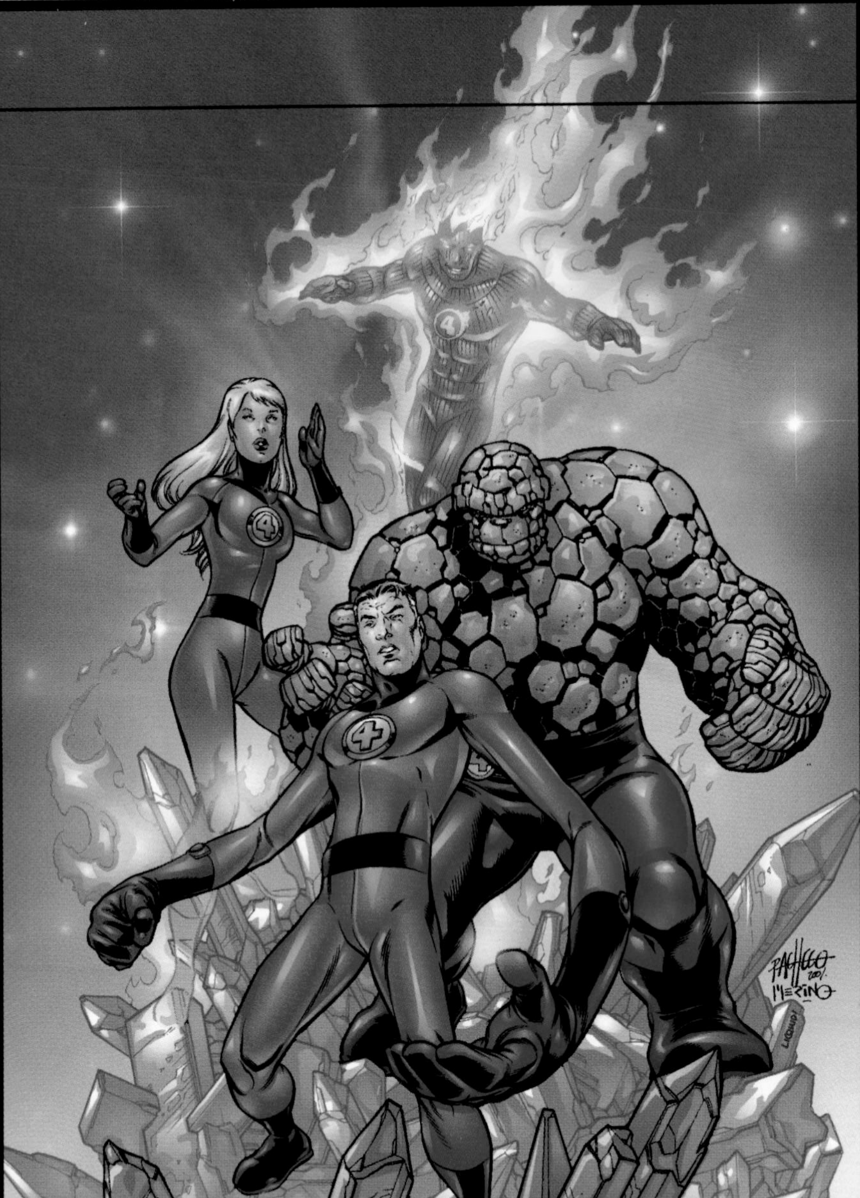

FANTASTIC FOUR #4

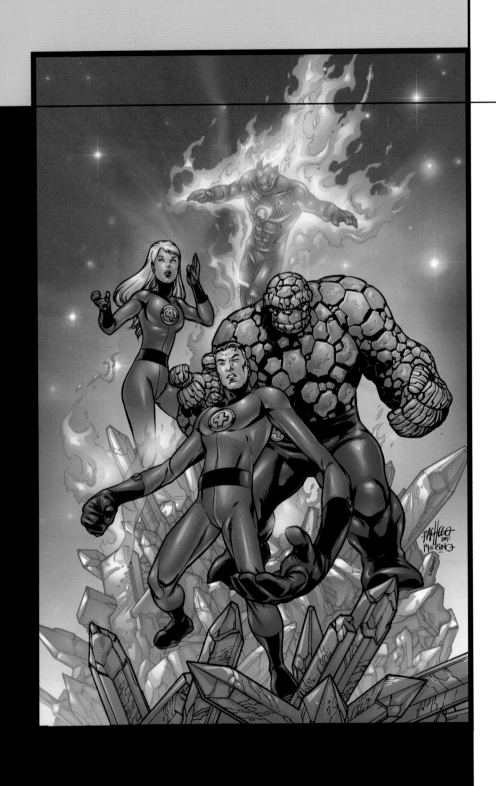

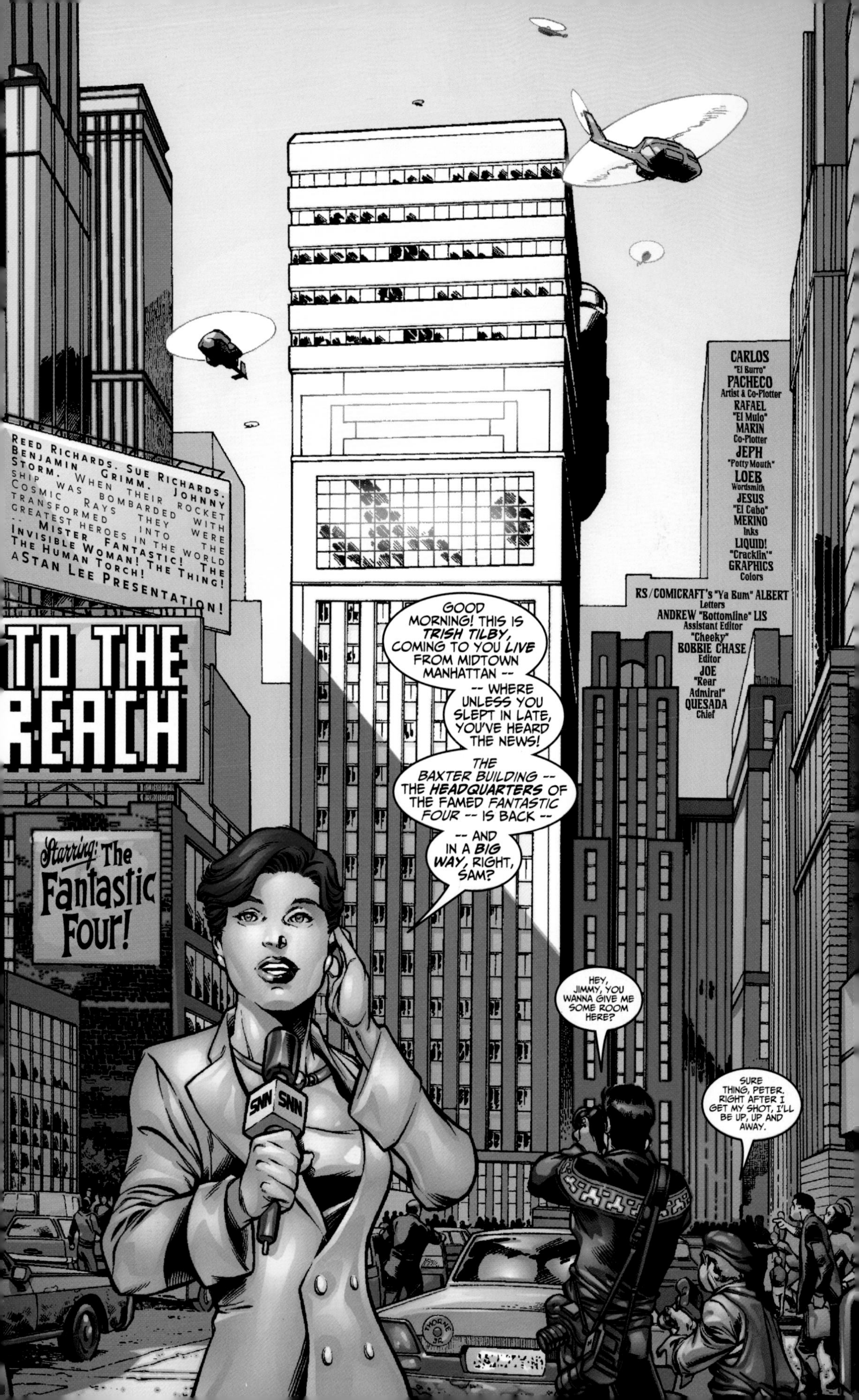

REED RICHARDS. SUE RICHARDS. BENJAMIN GRIMM. JOHNNY STORM. WHEN THEIR ROCKET SHIP WAS BOMBARDED WITH COSMIC RAYS THEY WERE TRANSFORMED INTO THE GREATEST HEROES IN THE WORLD -- MISTER FANTASTIC! THE INVISIBLE WOMAN! THE THING! THE HUMAN TORCH! A STAN LEE PRESENTATION!
TO THE REACH
Starring: The Fantastic Four!
CARLOS "El Burro" PACHECO Artist & Co-Plotter
RAFAEL "El Mulo" MARIN Co-Plotter
JEPH "Potty Mouth" LOEB Wordsmith
JESUS "El Cabo" MERINO Inks
LIQUID! "Cracklin'" GRAPHICS Colors
RS/COMICRAFT's "Ya Bum" ALBERT Letters
ANDREW "Bottomline" LIS Assistant Editor
"Cheeky" BOBBIE CHASE Editor
JOE "Rear Admiral" QUESADA Chief
GOOD MORNING! THIS IS TRISH TILBY, COMING TO YOU LIVE FROM MIDTOWN MANHATTAN --
-- WHERE UNLESS YOU SLEPT IN LATE, YOU'VE HEARD THE NEWS!
THE BAXTER BUILDING -- THE HEADQUARTERS OF THE FAMED FANTASTIC FOUR -- IS BACK --
-- AND IN A BIG WAY, RIGHT, SAM?
HEY, JIMMY, YOU WANNA GIVE ME SOME ROOM HERE?
SURE THING, PETER. RIGHT AFTER I GET MY SHOT, I'LL BE UP, UP AND AWAY.
SNN

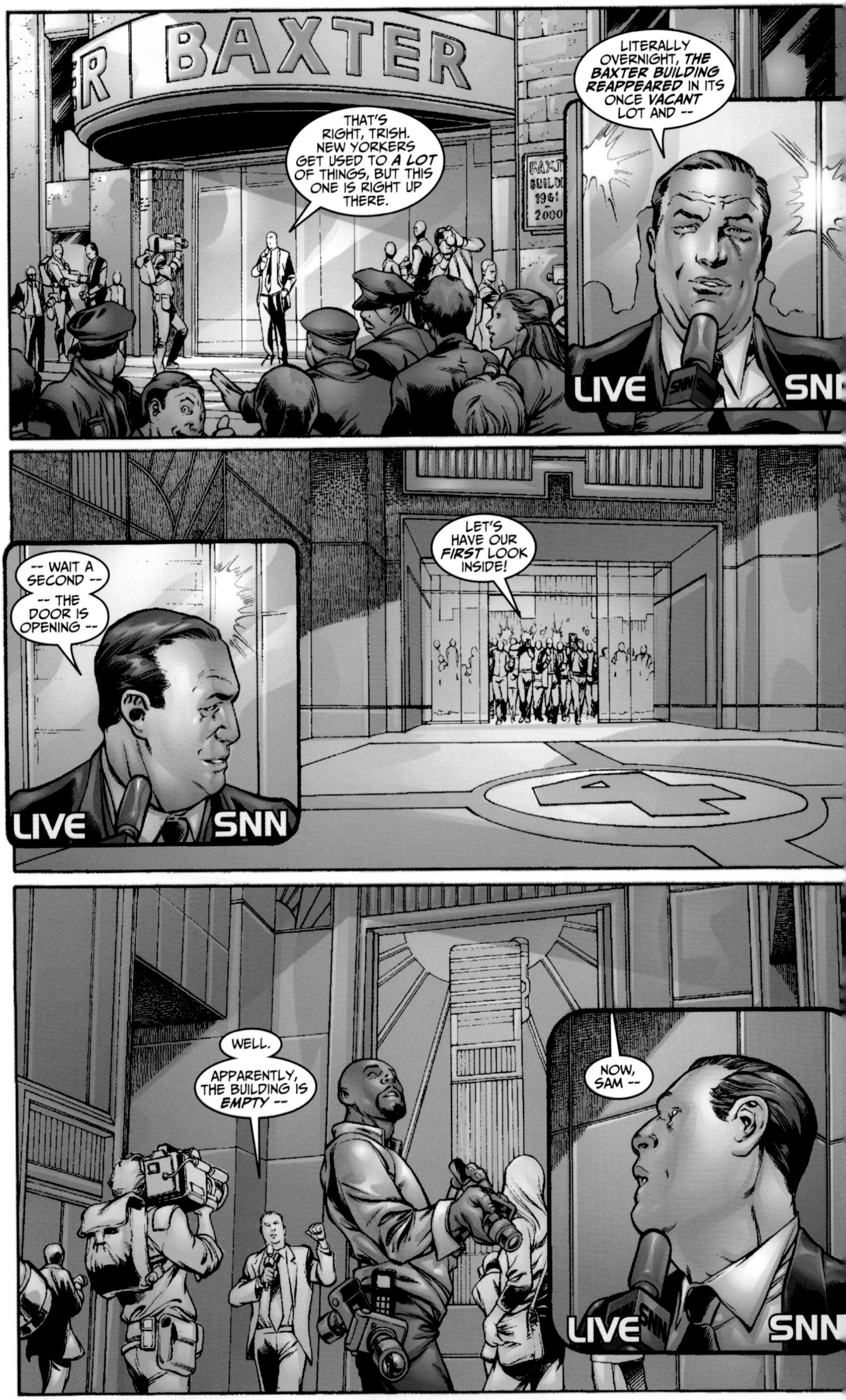
BAXTER
THAT'S RIGHT, TRISH. NEW YORKERS GET USED TO A LOT OF THINGS, BUT THIS ONE IS RIGHT UP THERE.
LITERALLY OVERNIGHT, THE BAXTER BUILDING REAPPEARED IN ITS ONCE VACANT LOT AND --
LIVE
-- WAIT A SECOND --
-- THE DOOR IS OPENING --
LIVE
SNN
LET'S HAVE OUR FIRST LOOK INSIDE!
WELL.
APPARENTLY, THE BUILDING IS EMPTY --
NOW, SAM --
LIVE
SNN

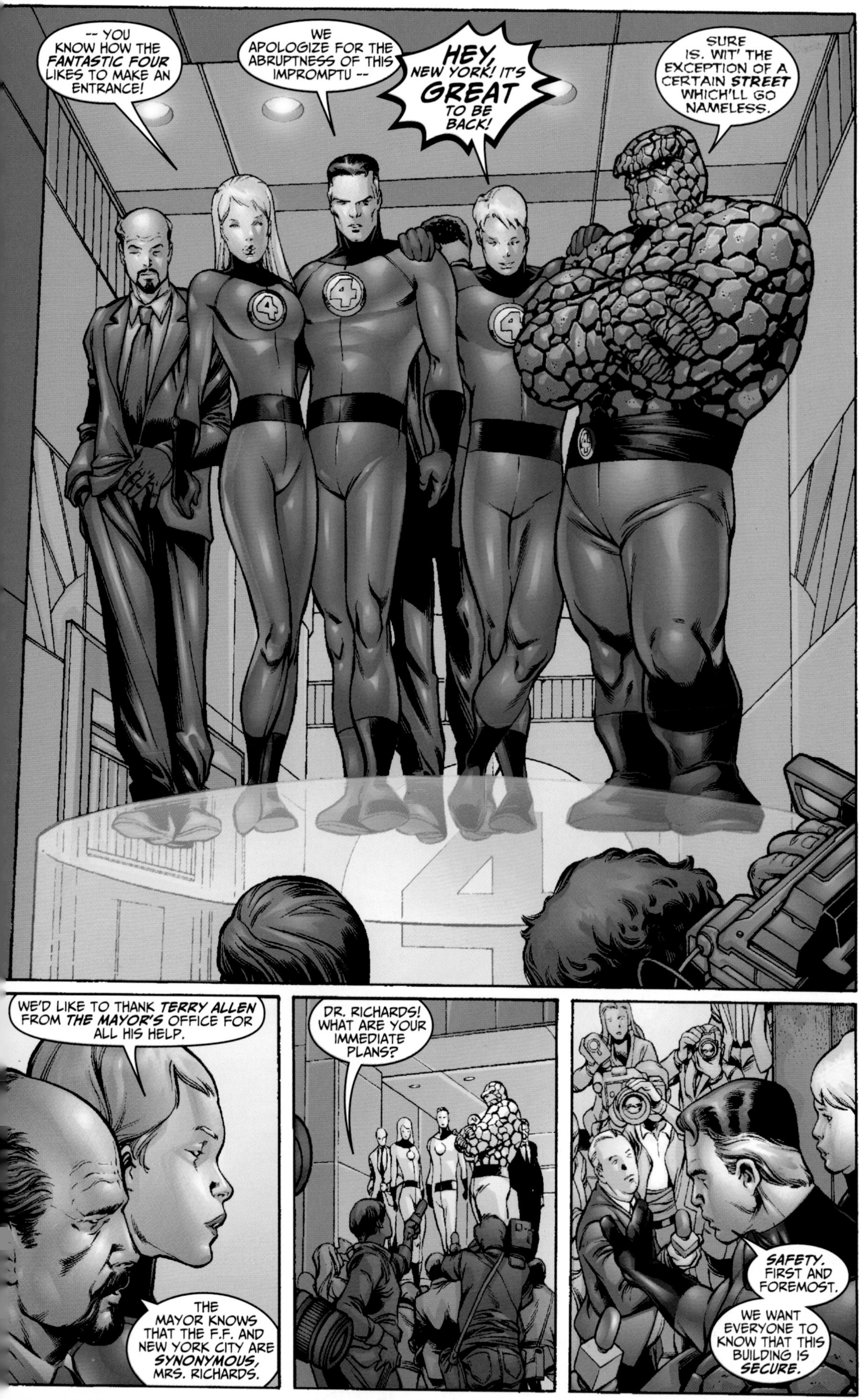
-- YOU KNOW HOW THE FANTASTIC FOUR LIKES TO MAKE AN ENTRANCE!
WE APOLOGIZE FOR THE ABRUPTNESS OF THIS IMPROMPTU --
HEY, NEW YORK! IT'S GREAT TO BE BACK!
SURE IS. WIT' THE EXCEPTION OF A CERTAIN STREET WHICH'LL GO NAMELESS.
WE'D LIKE TO THANK TERRY ALLEN FROM THE MAYOR'S OFFICE FOR ALL HIS HELP.
THE MAYOR KNOWS THAT THE F.F. AND NEW YORK CITY ARE SYNONYMOUS, MRS. RICHARDS.
DR. RICHARDS! WHAT ARE YOUR IMMEDIATE PLANS?
SAFETY. FIRST AND FOREMOST.
WE WANT EVERYONE TO KNOW THAT THIS BUILDING IS SECURE.

DOES THE MAYOR --

WHEN IT INVOLVES THE F.F. -- YES!

BOYS, PLEASE! LET'S TAKE THIS *OUTSIDE* WHERE I'LL BE HAPPY TO ANSWER ALL YOUR QUESTIONS!

WELL, REED, SUE SEEMS TO HAVE HER USUAL HANDLE ON THINGS.

SURE WE CAN'T GET HER TO DO SOME PR WORK FOR *DAMAGE CONTROL?*

APPRECIATE THE SENTIMENT, ALBERT, BUT *WE* NEED SUE MORE THAN ANYONE.

OH, AND BEN, I'M TO GIVE YOU A MESSAGE FROM SOMEONE AT THE OFFICE.

YEAH? WHAT'S MY PAL *LENNY* GOT TO SAY FER HIMSELF?

IT'S... UH... *NOT* FROM LENNY. SEEMS *MISS* KATHLEEN O'MEARA SAID IT'D BE OKAY IF YOU "*CALLED* ON HER."

A NOT-SO-SECRET ADMIRER, BEN?

KATHLEEN? WHO'DA THUNK?

SHE'S PROBABLY GOT YOU MIXED UP WITH SOME *OTHER* ORANGE-SKINNED *GORILLA!*

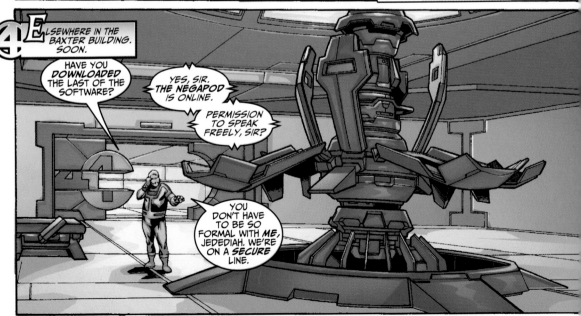

ELSEWHERE IN THE BAXTER BUILDING. SOON.

HAVE YOU *DOWNLOADED* THE LAST OF THE SOFTWARE?

YES, SIR. *THE NEGAPOD* IS ONLINE.

PERMISSION TO SPEAK FREELY, SIR?

YOU DON'T HAVE TO BE SO FORMAL WITH *ME,* JEDEDIAH. WE'RE ON A *SECURE* LINE.

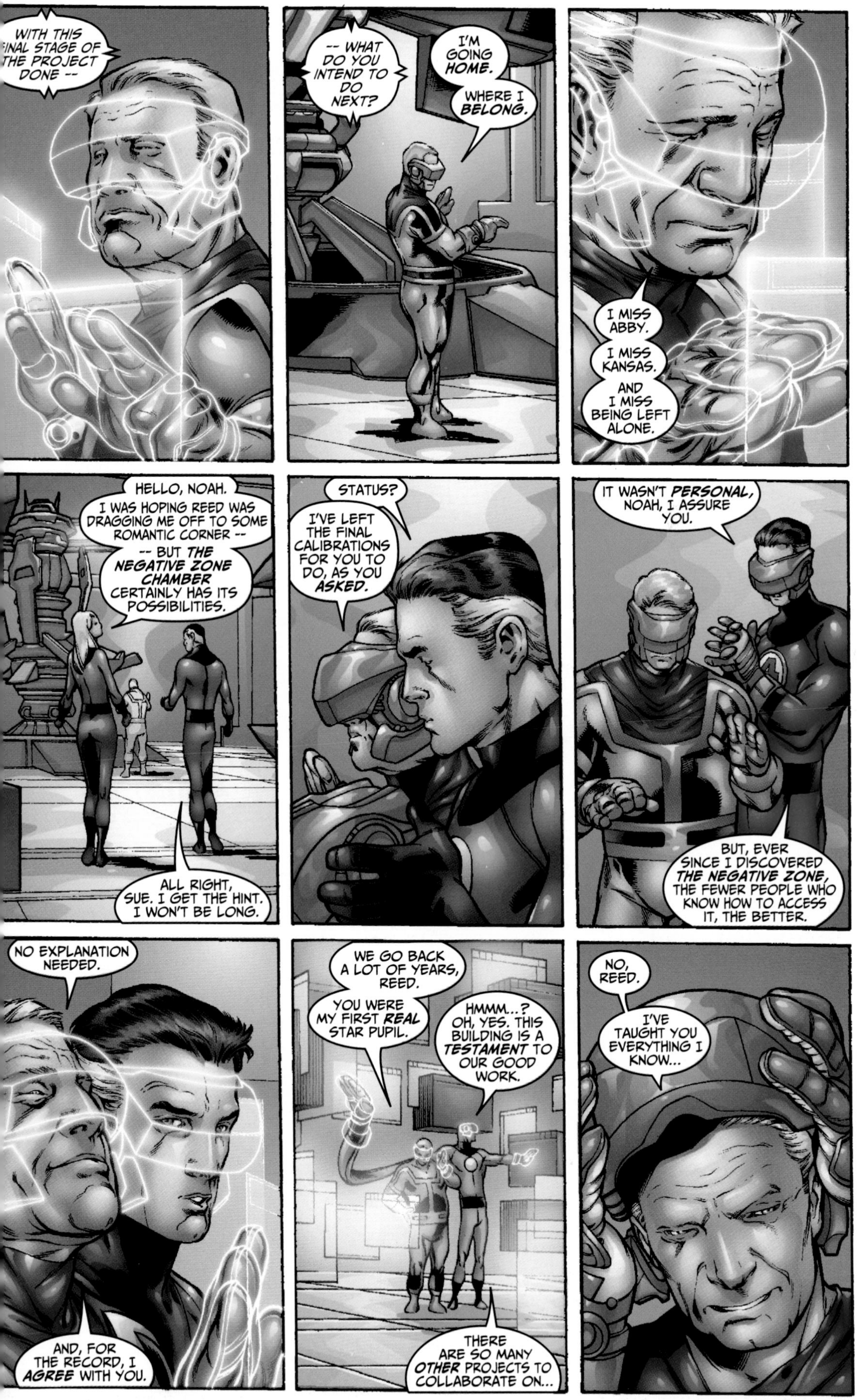
WITH THIS FINAL STAGE OF THE PROJECT DONE --
-- WHAT DO YOU INTEND TO DO NEXT?
I'M GOING HOME.
WHERE I BELONG.
I MISS ABBY.
I MISS KANSAS.
AND I MISS BEING LEFT ALONE.
HELLO, NOAH.
I WAS HOPING REED WAS DRAGGING ME OFF TO SOME ROMANTIC CORNER --
-- BUT THE NEGATIVE ZONE CHAMBER CERTAINLY HAS ITS POSSIBILITIES.
ALL RIGHT, SUE. I GET THE HINT. I WON'T BE LONG.
STATUS?
I'VE LEFT THE FINAL CALIBRATIONS FOR YOU TO DO, AS YOU ASKED.
IT WASN'T PERSONAL, NOAH, I ASSURE YOU.
BUT, EVER SINCE I DISCOVERED THE NEGATIVE ZONE, THE FEWER PEOPLE WHO KNOW HOW TO ACCESS IT, THE BETTER.
NO EXPLANATION NEEDED.
AND, FOR THE RECORD, I AGREE WITH YOU.
WE GO BACK A LOT OF YEARS, REED.
YOU WERE MY FIRST REAL STAR PUPIL.
HMMM...? OH, YES. THIS BUILDING IS A TESTAMENT TO OUR GOOD WORK.
THERE ARE SO MANY OTHER PROJECTS TO COLLABORATE ON...
NO, REED.
I'VE TAUGHT YOU EVERYTHING I KNOW...

NOAH. I'VE BEEN MARRIED TO THE MAN LONG ENOUGH TO KNOW WHEN HE *ISN'T* LISTENING.

BUT *I* WAS.

TAKE GOOD CARE OF HIM, SUSAN. HE'S -- HE'S ONE OF THE SPECIAL ONES.

OH. AND *PLEASE* DON'T UNDERESTIMATE *THE GIDEON TRUST.*

WILL YOU *STOP* WORRYING? WE'VE BEEN OVER IT --

NOAH, THANK YOU.

I KNOW. BUT MY *INSIDE* SOURCE TELLS ME THAT SOMETHING *BIG* IS COMING.

WE'LL BE ON THE LOOKOUT.

NO, SU THANK YC ALL OF YOU.

ALEXANDRI BEAM ME U

BEN GRIMM'S QUARTERS. NOW.

NEED A LITTLE HELP WITH THAT, BIG FELLA?

YOU SEE, THE ARMS GO *THROUGH* THE SLEEVES...

HARDY. HAR. HAR.

THE *GENIUSES* WHO THREW THIS JOINT TOGETHER LEFT CLOTHES FOR *THE THING.*

BUT, NUTHIN' FOR YERS TRULY, WHEN I CHANGE BACK TA BEN GRIMM.

IF YOU'RE ASKING ME TO TAKE YOU *SHOPPING* --

--FORGET IT!

COULDN'T STAND THE COMPETITION, HUH?

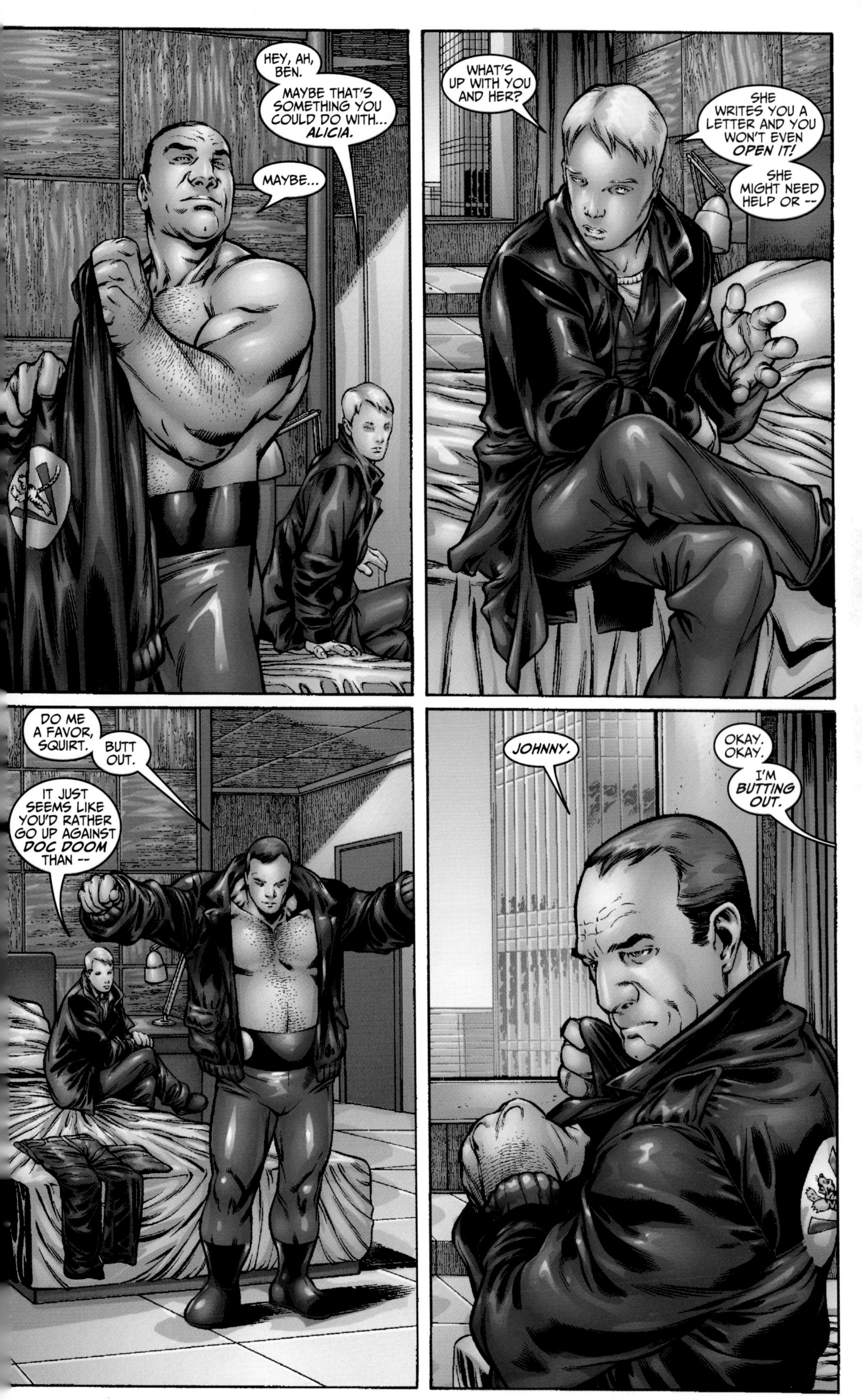
HEY, AH, BEN.
MAYBE THAT'S SOMETHING YOU COULD DO WITH... ALICIA.
MAYBE...
WHAT'S UP WITH YOU AND HER?
SHE WRITES YOU A LETTER AND YOU WON'T EVEN OPEN IT!
SHE MIGHT NEED HELP OR --
DO ME A FAVOR, SQUIRT.
BUTT OUT.
IT JUST SEEMS LIKE YOU'D RATHER GO UP AGAINST DOC DOOM THAN --
JOHNNY.
OKAY. OKAY. I'M BUTTING OUT.

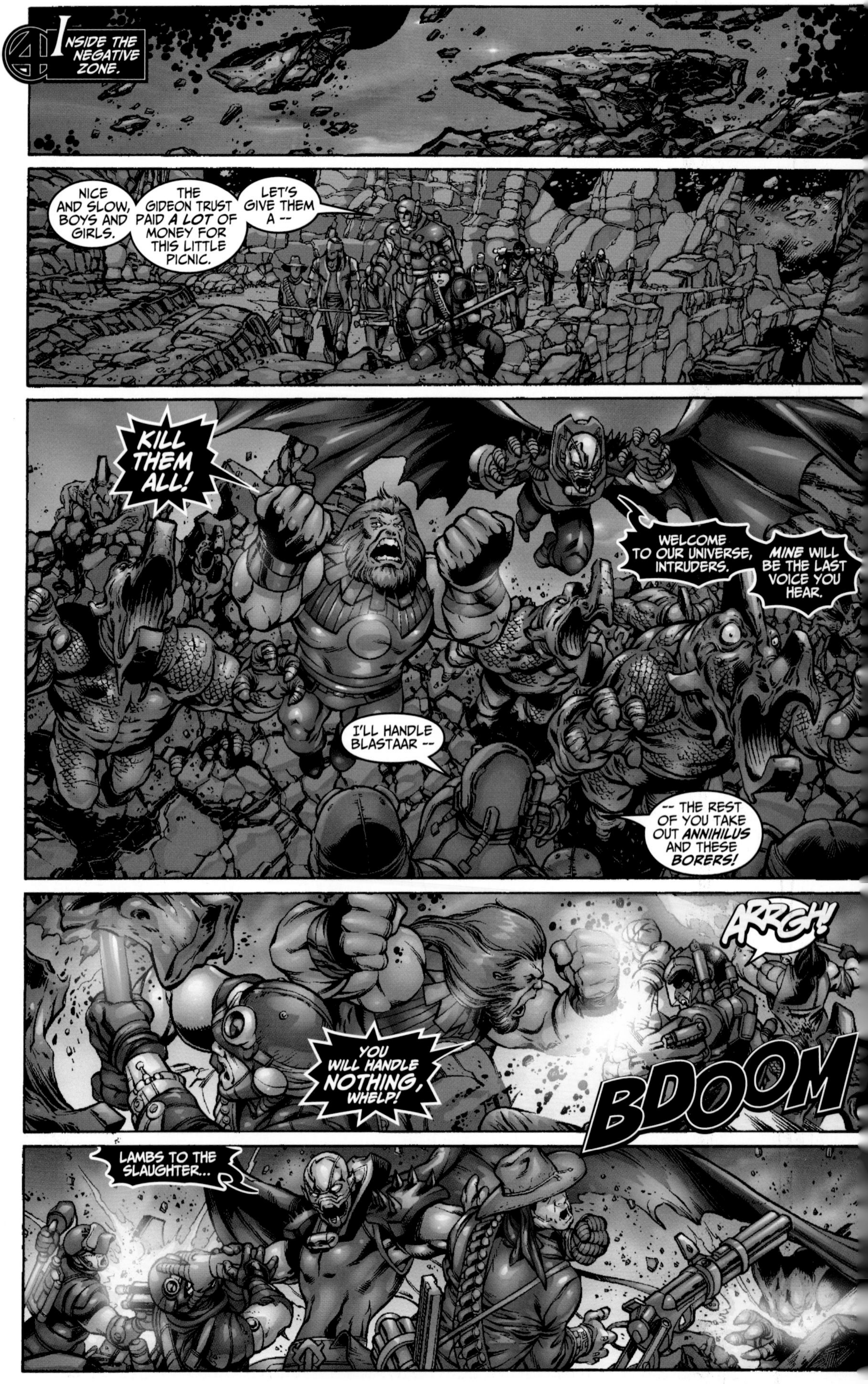
INSIDE THE NEGATIVE ZONE.
NICE AND SLOW, BOYS AND GIRLS.
THE GIDEON TRUST PAID A LOT OF MONEY FOR THIS LITTLE PICNIC.
LET'S GIVE THEM A --
KILL THEM ALL!
WELCOME TO OUR UNIVERSE, INTRUDERS.
MINE WILL BE THE LAST VOICE YOU HEAR.
I'LL HANDLE BLASTAAR --
-- THE REST OF YOU TAKE OUT ANNIHILUS AND THESE BORERS!
ARRGH!
YOU WILL HANDLE NOTHING, WHELP!
BDOOM
LAMBS TO THE SLAUGHTER...

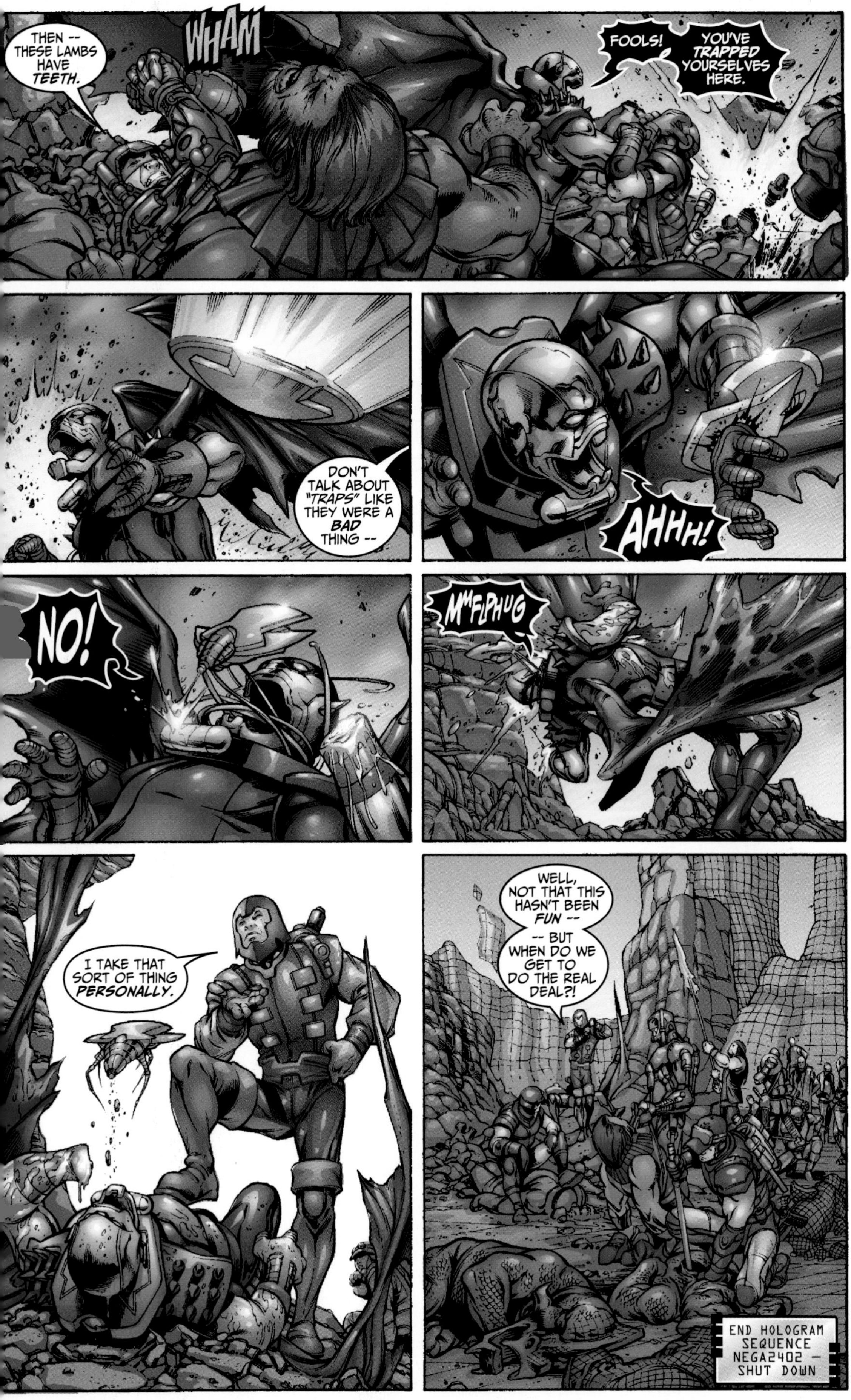
THEN -- THESE LAMBS HAVE TEETH.
WHAM
FOOLS!
YOU'VE TRAPPED YOURSELVES HERE.
DON'T TALK ABOUT "TRAPS" LIKE THEY WERE A BAD THING --
AHHH!
NO!
MMFLPHUG
I TAKE THAT SORT OF THING PERSONALLY.
WELL, NOT THAT THIS HASN'T BEEN FUN --
-- BUT WHEN DO WE GET TO DO THE REAL DEAL?!
END HOLOGRAM SEQUENCE NEGA2402 — SHUT DOWN

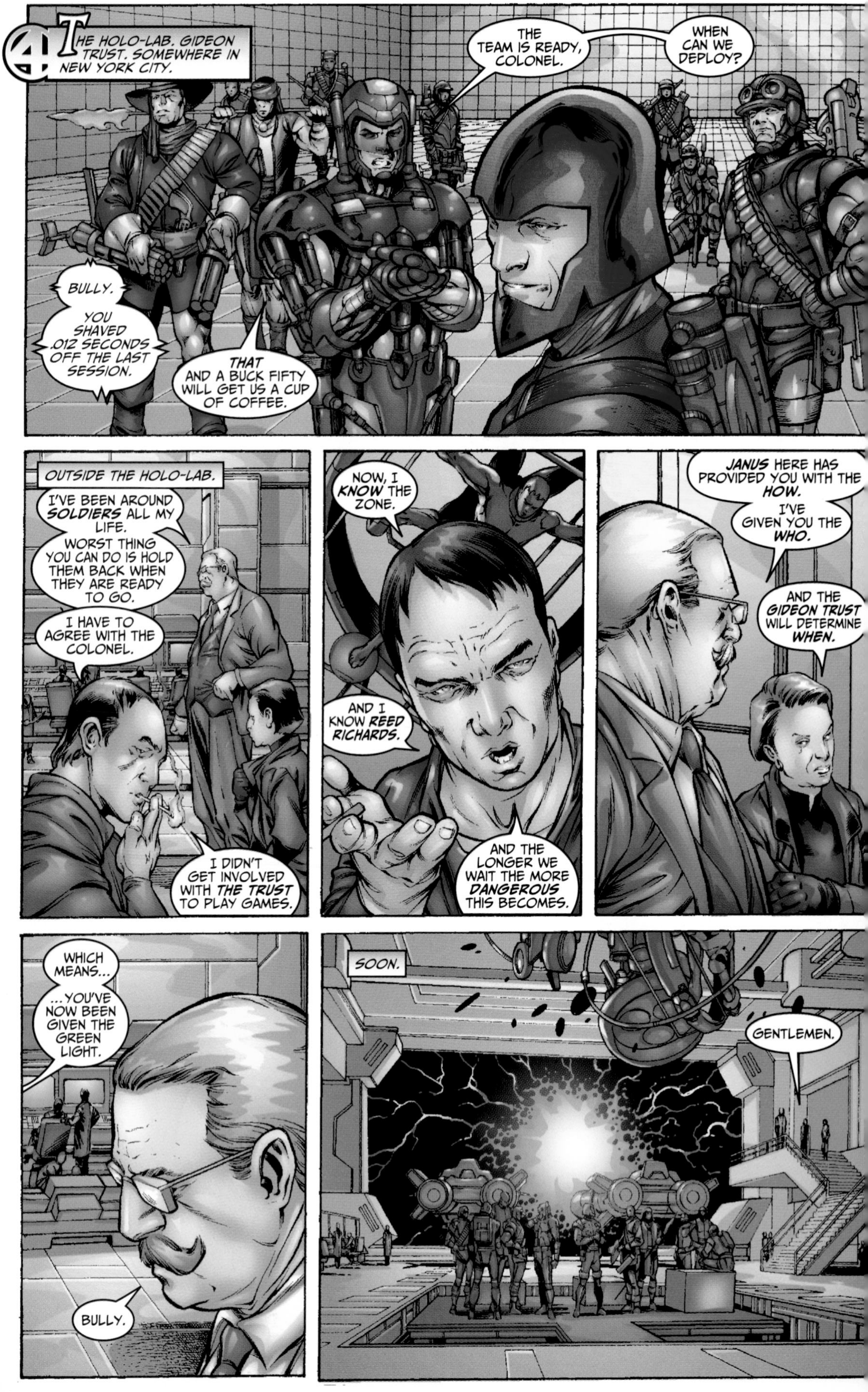

THE HOLO-LAB. GIDEON TRUST. SOMEWHERE IN NEW YORK CITY.
THE TEAM IS READY, COLONEL.
WHEN CAN WE DEPLOY?
BULLY.
YOU SHAVED .012 SECONDS OFF THE LAST SESSION.
THAT AND A BUCK FIFTY WILL GET US A CUP OF COFFEE.
OUTSIDE THE HOLO-LAB.
I'VE BEEN AROUND SOLDIERS ALL MY LIFE.
WORST THING YOU CAN DO IS HOLD THEM BACK WHEN THEY ARE READY TO GO.
I HAVE TO AGREE WITH THE COLONEL.
I DIDN'T GET INVOLVED WITH THE TRUST TO PLAY GAMES.
NOW, I KNOW THE ZONE.
AND I KNOW REED RICHARDS.
AND THE LONGER WE WAIT THE MORE DANGEROUS THIS BECOMES.
JANUS HERE HAS PROVIDED YOU WITH THE HOW.
I'VE GIVEN YOU THE WHO.
AND THE GIDEON TRUST WILL DETERMINE WHEN.
WHICH MEANS...
...YOU'VE NOW BEEN GIVEN THE GREEN LIGHT.
BULLY.
SOON.
GENTLEMEN.

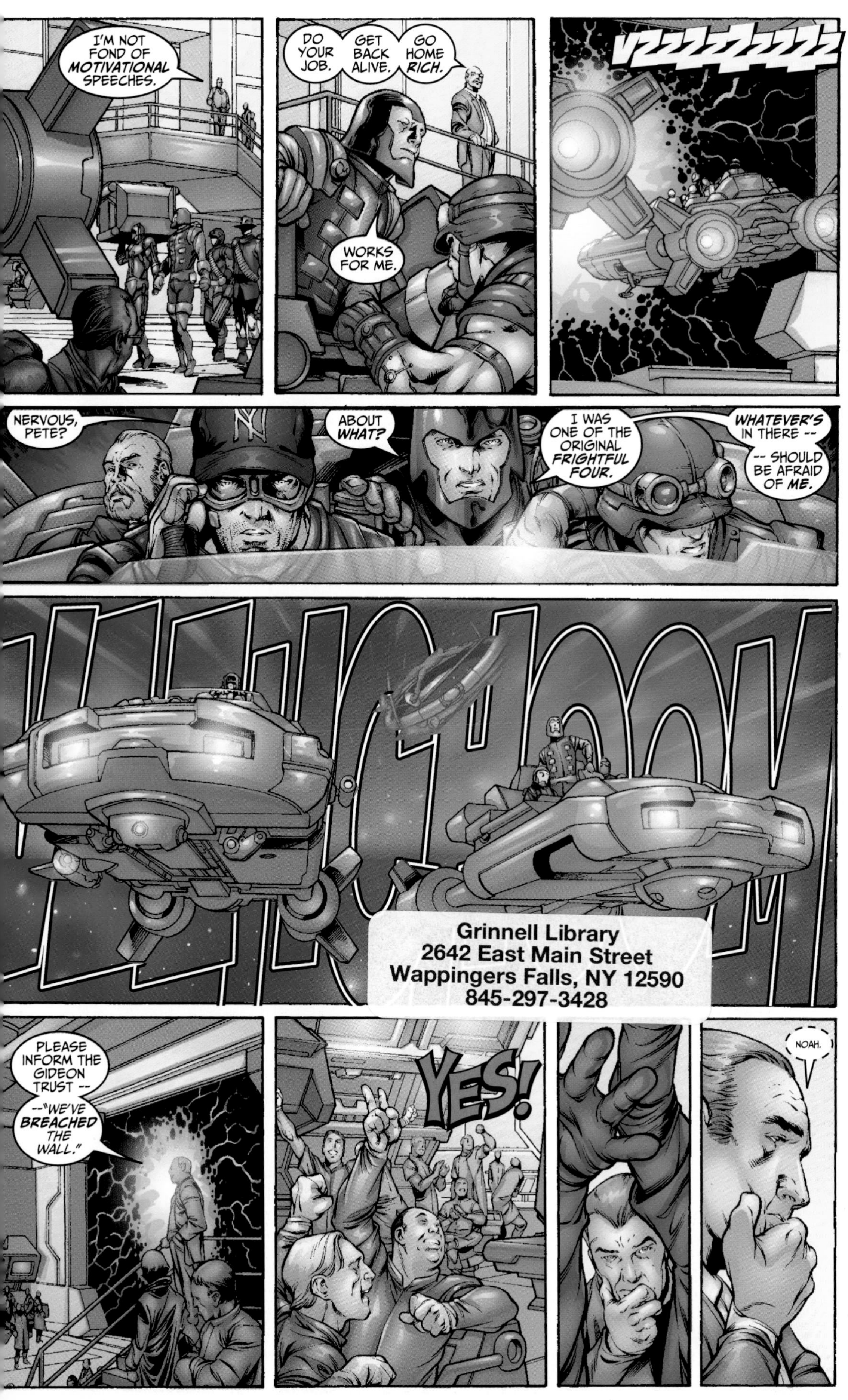
I'M NOT FOND OF MOTIVATIONAL SPEECHES.
DO YOUR JOB.
GET BACK ALIVE.
GO HOME RICH.
WORKS FOR ME.
VZZZZZZZZZ
NERVOUS, PETE?
ABOUT WHAT?
I WAS ONE OF THE ORIGINAL FRIGHTFUL FOUR.
WHATEVER'S IN THERE --
-- SHOULD BE AFRAID OF ME.
PLEASE INFORM THE GIDEON TRUST --
--"WE'VE BREACHED THE WALL."
YES!
NOAH.

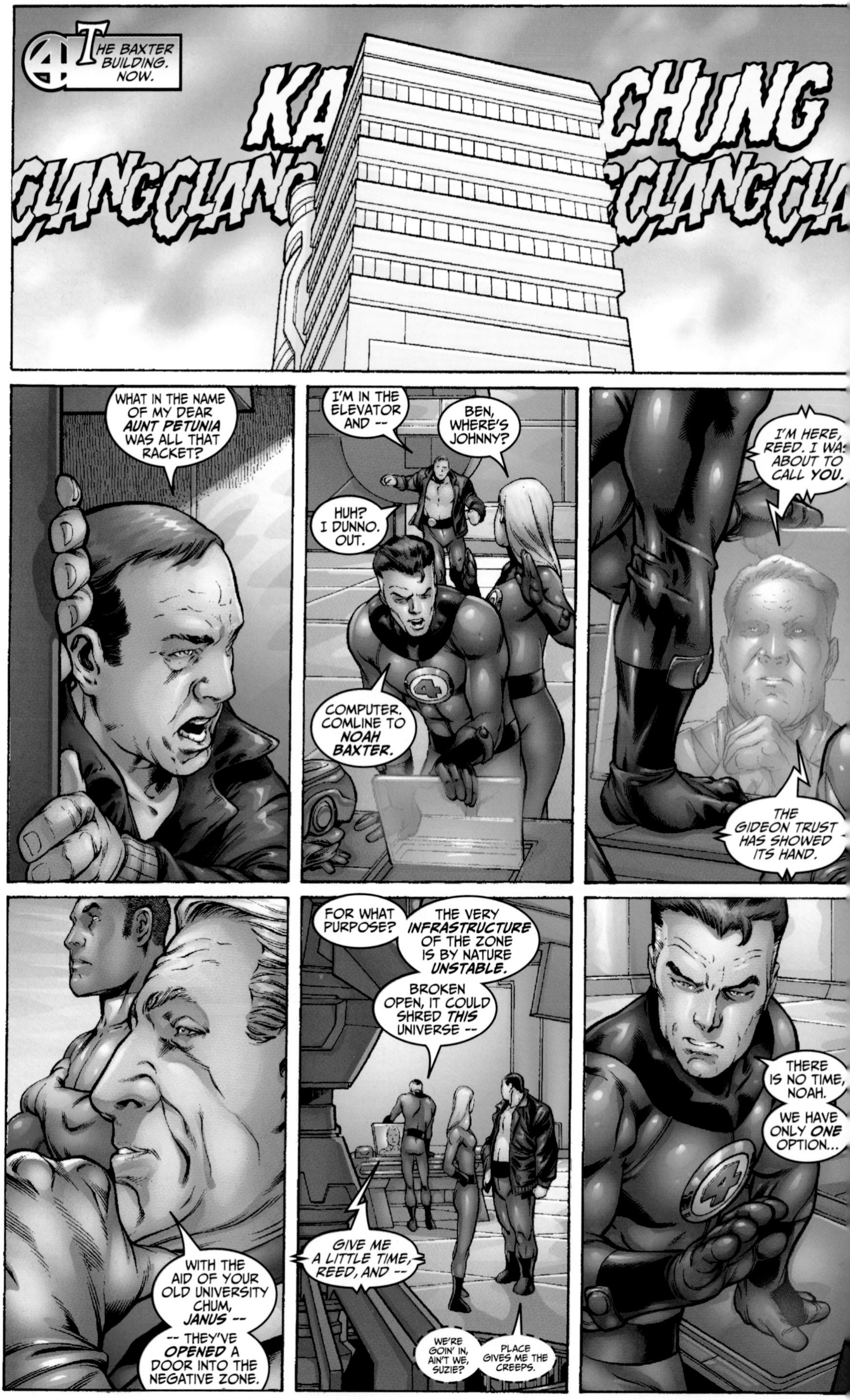
THE BAXTER BUILDING. NOW.
KA-CHUNG
CLANG CLANG CLANG CLANG CLANG CLA
WHAT IN THE NAME OF MY DEAR AUNT PETUNIA WAS ALL THAT RACKET?
I'M IN THE ELEVATOR AND --
BEN, WHERE'S JOHNNY?
HUH? I DUNNO. OUT.
COMPUTER. COMLINE TO NOAH BAXTER.
I'M HERE, REED. I WAS ABOUT TO CALL YOU.
THE GIDEON TRUST HAS SHOWED ITS HAND.
WITH THE AID OF YOUR OLD UNIVERSITY CHUM, JANUS --
-- THEY'VE OPENED A DOOR INTO THE NEGATIVE ZONE.
FOR WHAT PURPOSE?
THE VERY INFRASTRUCTURE OF THE ZONE IS BY NATURE UNSTABLE.
BROKEN OPEN, IT COULD SHRED THIS UNIVERSE --
GIVE ME A LITTLE TIME, REED, AND --
WE'RE GOIN' IN, AIN'T WE, SUZIE?
PLACE GIVES ME THE CREEPS.
THERE IS NO TIME, NOAH.
WE HAVE ONLY ONE OPTION...

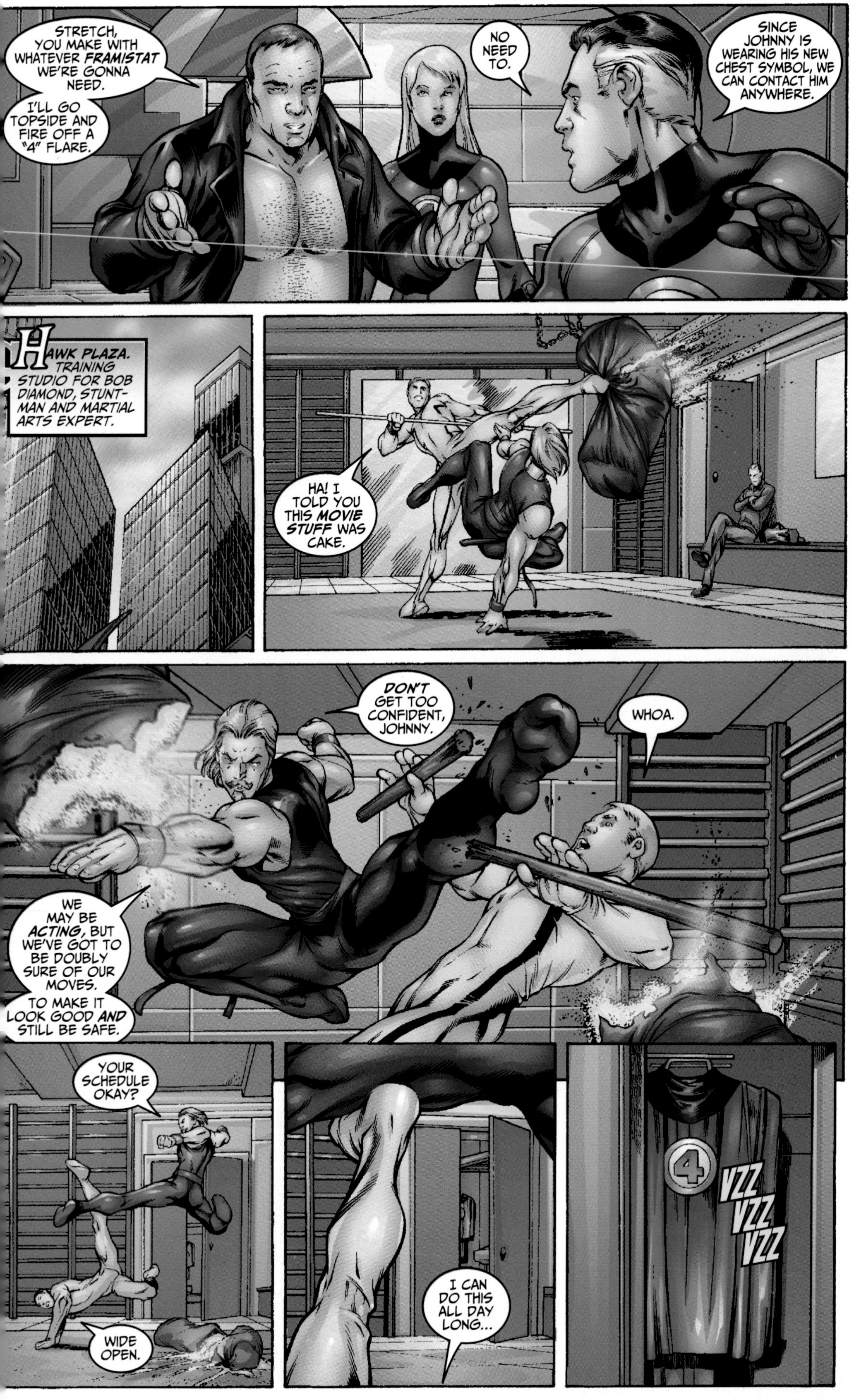
STRETCH, YOU MAKE WITH WHATEVER FRAMISTAT WE'RE GONNA NEED.
I'LL GO TOPSIDE AND FIRE OFF A "4" FLARE.
NO NEED TO.
SINCE JOHNNY IS WEARING HIS NEW CHEST SYMBOL, WE CAN CONTACT HIM ANYWHERE.
HAWK PLAZA. TRAINING STUDIO FOR BOB DIAMOND, STUNT-MAN AND MARTIAL ARTS EXPERT.
HA! I TOLD YOU THIS MOVIE STUFF WAS CAKE.
DON'T GET TOO CONFIDENT, JOHNNY.
WHOA.
WE MAY BE ACTING, BUT WE'VE GOT TO BE DOUBLY SURE OF OUR MOVES.
TO MAKE IT LOOK GOOD AND STILL BE SAFE.
YOUR SCHEDULE OKAY?
WIDE OPEN.
I CAN DO THIS ALL DAY LONG...
VZZ VZZ VZZ

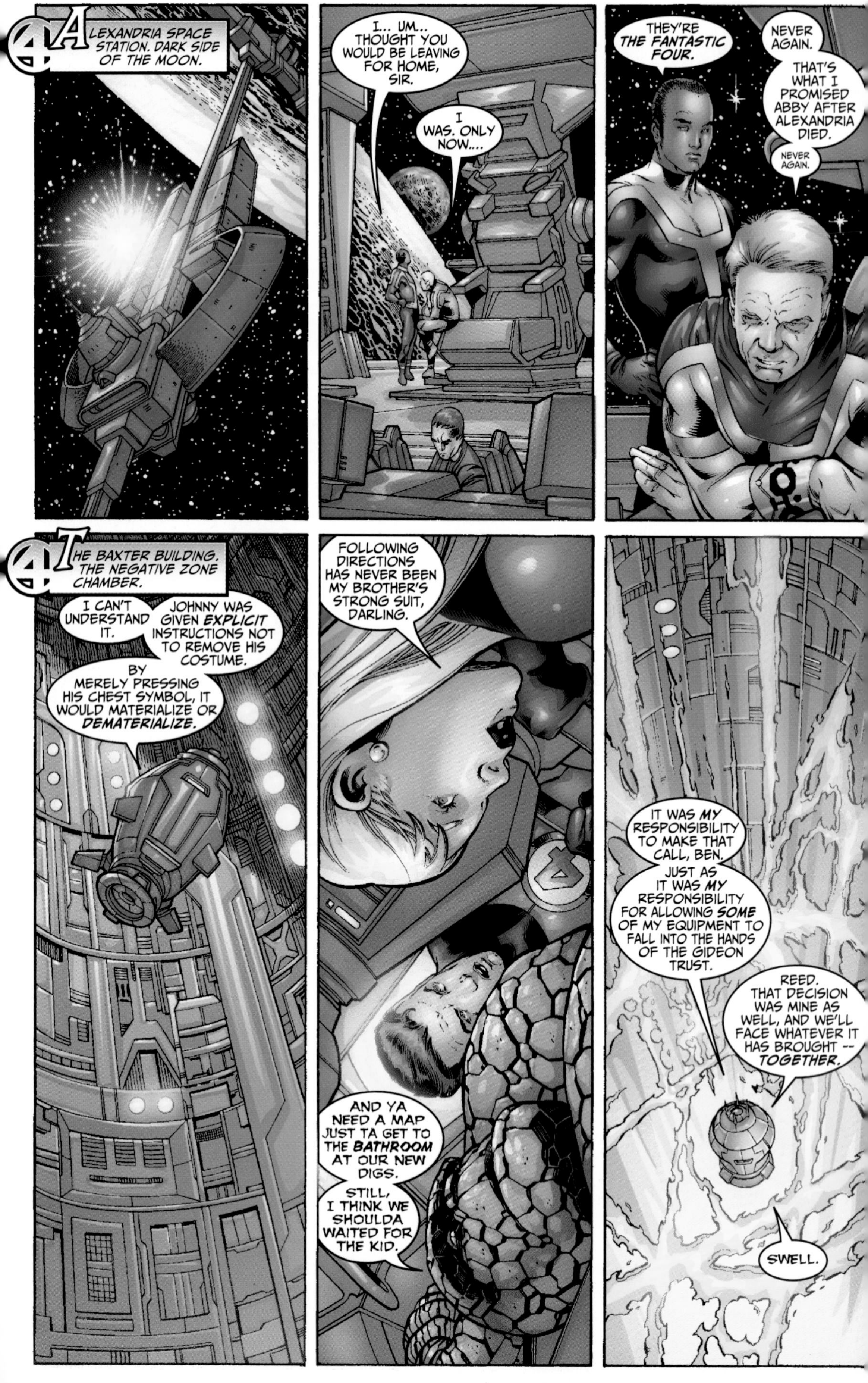
ALEXANDRIA SPACE STATION. DARK SIDE OF THE MOON.
I... UM... THOUGHT YOU WOULD BE LEAVING FOR HOME, SIR.
I WAS. ONLY NOW....
THEY'RE THE FANTASTIC FOUR.
NEVER AGAIN.
THAT'S WHAT I PROMISED ABBY AFTER ALEXANDRIA DIED.
NEVER AGAIN.
THE BAXTER BUILDING. THE NEGATIVE ZONE CHAMBER.
I CAN'T UNDERSTAND IT.
JOHNNY WAS GIVEN EXPLICIT INSTRUCTIONS NOT TO REMOVE HIS COSTUME.
BY MERELY PRESSING HIS CHEST SYMBOL, IT WOULD MATERIALIZE OR DEMATERIALIZE.
FOLLOWING DIRECTIONS HAS NEVER BEEN MY BROTHER'S STRONG SUIT, DARLING.
AND YA NEED A MAP JUST TA GET TO THE BATHROOM AT OUR NEW DIGS.
STILL, I THINK WE SHOULDA WAITED FOR THE KID.
IT WAS MY RESPONSIBILITY TO MAKE THAT CALL, BEN.
JUST AS IT WAS MY RESPONSIBILITY FOR ALLOWING SOME OF MY EQUIPMENT TO FALL INTO THE HANDS OF THE GIDEON TRUST.
REED. THAT DECISION WAS MINE AS WELL, AND WE'LL FACE WHATEVER IT HAS BROUGHT -- TOGETHER.
SWELL.

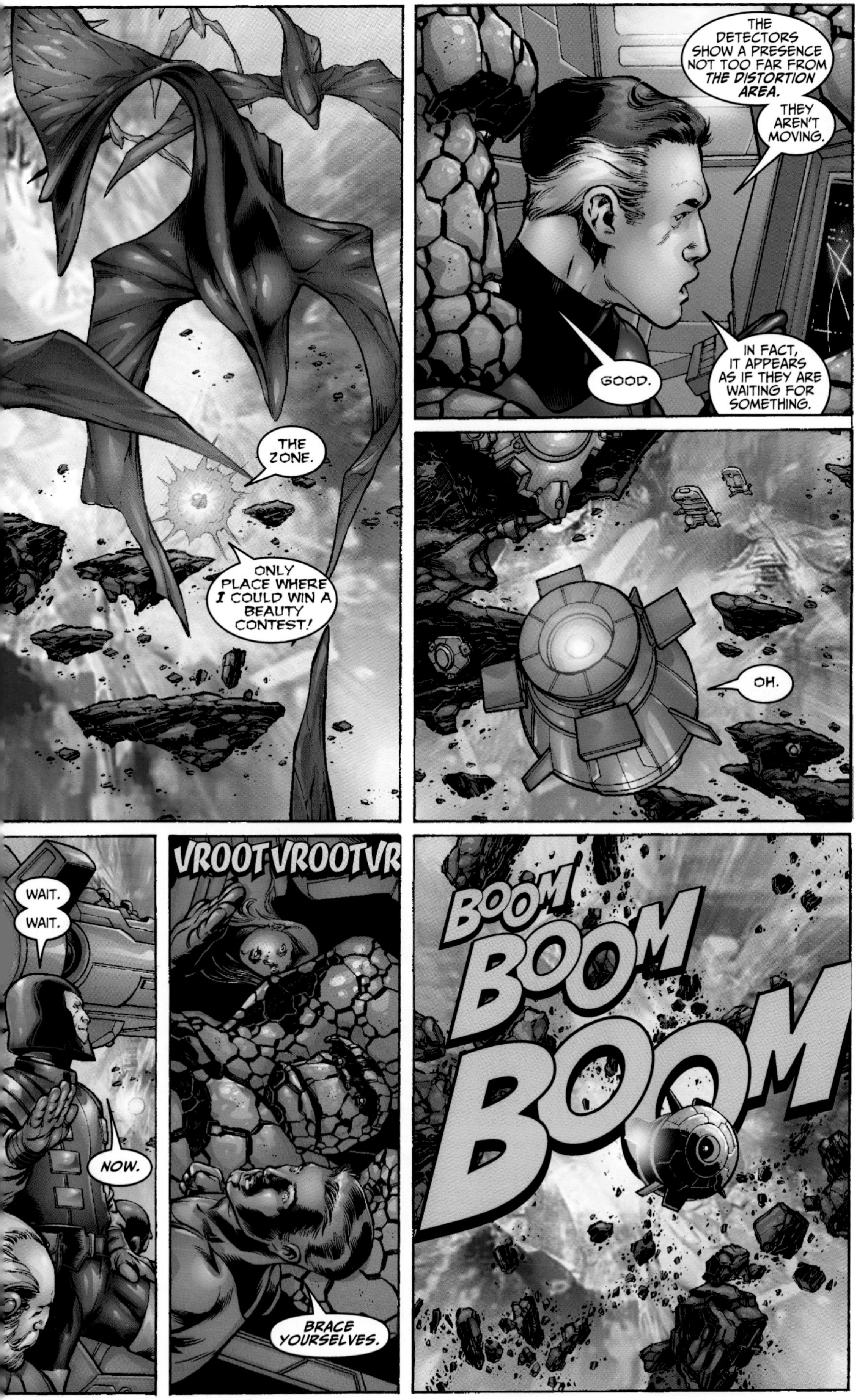
THE ZONE.
ONLY PLACE WHERE I COULD WIN A BEAUTY CONTEST!
THE DETECTORS SHOW A PRESENCE NOT TOO FAR FROM THE DISTORTION AREA.
THEY AREN'T MOVING.
GOOD.
IN FACT, IT APPEARS AS IF THEY ARE WAITING FOR SOMETHING.
OH.
WAIT.
WAIT.
NOW.
VROOT VROOTVR
BRACE YOURSELVES.
BOOM
BOOM
BOOM

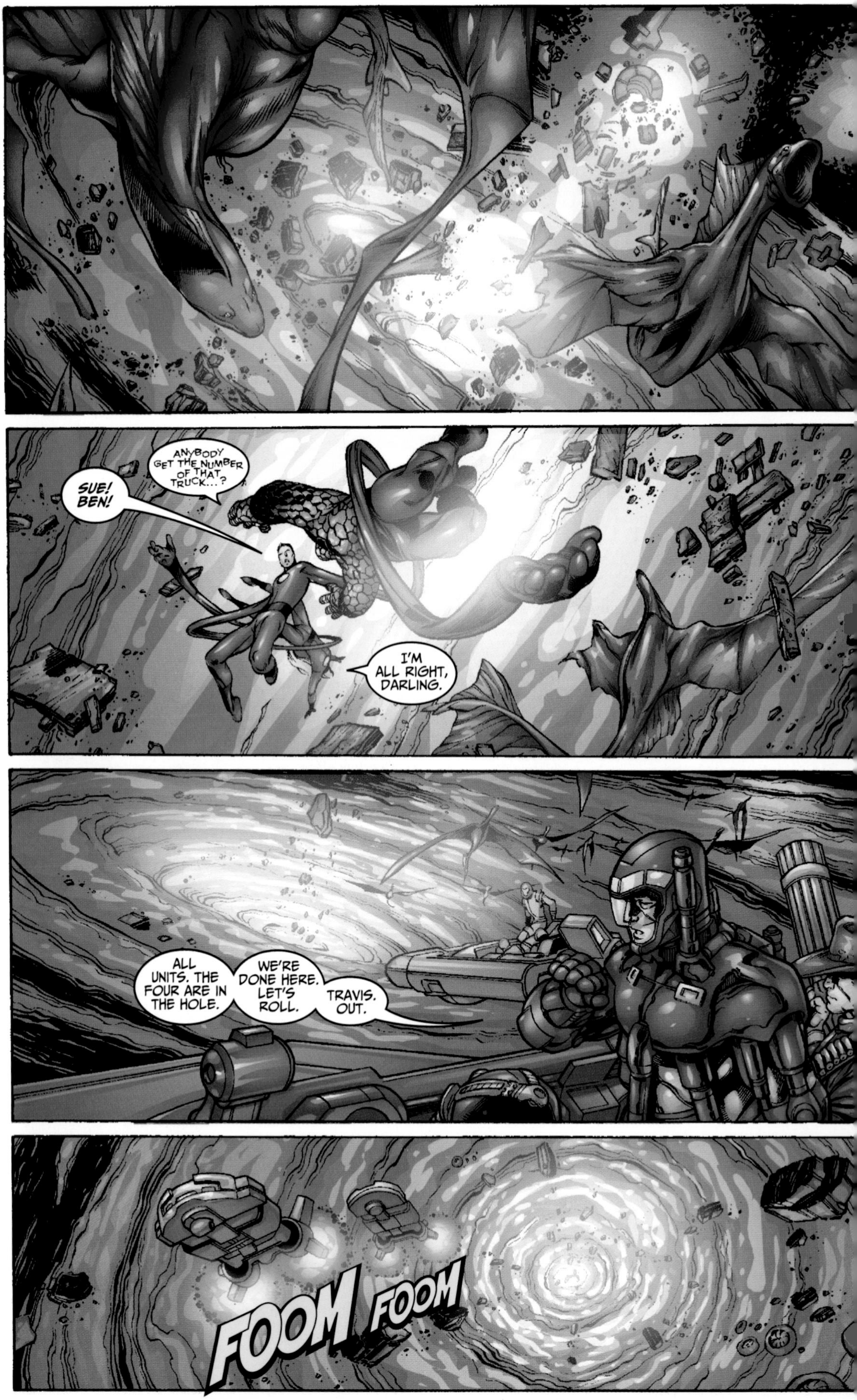
SUE! BEN!
ANYBODY GET THE NUMBER OF THAT TRUCK...?
I'M ALL RIGHT, DARLING.
ALL UNITS. THE FOUR ARE IN THE HOLE.
WE'RE DONE HERE. LET'S ROLL.
TRAVIS. OUT.
FOOM FOOM

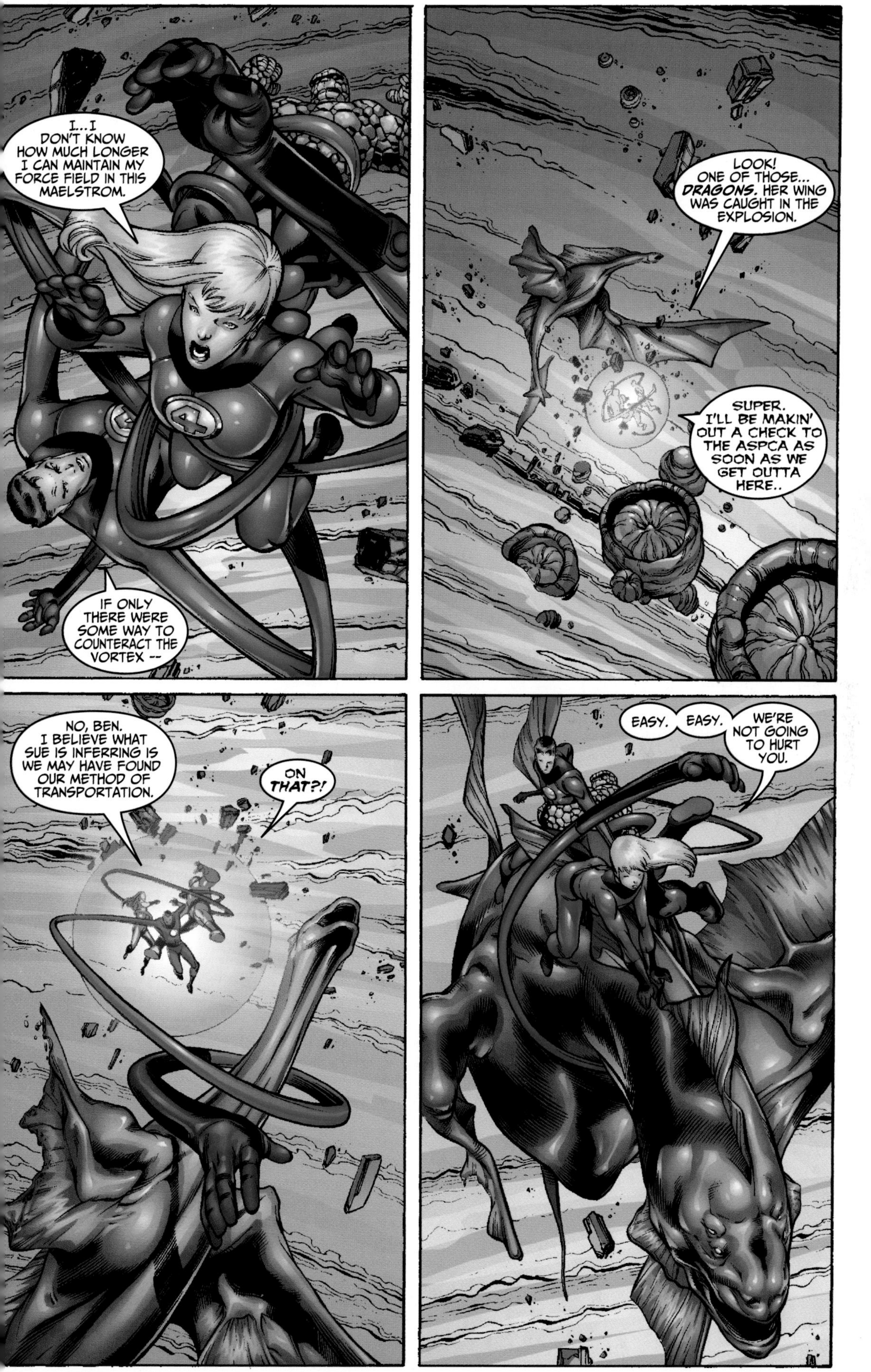
I...I DON'T KNOW HOW MUCH LONGER I CAN MAINTAIN MY FORCE FIELD IN THIS MAELSTROM.
IF ONLY THERE WERE SOME WAY TO COUNTERACT THE VORTEX --
LOOK! ONE OF THOSE... DRAGONS. HER WING WAS CAUGHT IN THE EXPLOSION.
SUPER. I'LL BE MAKIN' OUT A CHECK TO THE ASPCA AS SOON AS WE GET OUTTA HERE..
NO, BEN. I BELIEVE WHAT SUE IS INFERRING IS WE MAY HAVE FOUND OUR METHOD OF TRANSPORTATION.
ON THAT?!
EASY.
EASY.
WE'RE NOT GOING TO HURT YOU.

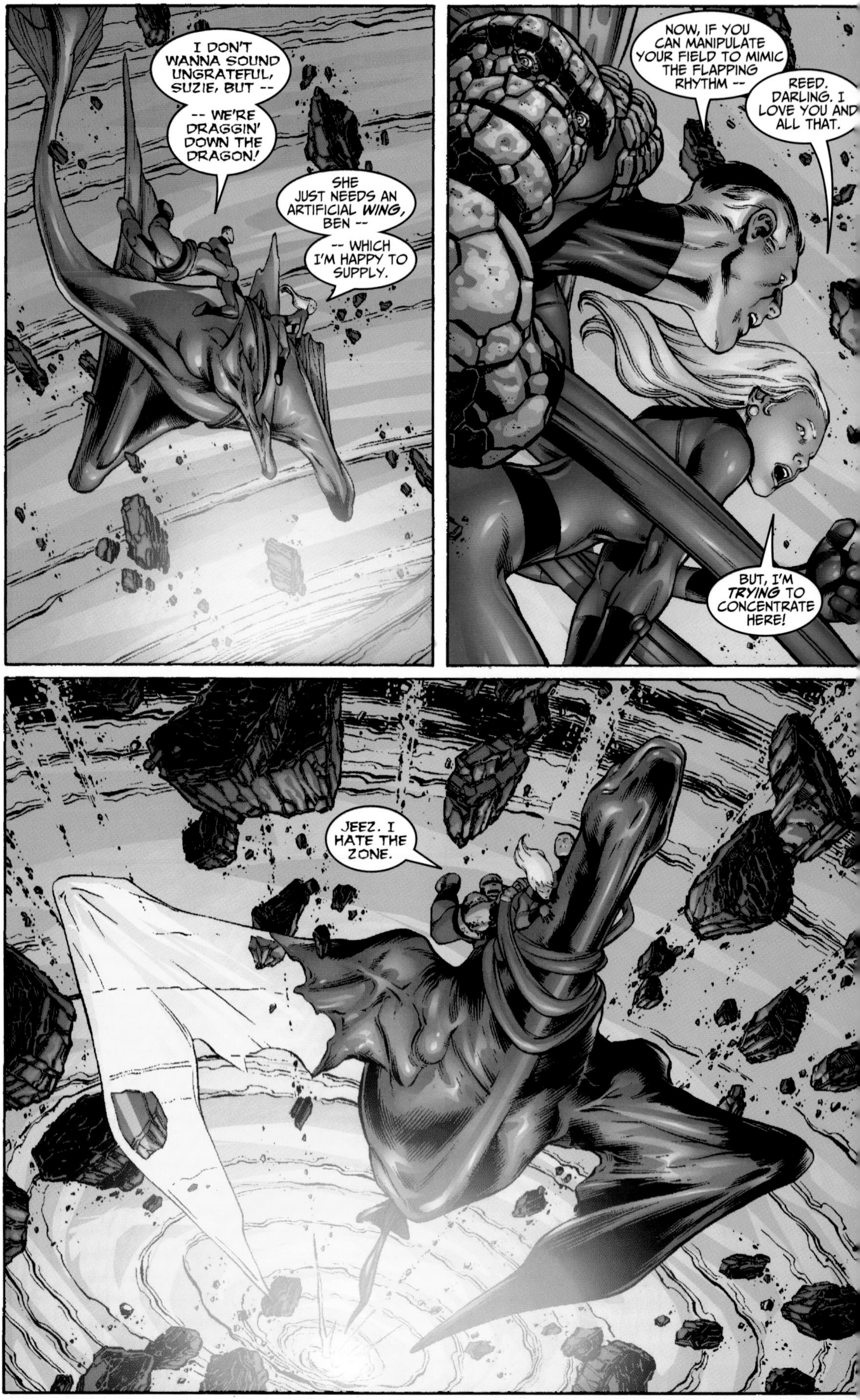
I DON'T WANNA SOUND UNGRATEFUL, SUZIE, BUT --
-- WE'RE DRAGGIN' DOWN THE DRAGON!
SHE JUST NEEDS AN ARTIFICIAL WING, BEN --
-- WHICH I'M HAPPY TO SUPPLY.
NOW, IF YOU CAN MANIPULATE YOUR FIELD TO MIMIC THE FLAPPING RHYTHM --
REED. DARLING. I LOVE YOU AND ALL THAT.
BUT, I'M TRYING TO CONCENTRATE HERE!
JEEZ. I HATE THE ZONE.

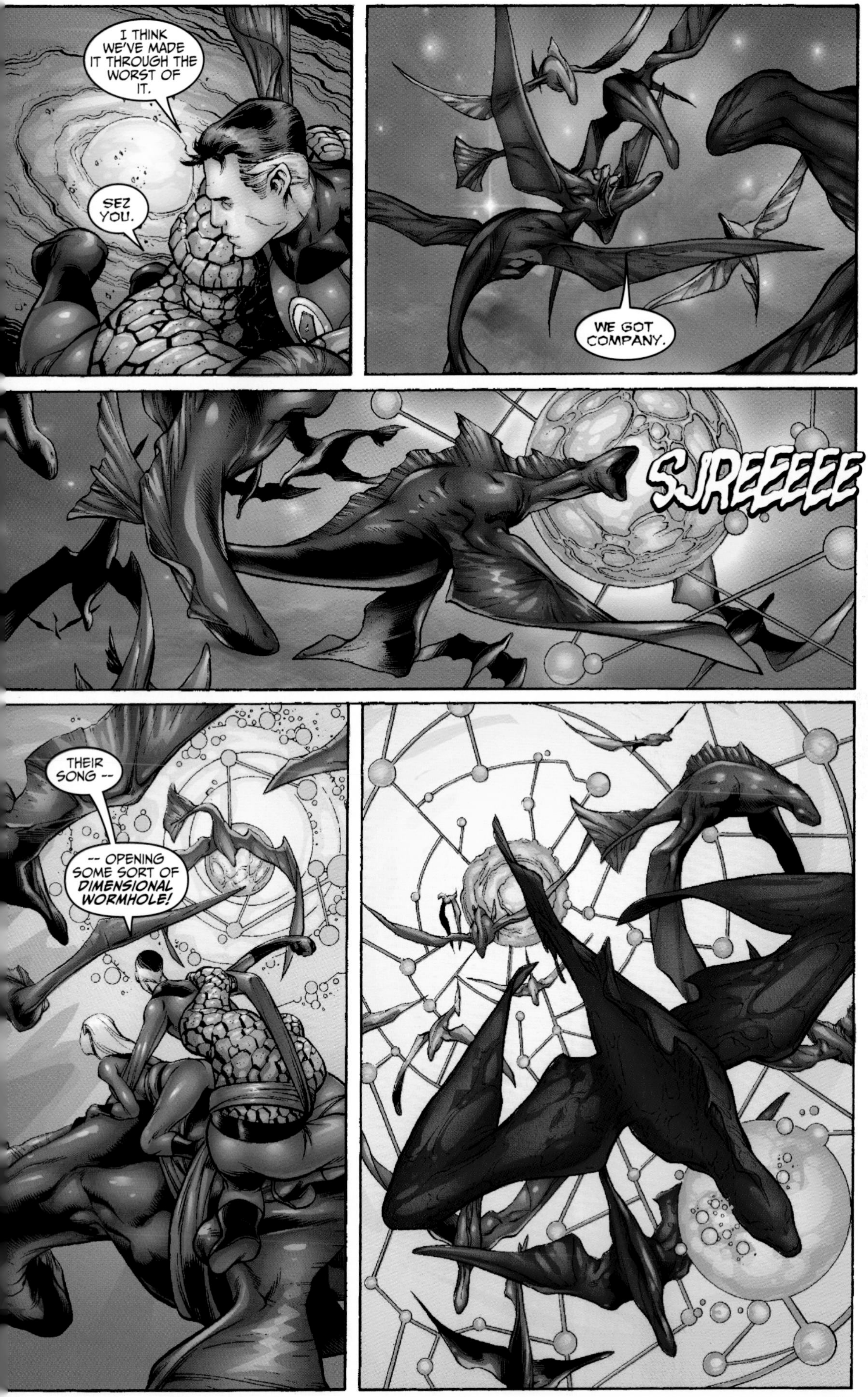
I THINK WE'VE MADE IT THROUGH THE WORST OF IT.
SEZ YOU.
WE GOT COMPANY.
SJREEEEEE
THEIR SONG --
-- OPENING SOME SORT OF *DIMENSIONAL WORMHOLE!*

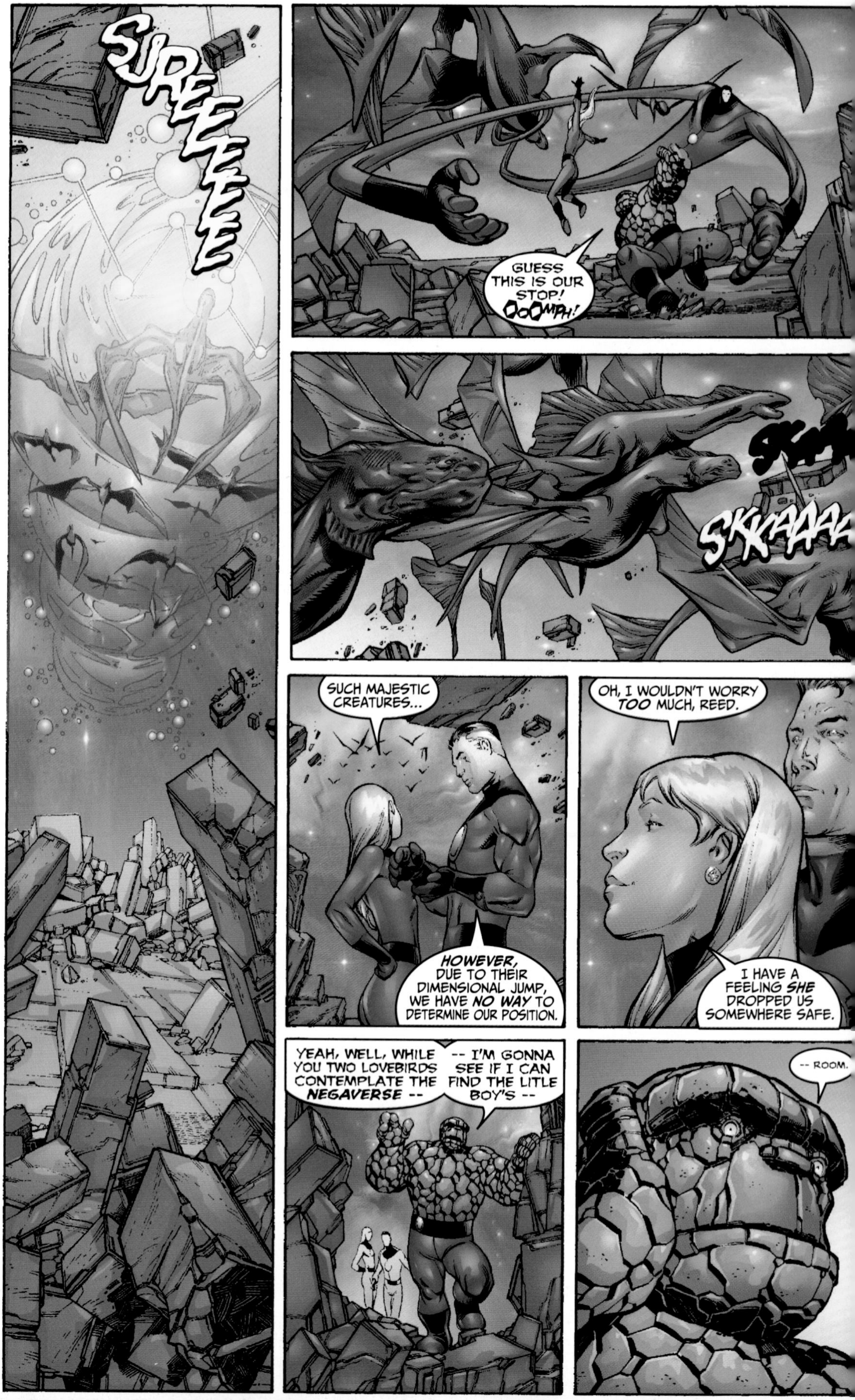
SJREEEEEE
GUESS THIS IS OUR STOP! OOOMPH!
SKKAAAA
SUCH MAJESTIC CREATURES...
HOWEVER, DUE TO THEIR DIMENSIONAL JUMP, WE HAVE NO WAY TO DETERMINE OUR POSITION.
OH, I WOULDN'T WORRY TOO MUCH, REED.
I HAVE A FEELING SHE DROPPED US SOMEWHERE SAFE.
YEAH, WELL, WHILE YOU TWO LOVEBIRDS CONTEMPLATE THE NEGAVERSE --
-- I'M GONNA SEE IF I CAN FIND THE LITLE BOY'S --
-- ROOM.

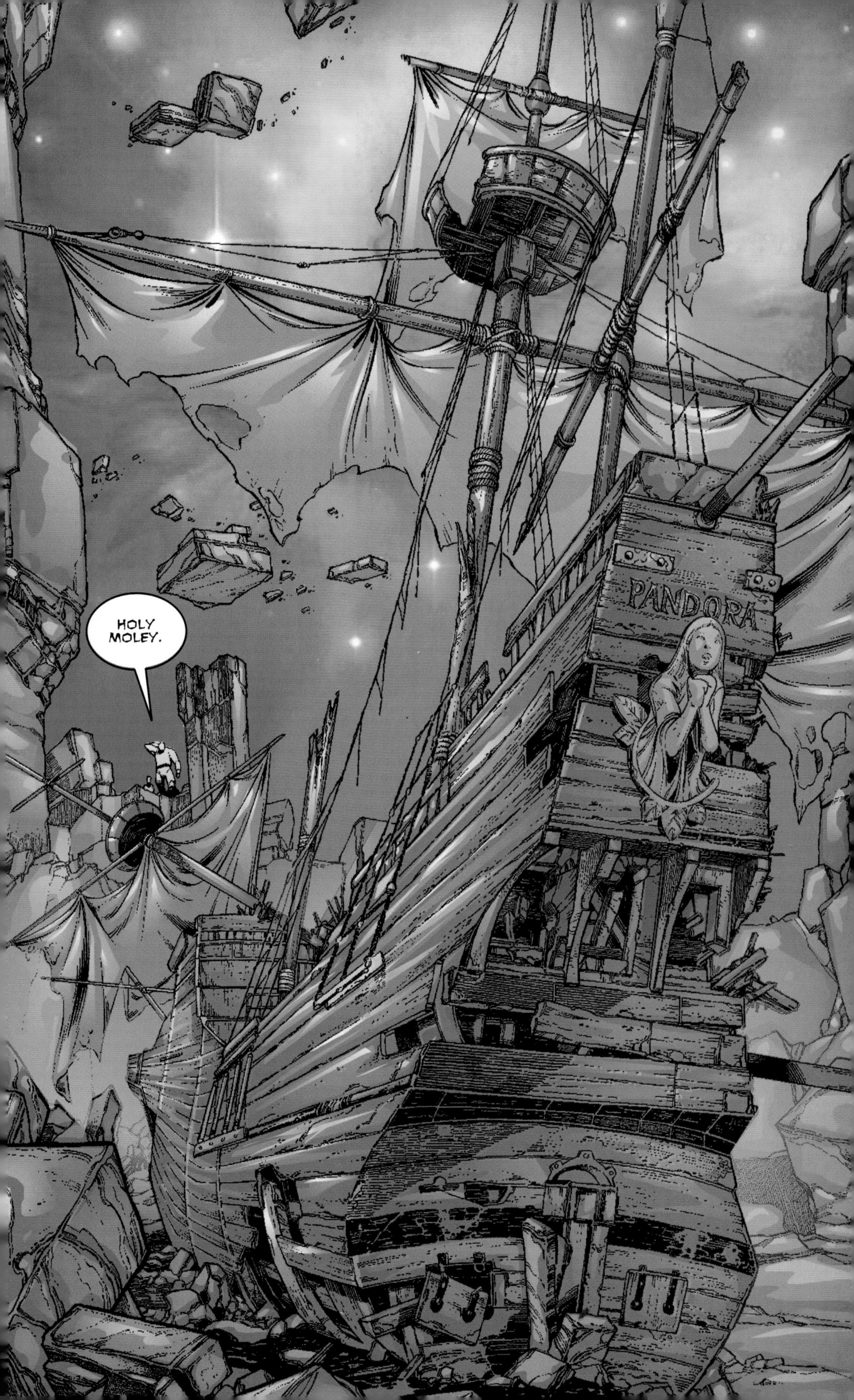
HOLY MOLEY.
PANDORA

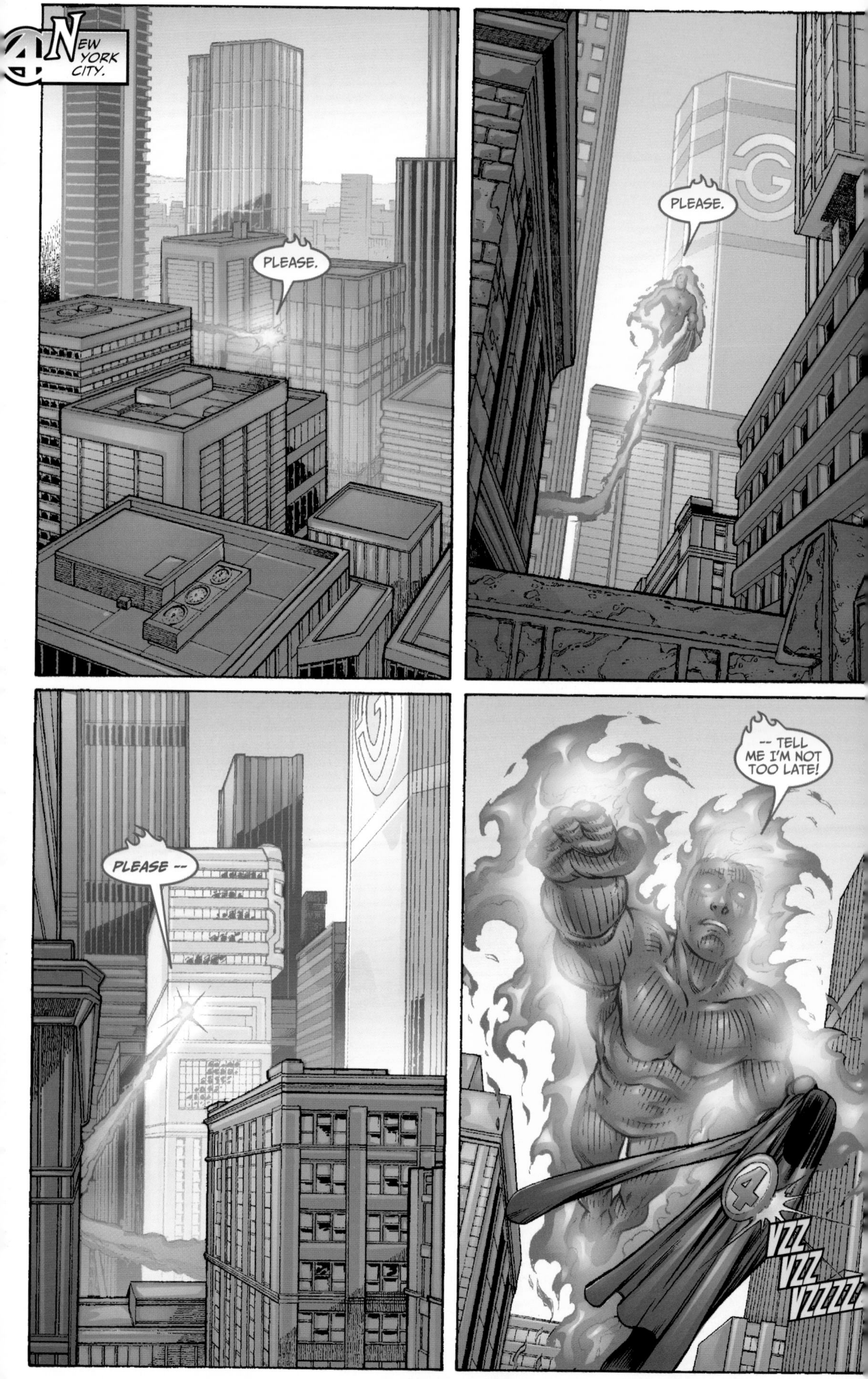
NEW YORK CITY.
PLEASE.
PLEASE.
PLEASE --
-- TELL ME I'M NOT TOO LATE!
VZZ VZZ VZZZZZ

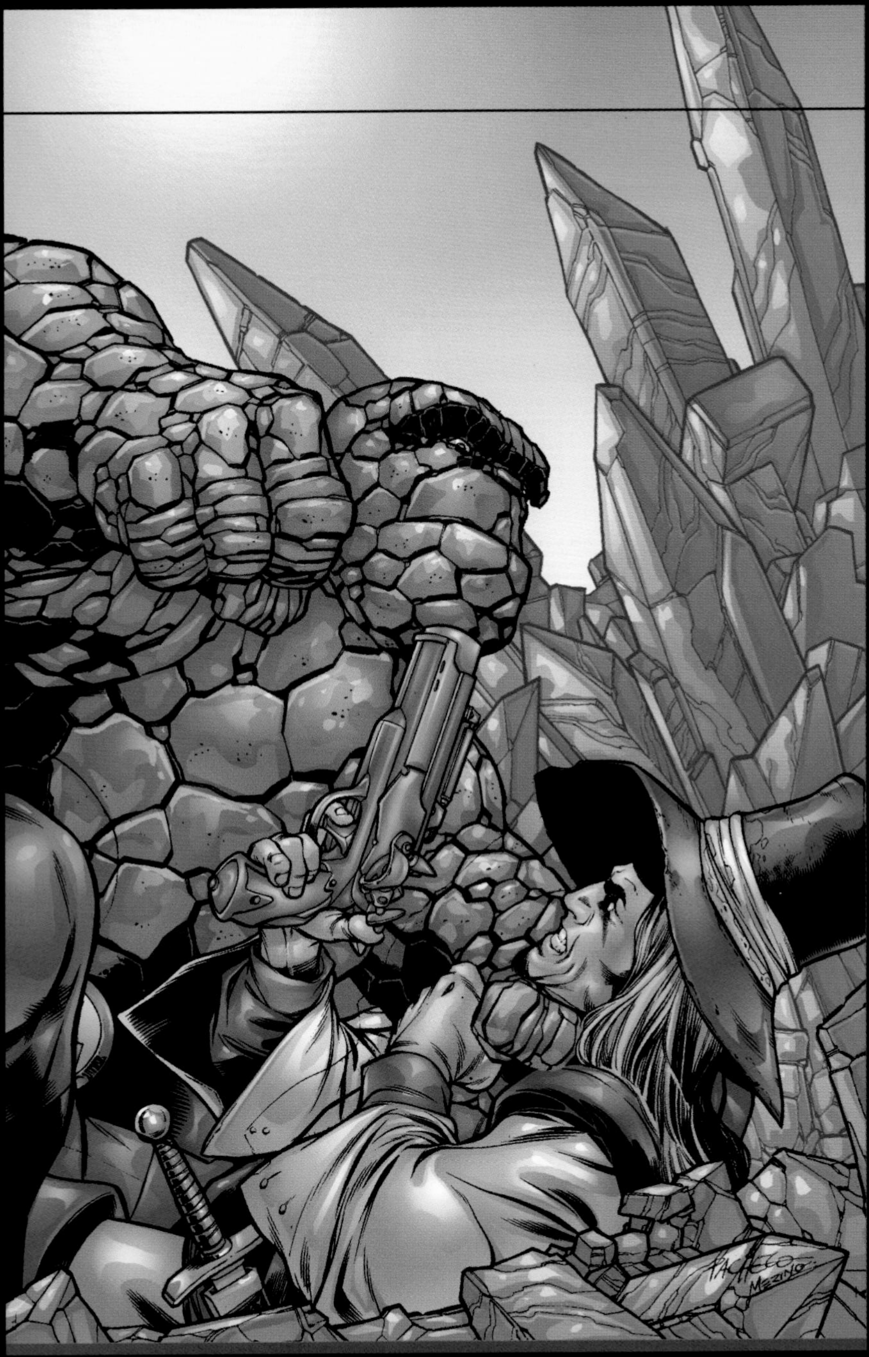

FANTASTIC FOUR #41

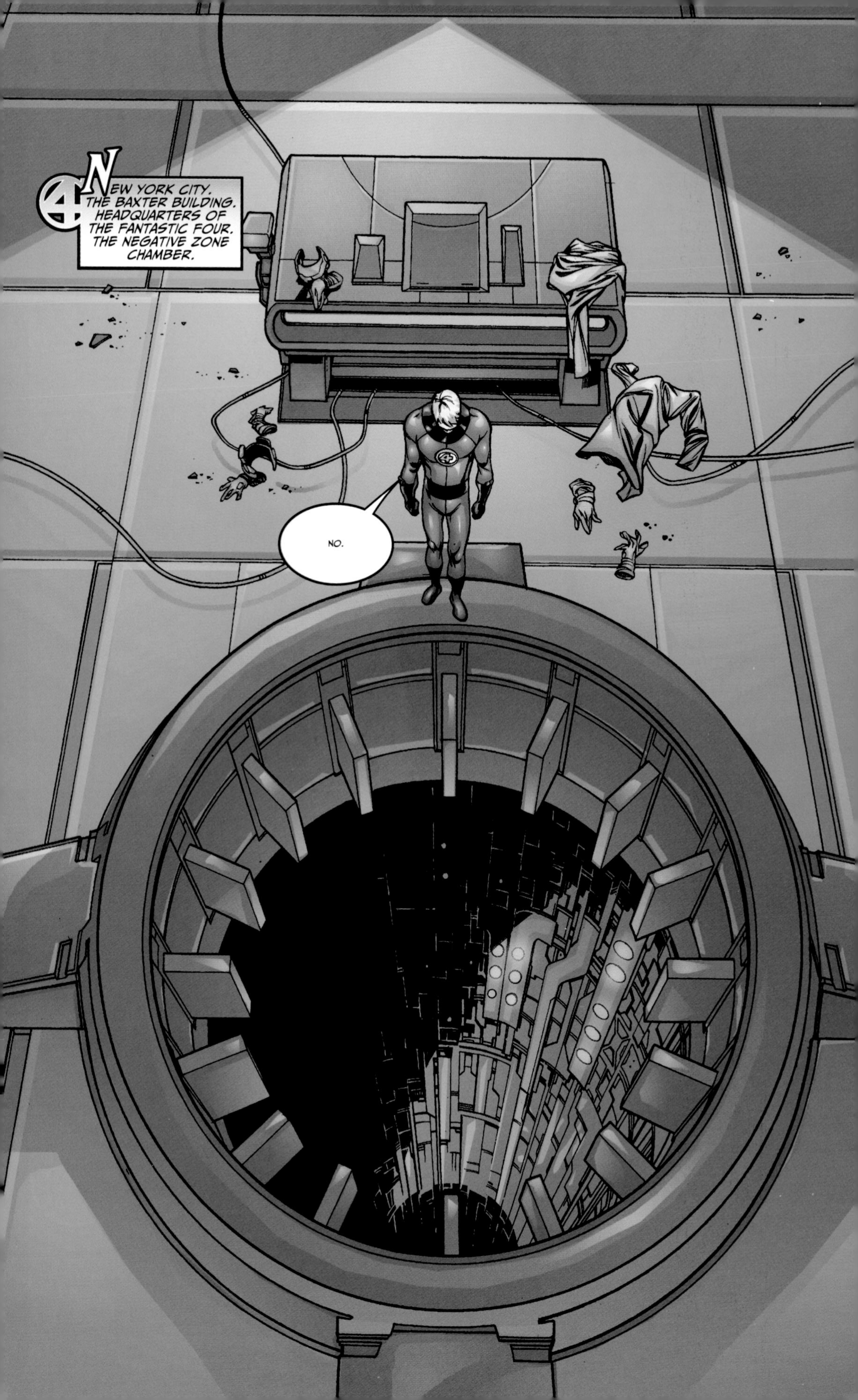
NEW YORK CITY. THE BAXTER BUILDING. HEADQUARTERS OF THE FANTASTIC FOUR. THE NEGATIVE ZONE CHAMBER.
NO.

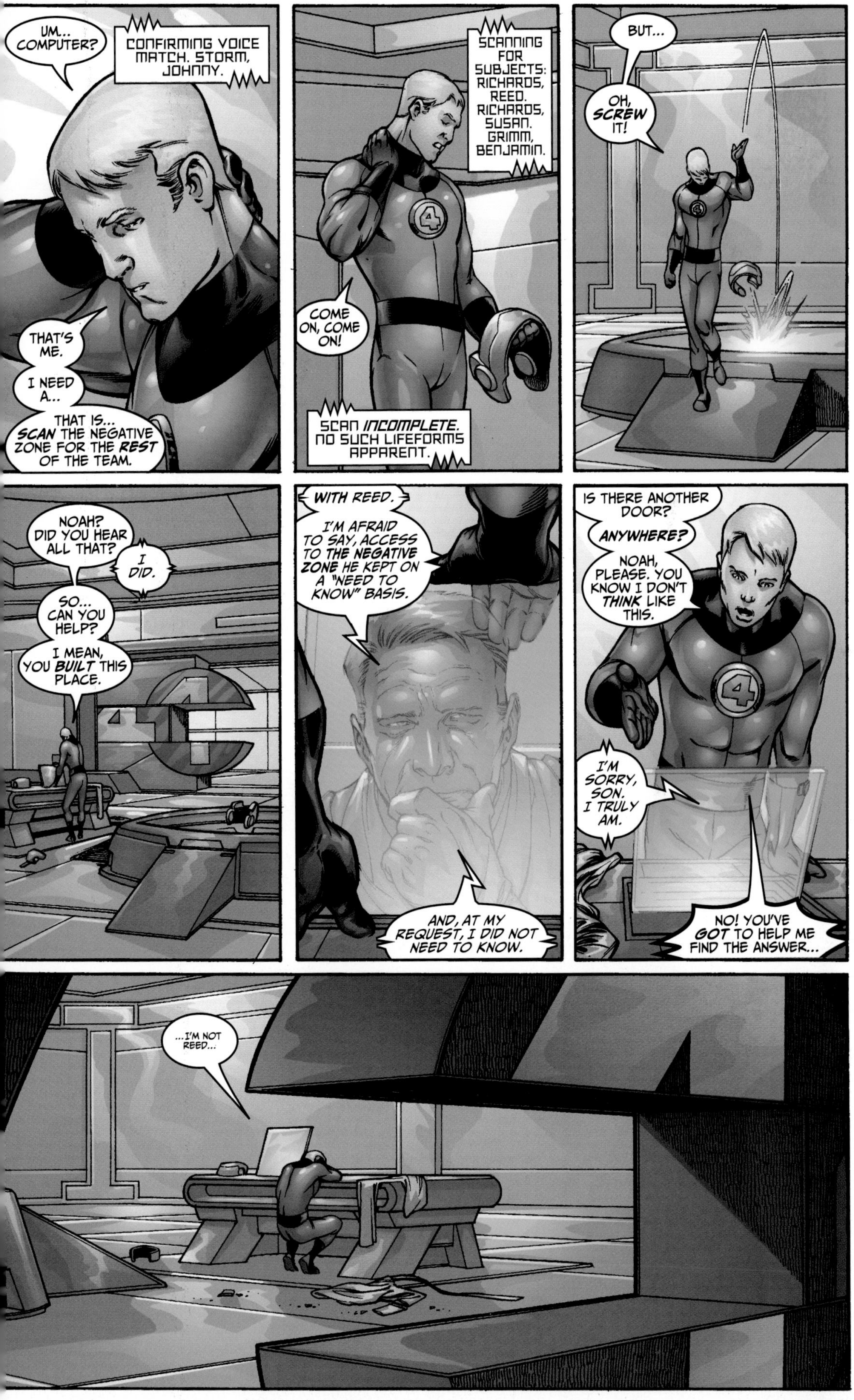
UM... COMPUTER?
CONFIRMING VOICE MATCH. STORM, JOHNNY.
THAT'S ME.
I NEED A...
THAT IS... SCAN THE NEGATIVE ZONE FOR THE REST OF THE TEAM.
SCANNING FOR SUBJECTS: RICHARDS, REED. RICHARDS, SUSAN. GRIMM, BENJAMIN.
COME ON, COME ON!
SCAN INCOMPLETE. NO SUCH LIFEFORMS APPARENT.
BUT...
OH, SCREW IT!
NOAH? DID YOU HEAR ALL THAT?
I DID.
SO... CAN YOU HELP?
I MEAN, YOU BUILT THIS PLACE.
WITH REED.
I'M AFRAID TO SAY, ACCESS TO THE NEGATIVE ZONE HE KEPT ON A "NEED TO KNOW" BASIS.
AND, AT MY REQUEST, I DID NOT NEED TO KNOW.
IS THERE ANOTHER DOOR?
ANYWHERE?
NOAH, PLEASE. YOU KNOW I DON'T THINK LIKE THIS.
I'M SORRY, SON. I TRULY AM.
NO! YOU'VE GOT TO HELP ME FIND THE ANSWER...
...I'M NOT REED...

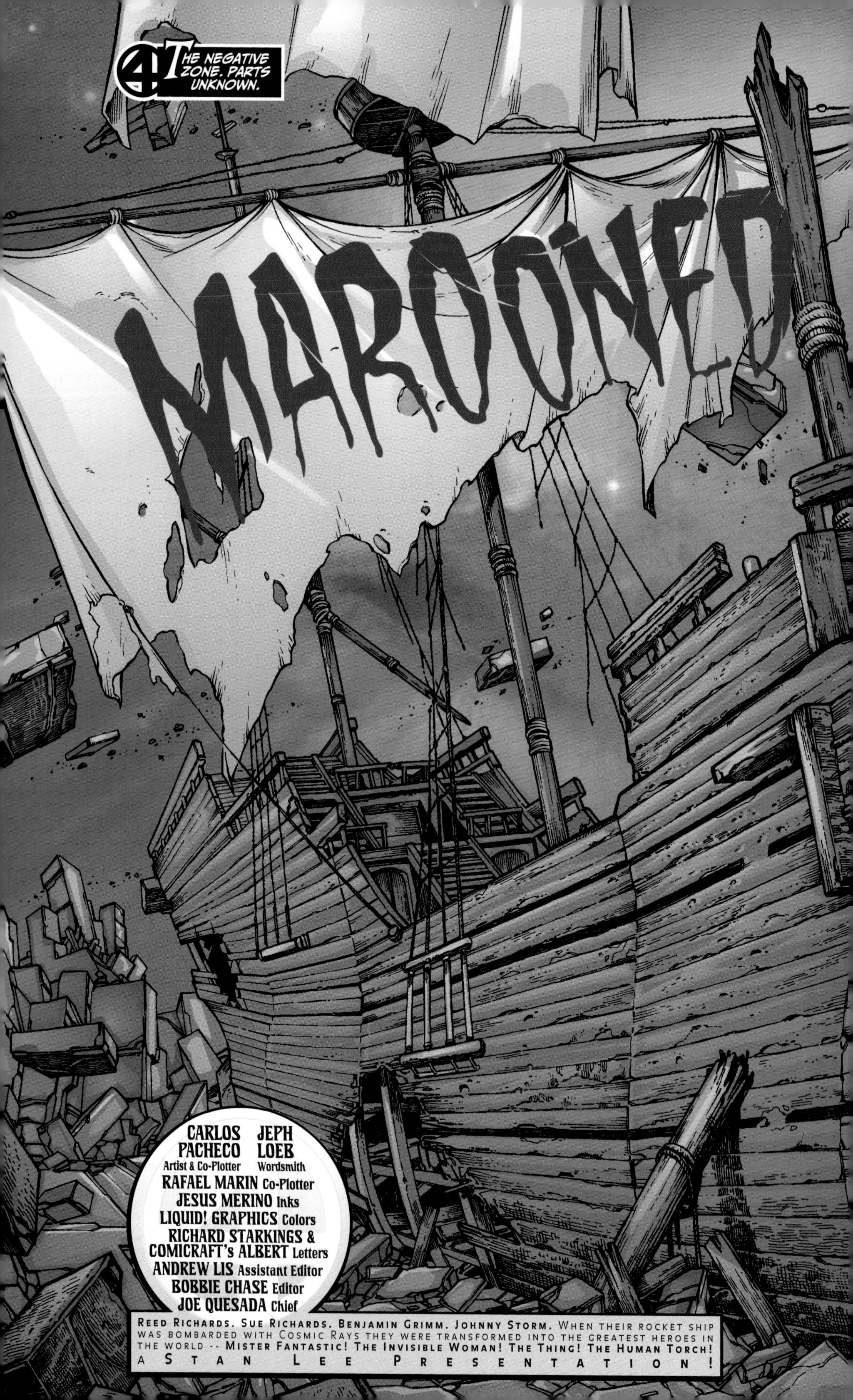

THE NEGATIVE ZONE. PARTS UNKNOWN.
MAROONED
CARLOS PACHECO Artist & Co-Plotter
JEPH LOEB Wordsmith
RAFAEL MARIN Co-Plotter
JESUS MERINO Inks
LIQUID! GRAPHICS Colors
RICHARD STARKINGS & COMICRAFT's ALBERT Letters
ANDREW LIS Assistant Editor
BOBBIE CHASE Editor
JOE QUESADA Chief
REED RICHARDS. SUE RICHARDS. BENJAMIN GRIMM. JOHNNY STORM. WHEN THEIR ROCKET SHIP WAS BOMBARDED WITH COSMIC RAYS THEY WERE TRANSFORMED INTO THE GREATEST HEROES IN THE WORLD -- MISTER FANTASTIC! THE INVISIBLE WOMAN! THE THING! THE HUMAN TORCH!
A STAN LEE PRESENTATION!

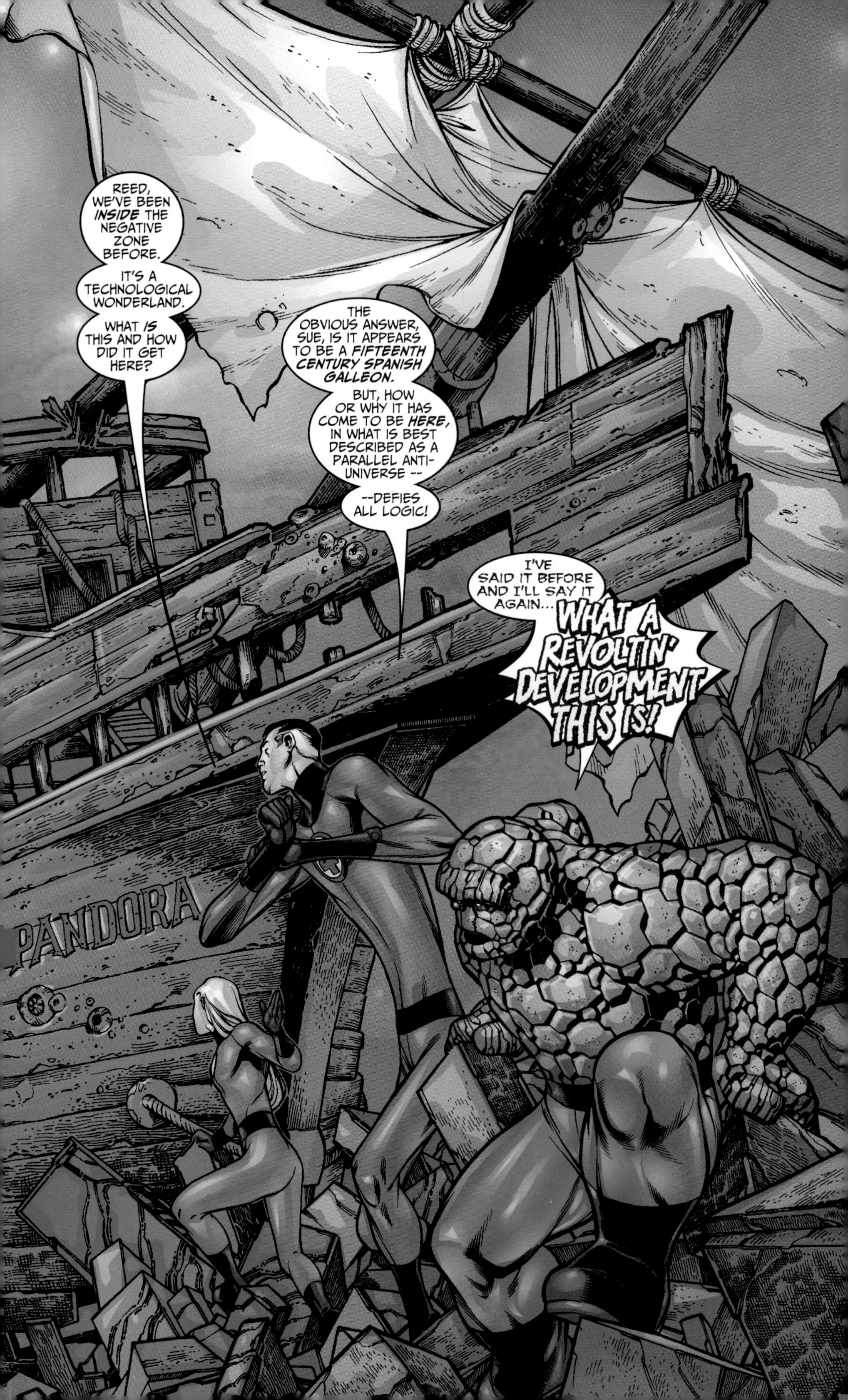

REED, WE'VE BEEN *INSIDE* THE NEGATIVE ZONE BEFORE.
IT'S A TECHNOLOGICAL WONDERLAND.
WHAT *IS* THIS AND HOW DID IT GET HERE?
THE OBVIOUS ANSWER, SUE, IS IT APPEARS TO BE A ***FIFTEENTH CENTURY SPANISH GALLEON.***
BUT, HOW OR WHY IT HAS COME TO BE *HERE,* IN WHAT IS BEST DESCRIBED AS A PARALLEL ANTI-UNIVERSE --
--DEFIES ALL LOGIC!
I'VE SAID IT BEFORE AND I'LL SAY IT AGAIN...
WHAT A REVOLTIN' DEVELOPMENT THIS IS!
PANDORA

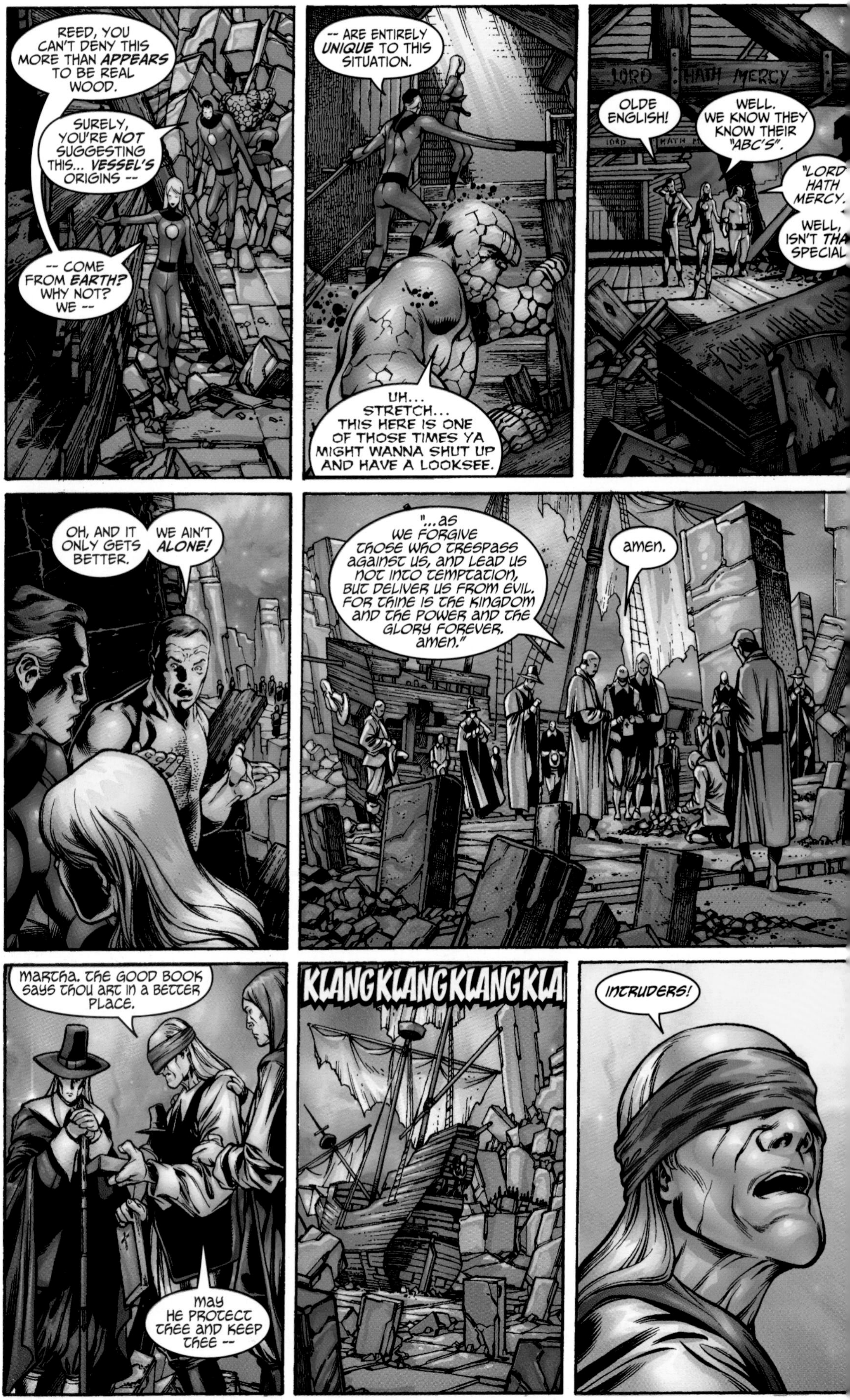
REED, YOU CAN'T DENY THIS MORE THAN APPEARS TO BE REAL WOOD.
SURELY, YOU'RE NOT SUGGESTING THIS... VESSEL'S ORIGINS --
-- COME FROM EARTH? WHY NOT? WE --
-- ARE ENTIRELY UNIQUE TO THIS SITUATION.
UH... STRETCH... THIS HERE IS ONE OF THOSE TIMES YA MIGHT WANNA SHUT UP AND HAVE A LOOKSEE.
LORD HATH MERCY
OLDE ENGLISH!
WELL. WE KNOW THEY KNOW THEIR "ABC'S".
"LORD HATH MERCY."
WELL, ISN'T THA SPECIAL
OH, AND IT ONLY GETS BETTER.
WE AIN'T ALONE!
"...as we forgive those who trespass against us, and lead us not into temptation, but deliver us from evil. For thine is the kingdom and the power and the glory forever. amen."
amen.
martha. the good book says thou art in a better place.
may he protect thee and keep thee --
KLANGKLANGKLANGKLA
intruders!

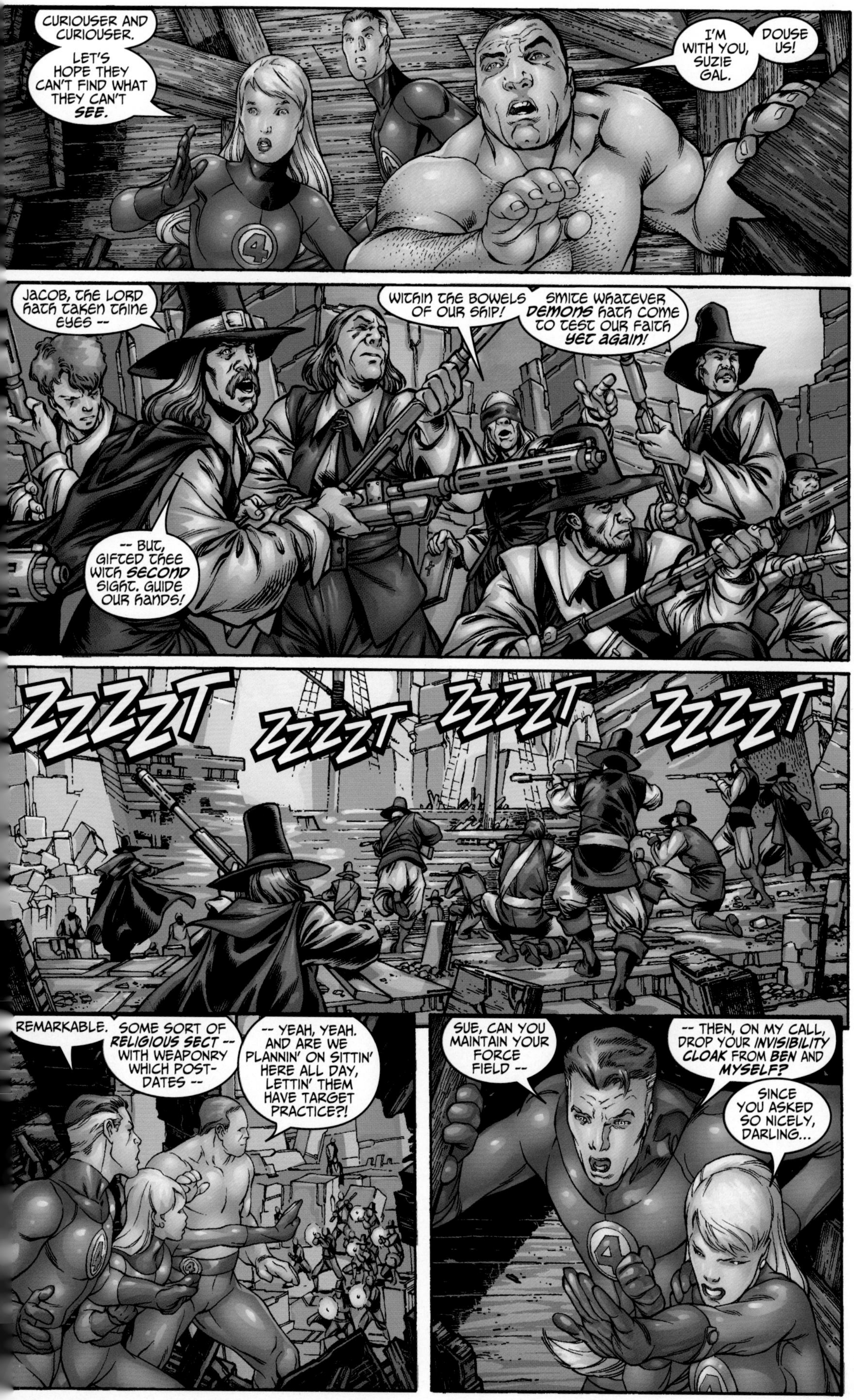
CURIOUSER AND CURIOUSER.
LET'S HOPE THEY CAN'T FIND WHAT THEY CAN'T SEE.
I'M WITH YOU, SUZIE GAL.
DOUSE US!
JACOB, THE LORD HATH TAKEN THINE EYES --
-- BUT, GIFTED THEE WITH SECOND SIGHT. GUIDE OUR HANDS!
WITHIN THE BOWELS OF OUR SHIP!
SMITE WHATEVER DEMONS HATH COME TO TEST OUR FAITH YET AGAIN!
ZZZZZT
ZZZZZT
ZZZZZT
ZZZZZT
REMARKABLE.
SOME SORT OF RELIGIOUS SECT -- WITH WEAPONRY WHICH POST-DATES --
-- YEAH, YEAH. AND ARE WE PLANNIN' ON SITTIN' HERE ALL DAY, LETTIN' THEM HAVE TARGET PRACTICE?!
SUE, CAN YOU MAINTAIN YOUR FORCE FIELD --
-- THEN, ON MY CALL, DROP YOUR INVISIBILITY CLOAK FROM BEN AND MYSELF?
SINCE YOU ASKED SO NICELY, DARLING...

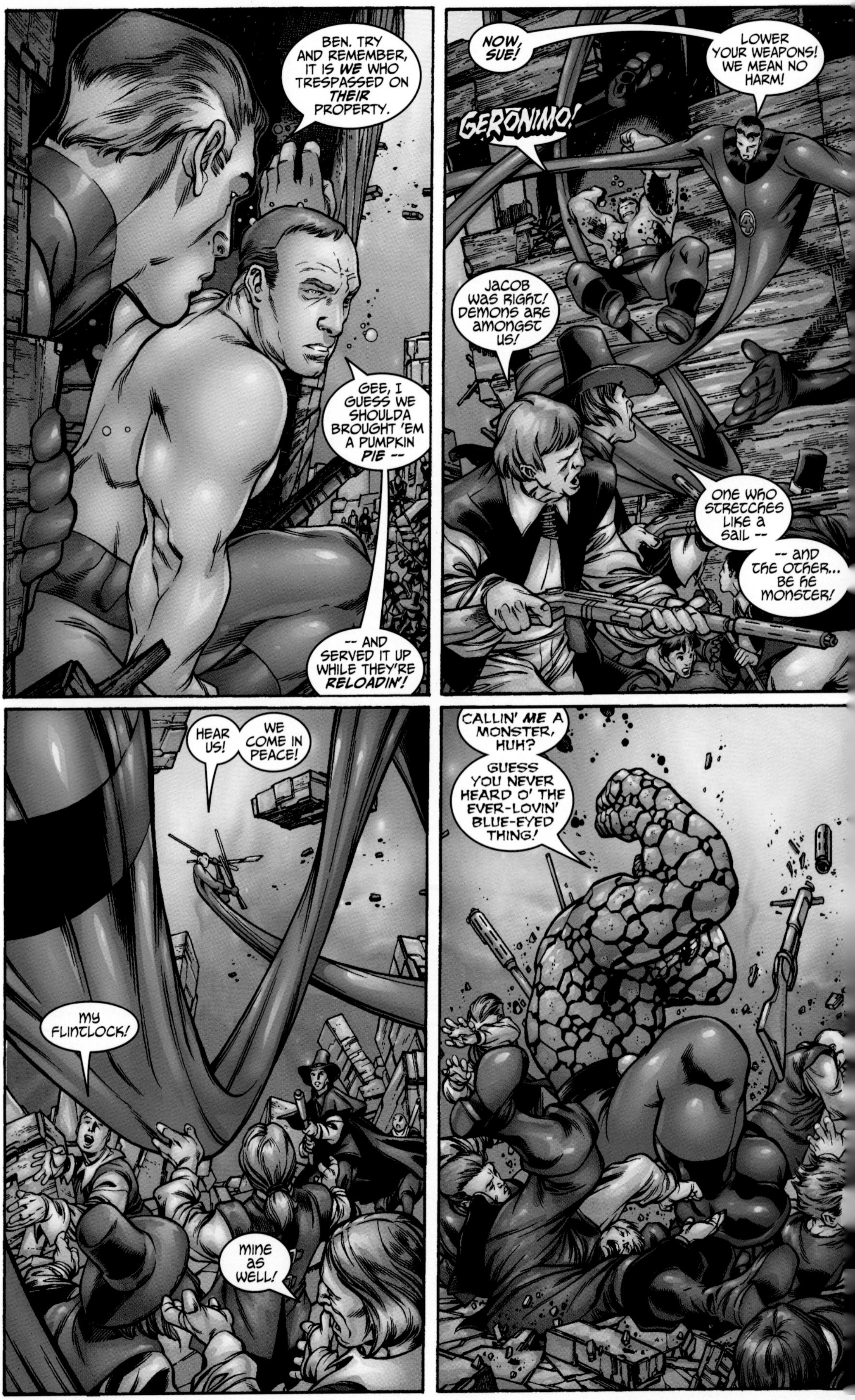
BEN. TRY AND REMEMBER, IT IS WE WHO TRESPASSED ON THEIR PROPERTY.
GEE, I GUESS WE SHOULDA BROUGHT 'EM A PUMPKIN PIE --
-- AND SERVED IT UP WHILE THEY'RE RELOADIN'!
NOW, SUE!
LOWER YOUR WEAPONS! WE MEAN NO HARM!
GERONIMO!
JACOB WAS RIGHT! DEMONS ARE AMONGST US!
ONE WHO STRETCHES LIKE A SAIL --
-- AND THE OTHER... BE HE MONSTER!
HEAR US!
WE COME IN PEACE!
MY FLINTLOCK!
MINE AS WELL!
CALLIN' ME A MONSTER, HUH?
GUESS YOU NEVER HEARD O' THE EVER-LOVIN' BLUE-EYED THING!

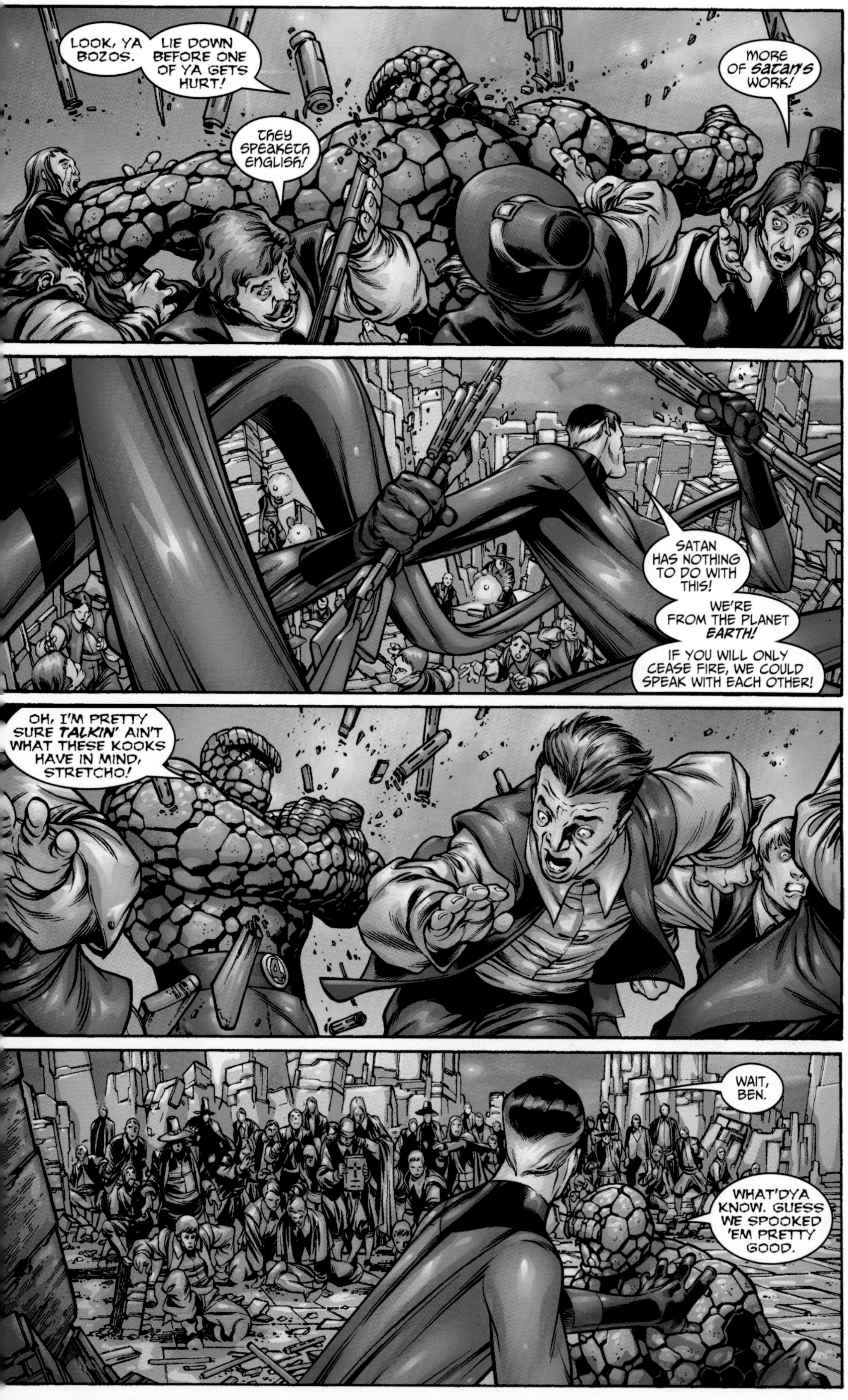
LOOK, YA BOZOS.
LIE DOWN BEFORE ONE OF YA GETS HURT!
THEY SPEAKETH ENGLISH!
MORE OF SATAN'S WORK!
SATAN HAS NOTHING TO DO WITH THIS!
WE'RE FROM THE PLANET EARTH!
IF YOU WILL ONLY CEASE FIRE, WE COULD SPEAK WITH EACH OTHER!
OH, I'M PRETTY SURE TALKIN' AIN'T WHAT THESE KOOKS HAVE IN MIND, STRETCHO!
WAIT, BEN.
WHAT'DYA KNOW. GUESS WE SPOOKED 'EM PRETTY GOOD.

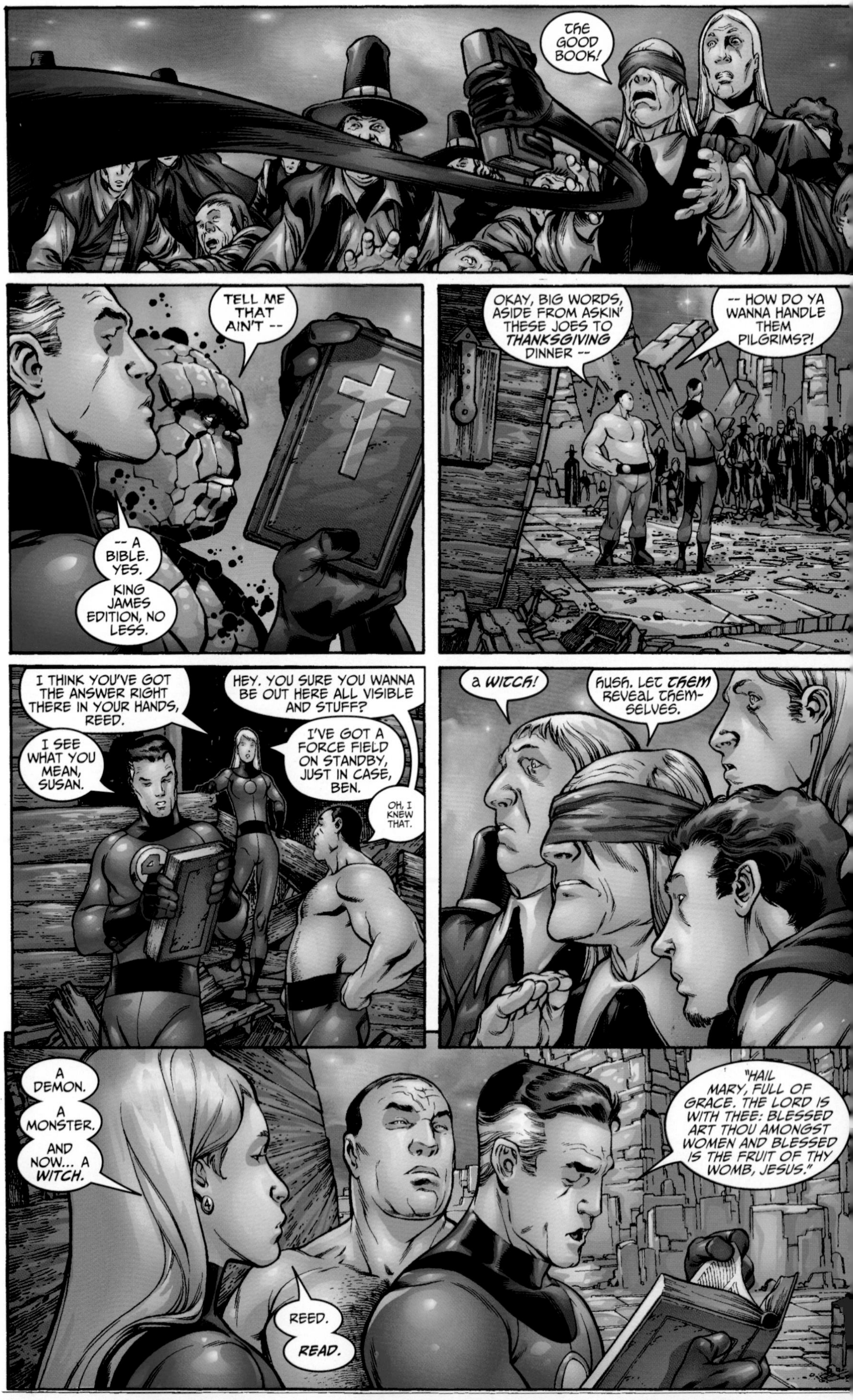
THE GOOD BOOK!
TELL ME THAT AIN'T --
-- A BIBLE. YES.
KING JAMES EDITION, NO LESS.
OKAY, BIG WORDS, ASIDE FROM ASKIN' THESE JOES TO THANKSGIVING DINNER --
-- HOW DO YA WANNA HANDLE THEM PILGRIMS?!
I THINK YOU'VE GOT THE ANSWER RIGHT THERE IN YOUR HANDS, REED.
I SEE WHAT YOU MEAN, SUSAN.
HEY. YOU SURE YOU WANNA BE OUT HERE ALL VISIBLE AND STUFF?
I'VE GOT A FORCE FIELD ON STANDBY, JUST IN CASE, BEN.
OH, I KNEW THAT.
A WITCH!
HUSH. LET THEM REVEAL THEMSELVES.
A DEMON.
A MONSTER.
AND NOW... A WITCH.
"HAIL MARY, FULL OF GRACE. THE LORD IS WITH THEE: BLESSED ART THOU AMONGST WOMEN AND BLESSED IS THE FRUIT OF THY WOMB, JESUS."
REED.
READ.

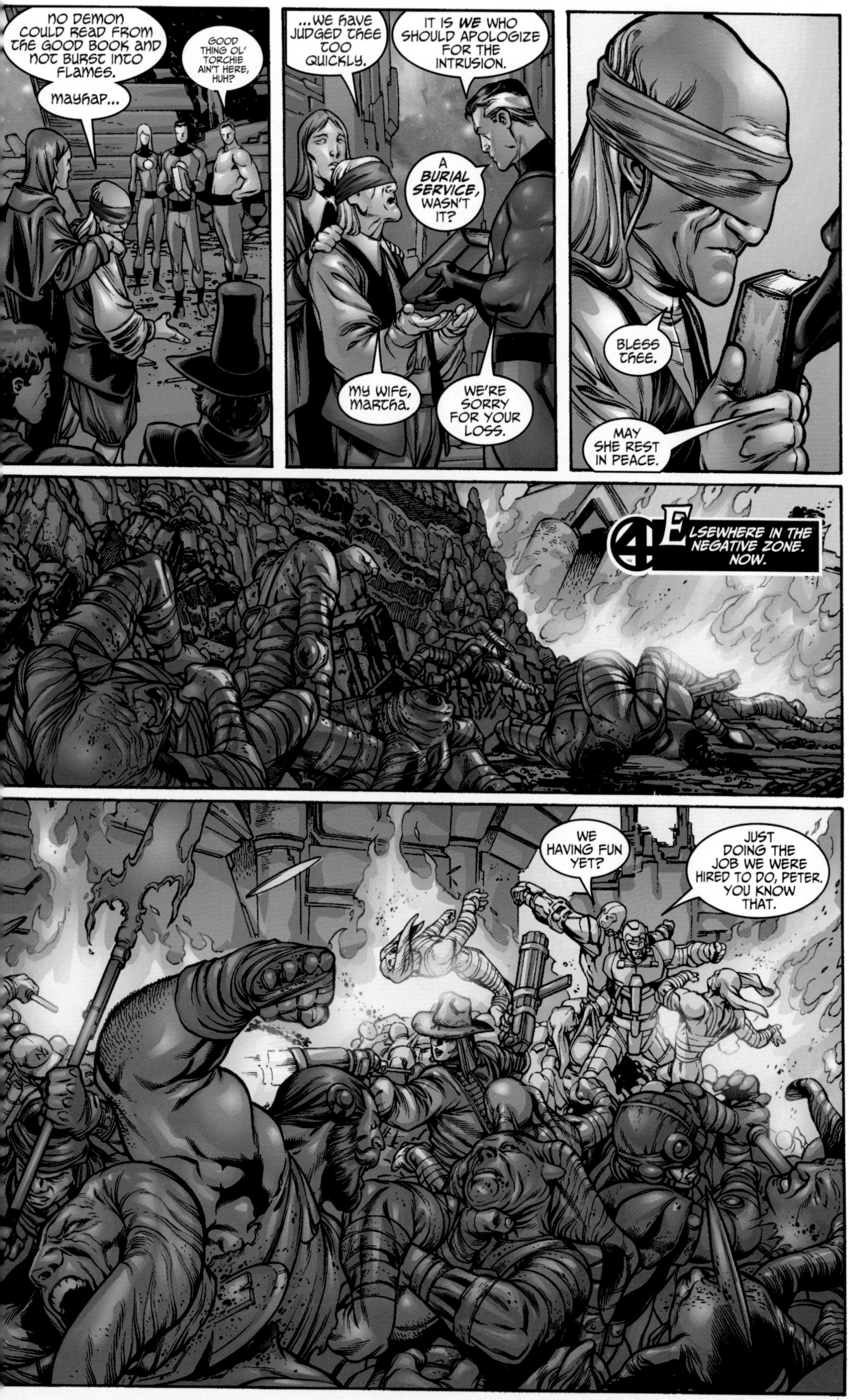
NO DEMON COULD READ FROM THE GOOD BOOK AND NOT BURST INTO FLAMES.
MAYHAP...
GOOD THING OL' TORCHIE AIN'T HERE, HUH?
...WE HAVE JUDGED THEE TOO QUICKLY.
IT IS WE WHO SHOULD APOLOGIZE FOR THE INTRUSION.
A BURIAL SERVICE, WASN'T IT?
MY WIFE, MARTHA.
WE'RE SORRY FOR YOUR LOSS.
BLESS THEE.
MAY SHE REST IN PEACE.
ELSEWHERE IN THE NEGATIVE ZONE. NOW.
WE HAVING FUN YET?
JUST DOING THE JOB WE WERE HIRED TO DO, PETER. YOU KNOW THAT.

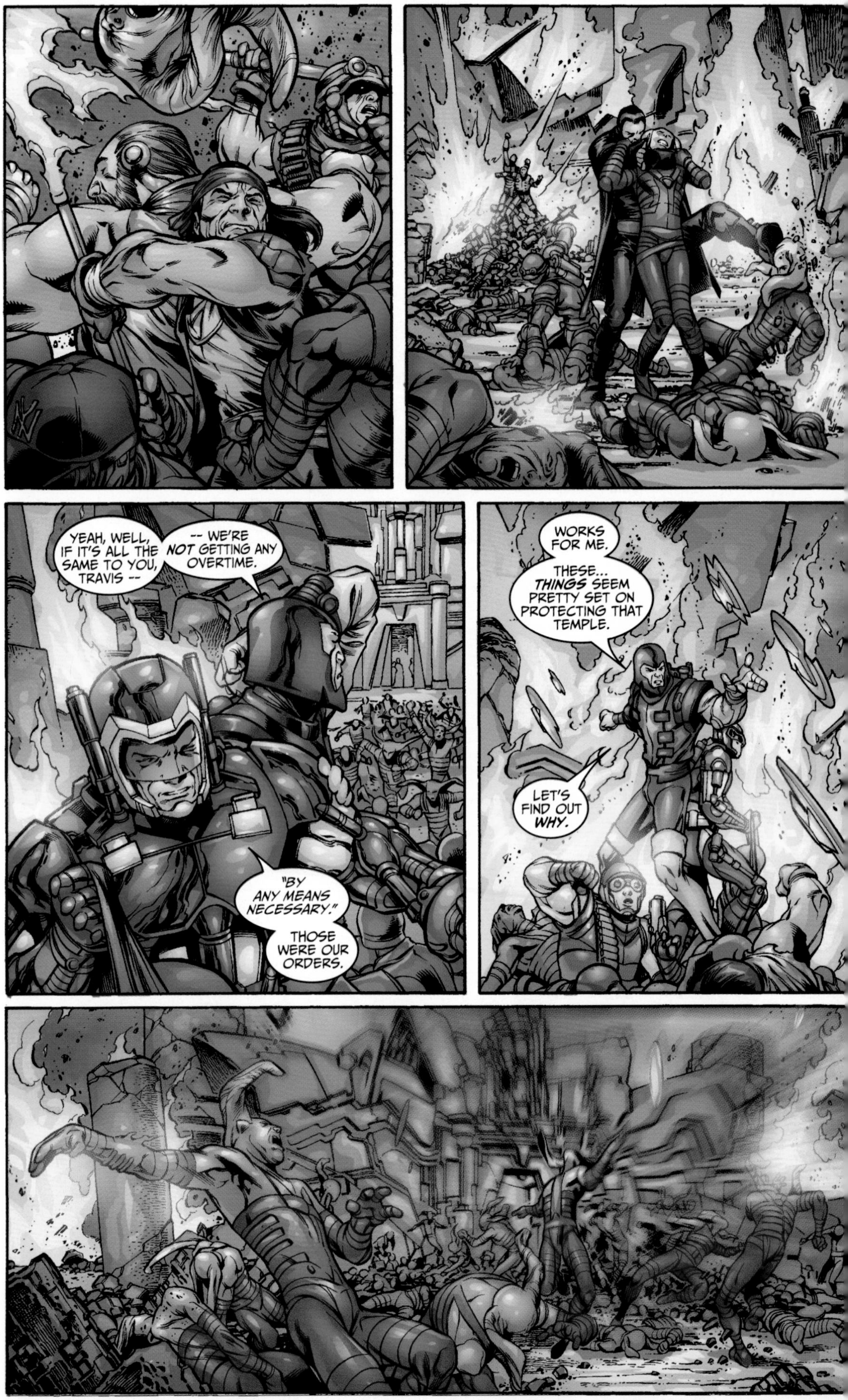

YEAH, WELL, IF IT'S ALL THE SAME TO YOU, TRAVIS --
-- WE'RE NOT GETTING ANY OVERTIME.
"BY ANY MEANS NECESSARY."
THOSE WERE OUR ORDERS.
WORKS FOR ME.
THESE... THINGS SEEM PRETTY SET ON PROTECTING THAT TEMPLE.
LET'S FIND OUT WHY.

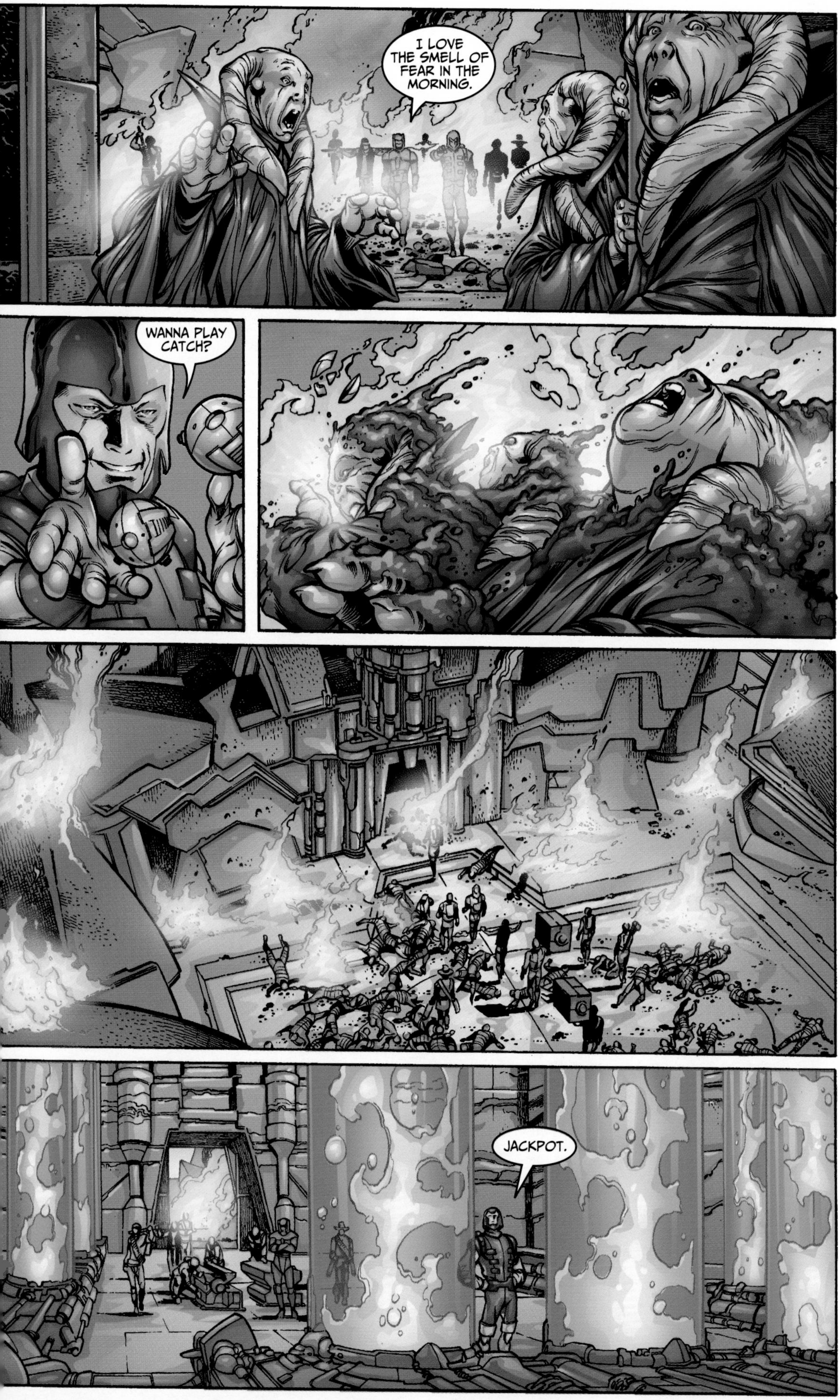

I LOVE THE SMELL OF FEAR IN THE MORNING.
WANNA PLAY CATCH?
JACKPOT.

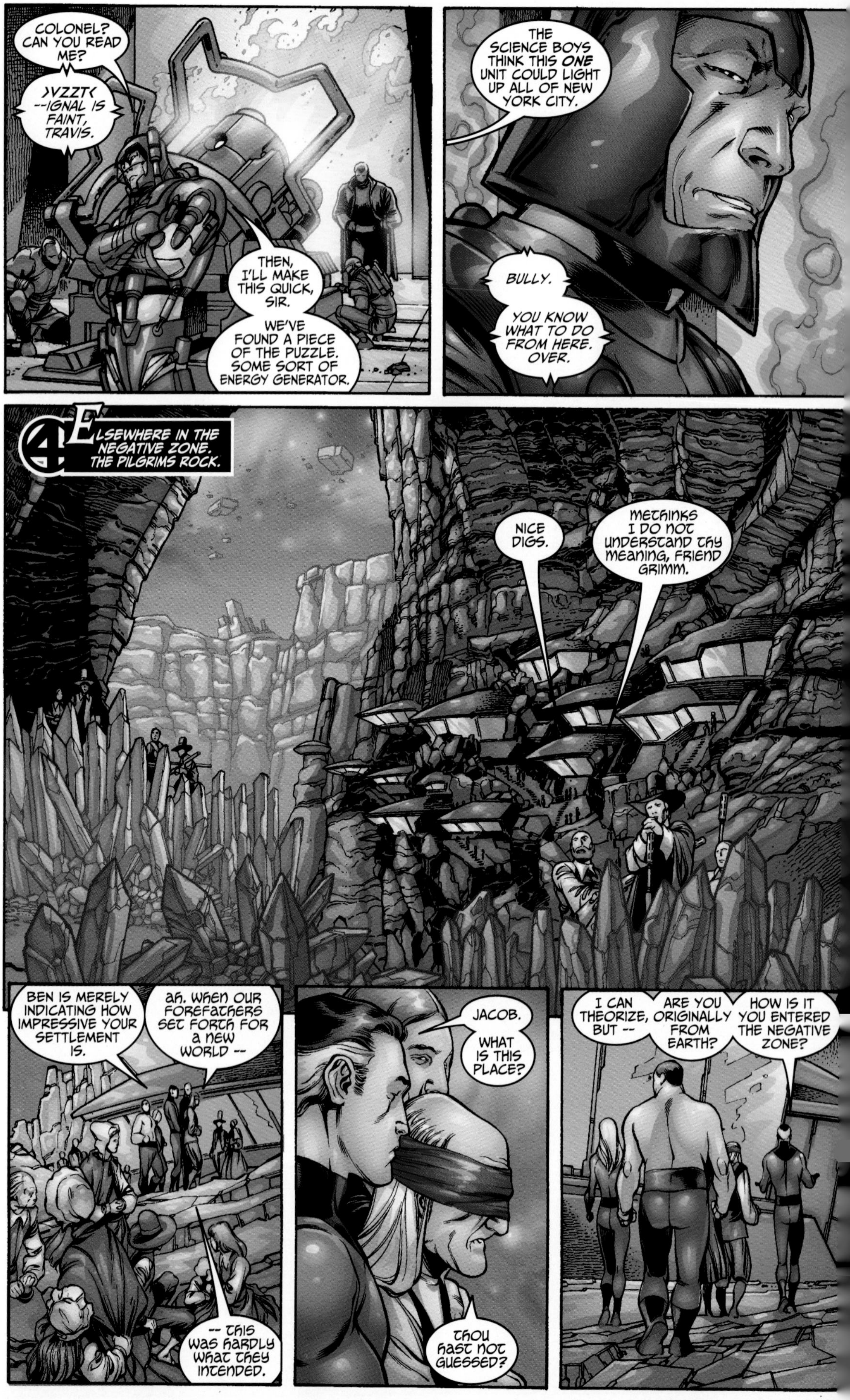
COLONEL? CAN YOU READ ME?
>VZZT< --IGNAL IS FAINT, TRAVIS.
THEN, I'LL MAKE THIS QUICK, SIR.
WE'VE FOUND A PIECE OF THE PUZZLE. SOME SORT OF ENERGY GENERATOR.
THE SCIENCE BOYS THINK THIS ONE UNIT COULD LIGHT UP ALL OF NEW YORK CITY.
BULLY.
YOU KNOW WHAT TO DO FROM HERE. OVER.
ELSEWHERE IN THE NEGATIVE ZONE. THE PILGRIMS ROCK.
NICE DIGS.
METHINKS I DO NOT UNDERSTAND THY MEANING, FRIEND GRIMM.
BEN IS MERELY INDICATING HOW IMPRESSIVE YOUR SETTLEMENT IS.
AH. WHEN OUR FOREFATHERS SET FORTH FOR A NEW WORLD --
-- THIS WAS HARDLY WHAT THEY INTENDED.
JACOB. WHAT IS THIS PLACE?
THOU HAST NOT GUESSED?
I CAN THEORIZE, BUT --
ARE YOU ORIGINALLY FROM EARTH?
HOW IS IT YOU ENTERED THE NEGATIVE ZONE?

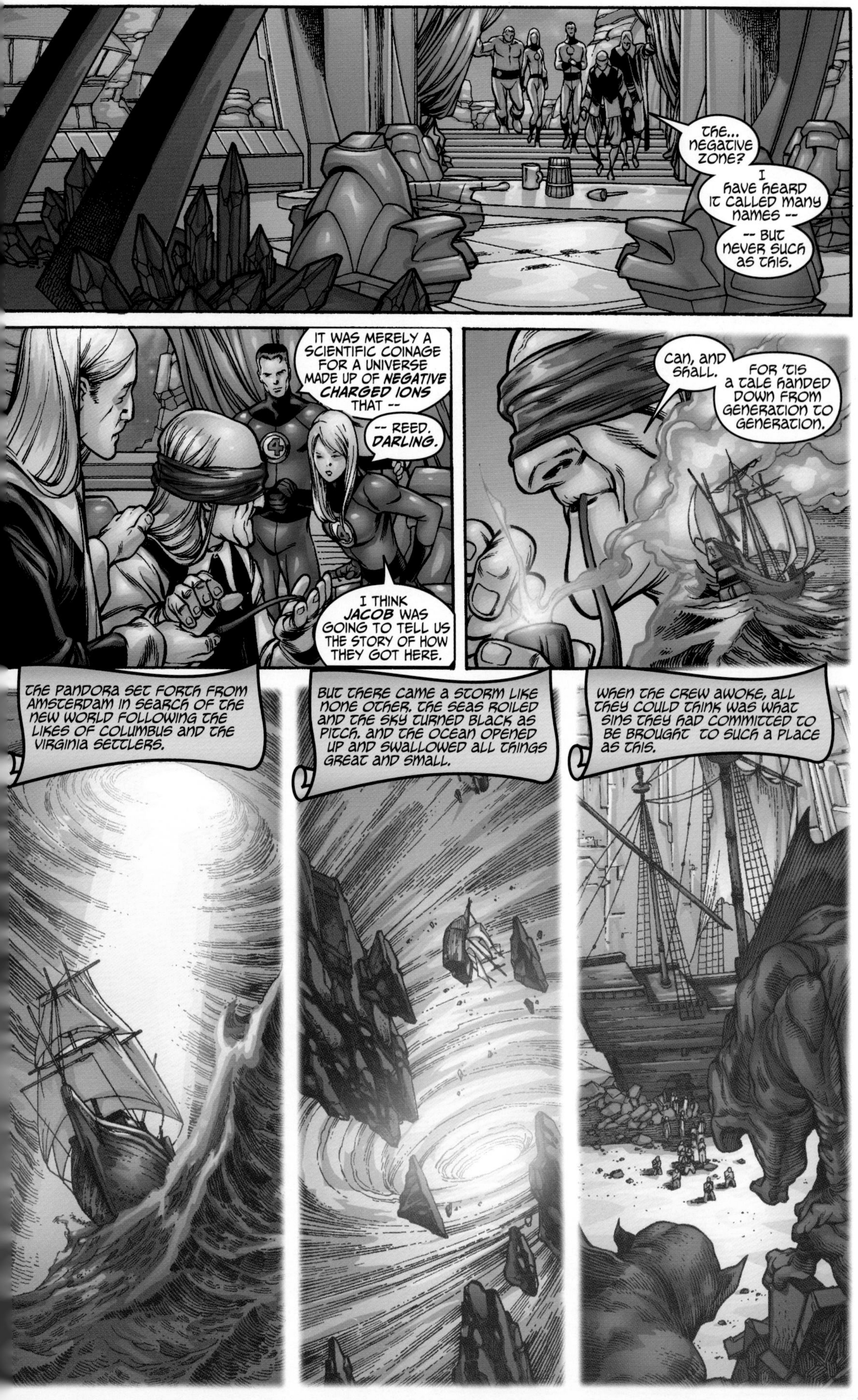
THE... NEGATIVE ZONE?
I HAVE HEARD IT CALLED MANY NAMES --
-- BUT NEVER SUCH AS THIS.
IT WAS MERELY A SCIENTIFIC COINAGE FOR A UNIVERSE MADE UP OF NEGATIVE CHARGED IONS THAT --
-- REED. DARLING.
I THINK JACOB WAS GOING TO TELL US THE STORY OF HOW THEY GOT HERE.
CAN, AND SHALL.
FOR 'TIS A TALE HANDED DOWN FROM GENERATION TO GENERATION.
THE PANDORA SET FORTH FROM AMSTERDAM IN SEARCH OF THE NEW WORLD FOLLOWING THE LIKES OF COLUMBUS AND THE VIRGINIA SETTLERS.
BUT THERE CAME A STORM LIKE NONE OTHER. THE SEAS ROILED AND THE SKY TURNED BLACK AS PITCH. AND THE OCEAN OPENED UP AND SWALLOWED ALL THINGS GREAT AND SMALL.
WHEN THE CREW AWOKE, ALL THEY COULD THINK WAS WHAT SINS THEY HAD COMMITTED TO BE BROUGHT TO SUCH A PLACE AS THIS.

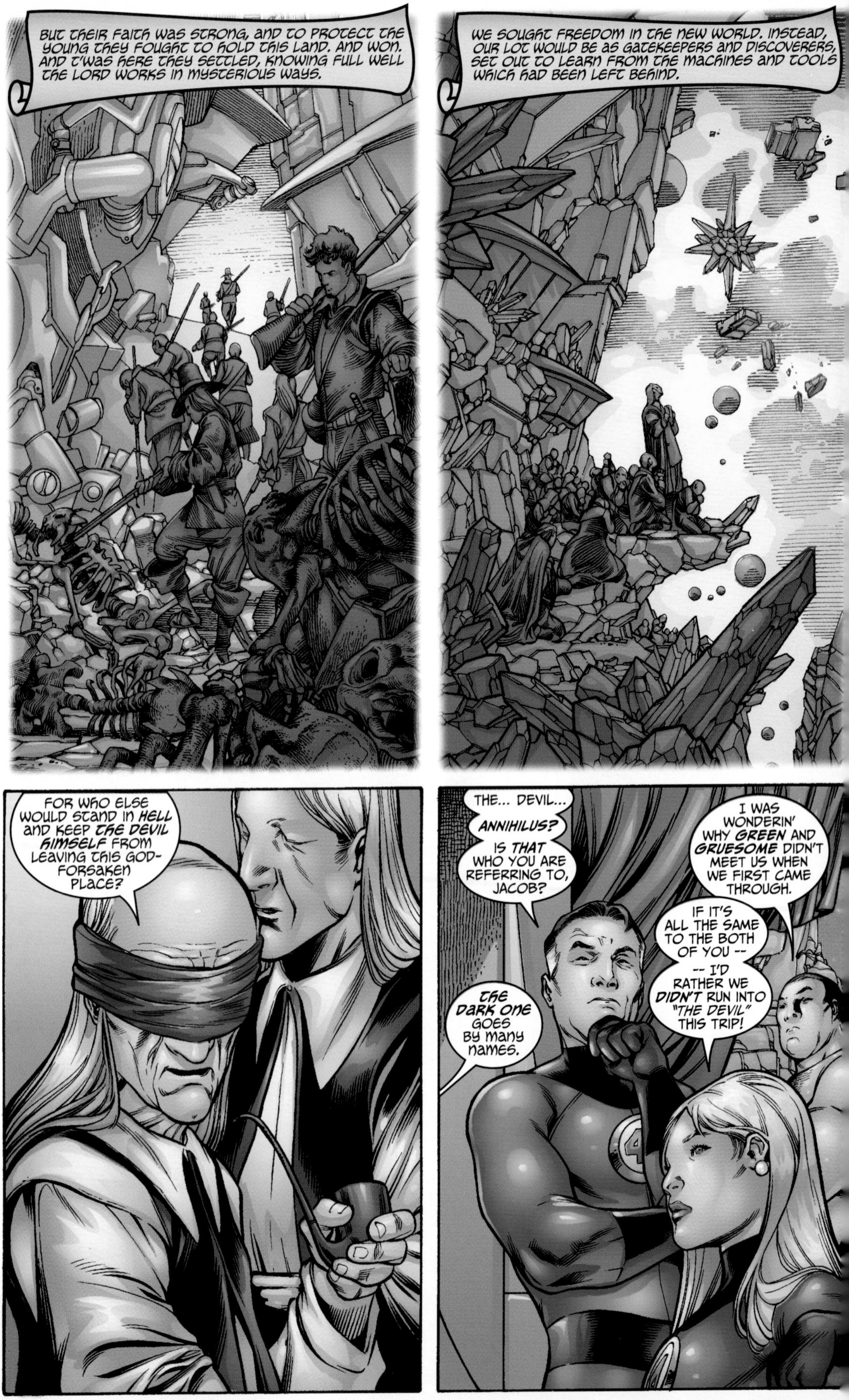
BUT THEIR FAITH WAS STRONG, AND TO PROTECT THE YOUNG THEY FOUGHT TO HOLD THIS LAND. AND WON. AND T'WAS HERE THEY SETTLED, KNOWING FULL WELL THE LORD WORKS IN MYSTERIOUS WAYS.
WE SOUGHT FREEDOM IN THE NEW WORLD. INSTEAD, OUR LOT WOULD BE AS GATEKEEPERS AND DISCOVERERS, SET OUT TO LEARN FROM THE MACHINES AND TOOLS WHICH HAD BEEN LEFT BEHIND.
FOR WHO ELSE WOULD STAND IN HELL AND KEEP THE DEVIL HIMSELF FROM LEAVING THIS GOD-FORSAKEN PLACE?
THE... DEVIL...
ANNIHILUS?
IS THAT WHO YOU ARE REFERRING TO, JACOB?
THE DARK ONE GOES BY MANY NAMES.
I WAS WONDERIN' WHY GREEN AND GRUESOME DIDN'T MEET US WHEN WE FIRST CAME THROUGH.
IF IT'S ALL THE SAME TO THE BOTH OF YOU --
-- I'D RATHER WE DIDN'T RUN INTO "THE DEVIL" THIS TRIP!

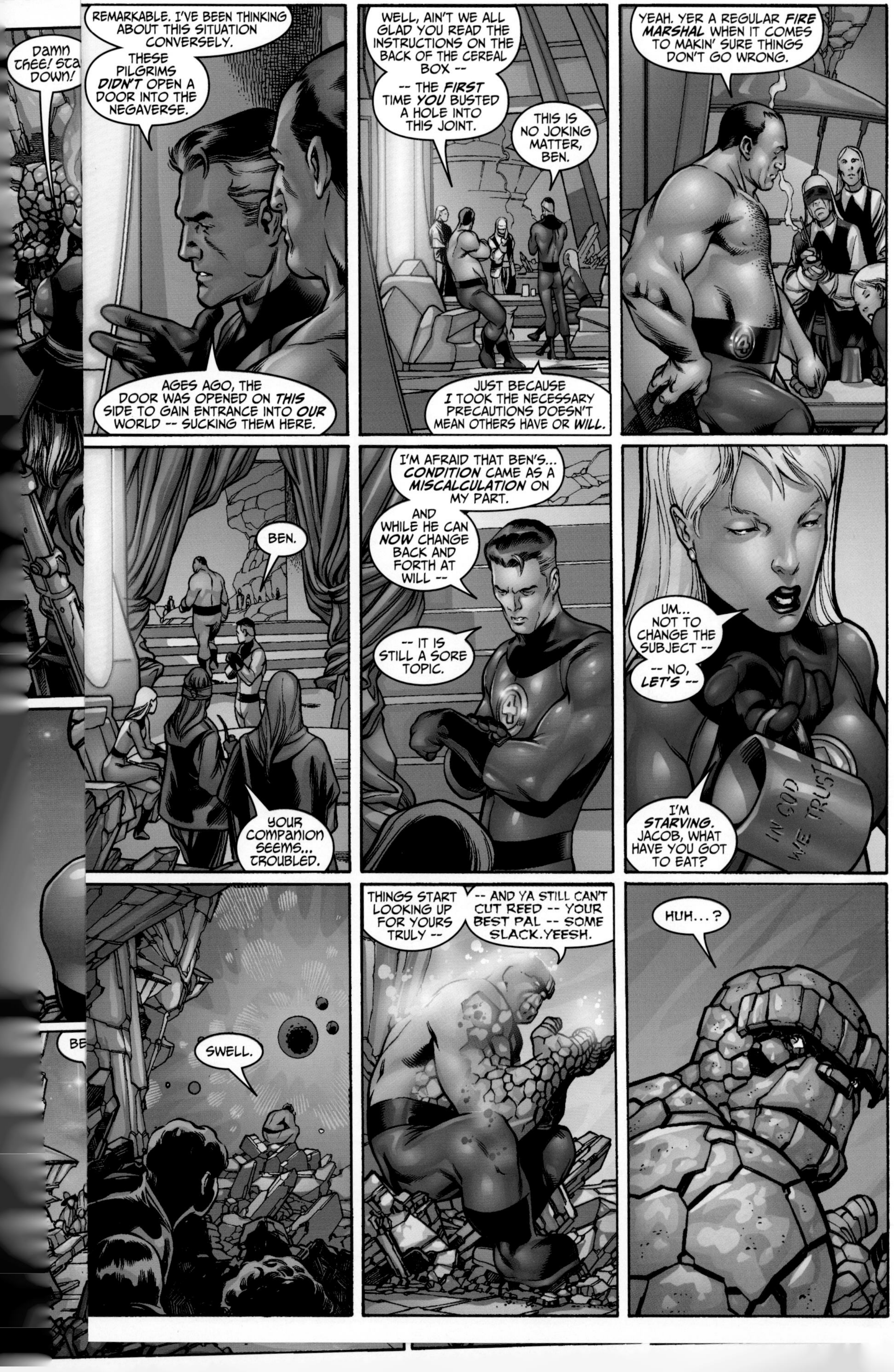
REMARKABLE. I'VE BEEN THINKING ABOUT THIS SITUATION CONVERSELY.
THESE PILGRIMS *DIDN'T* OPEN A DOOR INTO THE NEGAVERSE.
AGES AGO, THE DOOR WAS OPENED ON *THIS* SIDE TO GAIN ENTRANCE INTO *OUR* WORLD -- SUCKING THEM HERE.
WELL, AIN'T WE ALL GLAD YOU READ THE INSTRUCTIONS ON THE BACK OF THE CEREAL BOX --
-- THE *FIRST* TIME *YOU* BUSTED A HOLE INTO THIS JOINT.
THIS IS NO JOKING MATTER, BEN.
JUST BECAUSE *I* TOOK THE NECESSARY PRECAUTIONS DOESN'T MEAN OTHERS HAVE OR *WILL*.
YEAH. YER A REGULAR *FIRE MARSHAL* WHEN IT COMES TO MAKIN' SURE THINGS DON'T GO WRONG.
BEN.
YOUR COMPANION SEEMS... TROUBLED.
I'M AFRAID THAT BEN'S... *CONDITION* CAME AS A *MISCALCULATION* ON MY PART.
AND WHILE HE CAN *NOW* CHANGE BACK AND FORTH AT WILL --
-- IT IS STILL A SORE TOPIC.
UM... NOT TO CHANGE THE SUBJECT --
-- NO, *LET'S* --
IN GOD WE TRUST
I'M *STARVING.* JACOB, WHAT HAVE YOU GOT TO EAT?
SWELL.
THINGS START LOOKING UP FOR YOURS TRULY --
-- AND YA STILL CAN'T CUT REED -- YOUR BEST PAL -- SOME SLACK. YEESH.
HUH...?

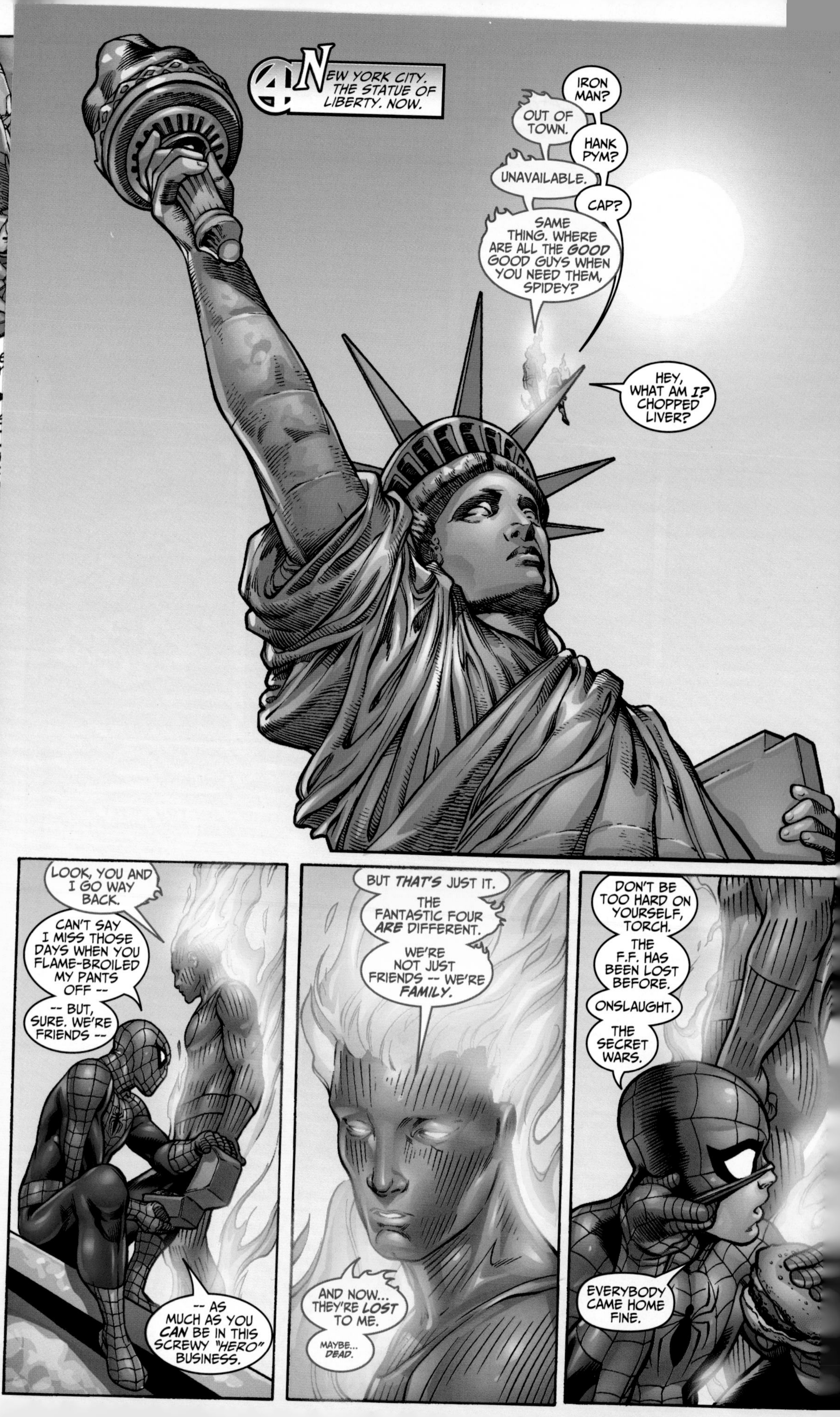
NEW YORK CITY. THE STATUE OF LIBERTY. NOW.
IRON MAN?
OUT OF TOWN.
HANK PYM?
UNAVAILABLE.
CAP?
SAME THING. WHERE ARE ALL THE GOOD GOOD GUYS WHEN YOU NEED THEM, SPIDEY?
HEY, WHAT AM I? CHOPPED LIVER?
LOOK, YOU AND I GO WAY BACK.
CAN'T SAY I MISS THOSE DAYS WHEN YOU FLAME-BROILED MY PANTS OFF --
-- BUT, SURE. WE'RE FRIENDS --
-- AS MUCH AS YOU CAN BE IN THIS SCREWY "HERO" BUSINESS.
BUT THAT'S JUST IT.
THE FANTASTIC FOUR ARE DIFFERENT.
WE'RE NOT JUST FRIENDS -- WE'RE FAMILY.
AND NOW... THEY'RE LOST TO ME.
MAYBE... DEAD.
DON'T BE TOO HARD ON YOURSELF, TORCH.
THE F.F. HAS BEEN LOST BEFORE.
ONSLAUGHT.
THE SECRET WARS.
EVERYBODY CAME HOME FINE.

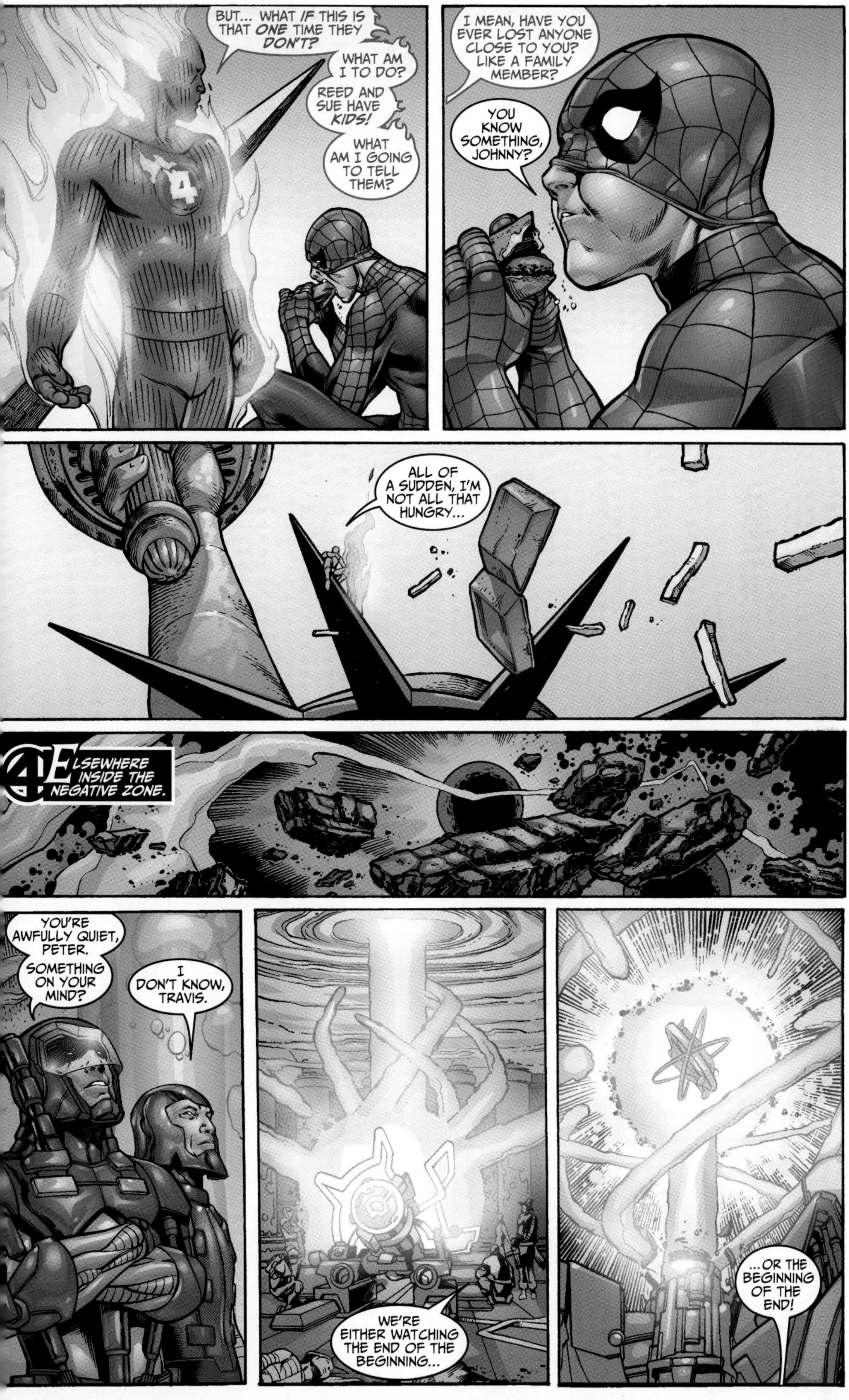
BUT... WHAT IF THIS IS THAT ONE TIME THEY DON'T?
WHAT AM I TO DO?
REED AND SUE HAVE KIDS!
WHAT AM I GOING TO TELL THEM?
I MEAN, HAVE YOU EVER LOST ANYONE CLOSE TO YOU? LIKE A FAMILY MEMBER?
YOU KNOW SOMETHING, JOHNNY?
ALL OF A SUDDEN, I'M NOT ALL THAT HUNGRY...
ELSEWHERE INSIDE THE NEGATIVE ZONE.
YOU'RE AWFULLY QUIET, PETER. SOMETHING ON YOUR MIND?
I DON'T KNOW, TRAVIS.
WE'RE EITHER WATCHING THE END OF THE BEGINNING...
...OR THE BEGINNING OF THE END!

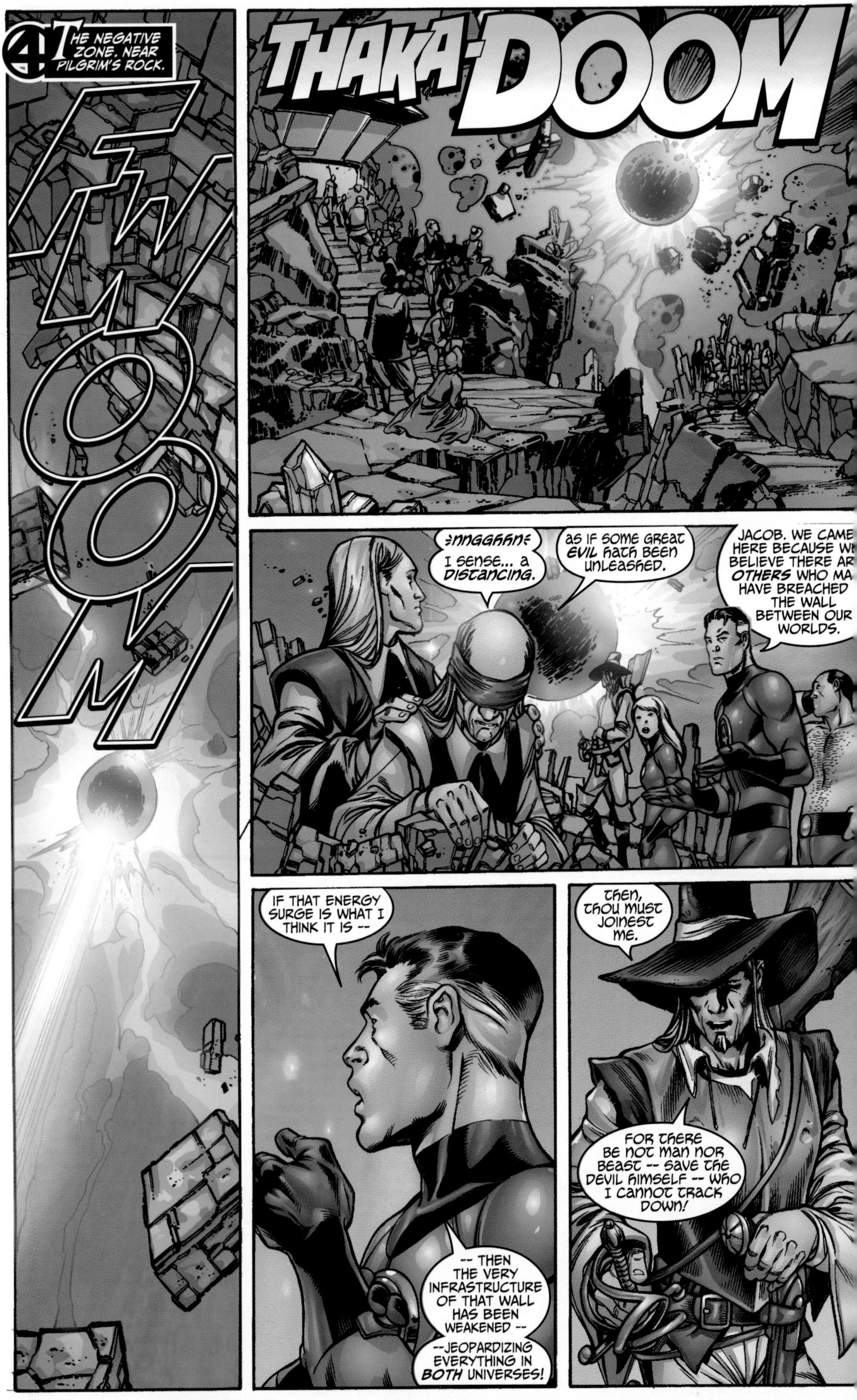

THE NEGATIVE ZONE. NEAR PILGRIM'S ROCK.
FWOOOM
THAKA-DOOM
=NNGGHHN= I SENSE... A DISTANCING.
AS IF SOME GREAT EVIL HATH BEEN UNLEASHED.
JACOB. WE CAME HERE BECAUSE W BELIEVE THERE AR OTHERS WHO MA HAVE BREACHED THE WALL BETWEEN OUR WORLDS.
IF THAT ENERGY SURGE IS WHAT I THINK IT IS --
-- THEN THE VERY INFRASTRUCTURE OF THAT WALL HAS BEEN WEAKENED --
--JEOPARDIZING EVERYTHING IN BOTH UNIVERSES!
THEN, THOU MUST JOINEST ME.
FOR THERE BE NOT MAN NOR BEAST -- SAVE THE DEVIL HIMSELF -- WHO I CANNOT TRACK DOWN!

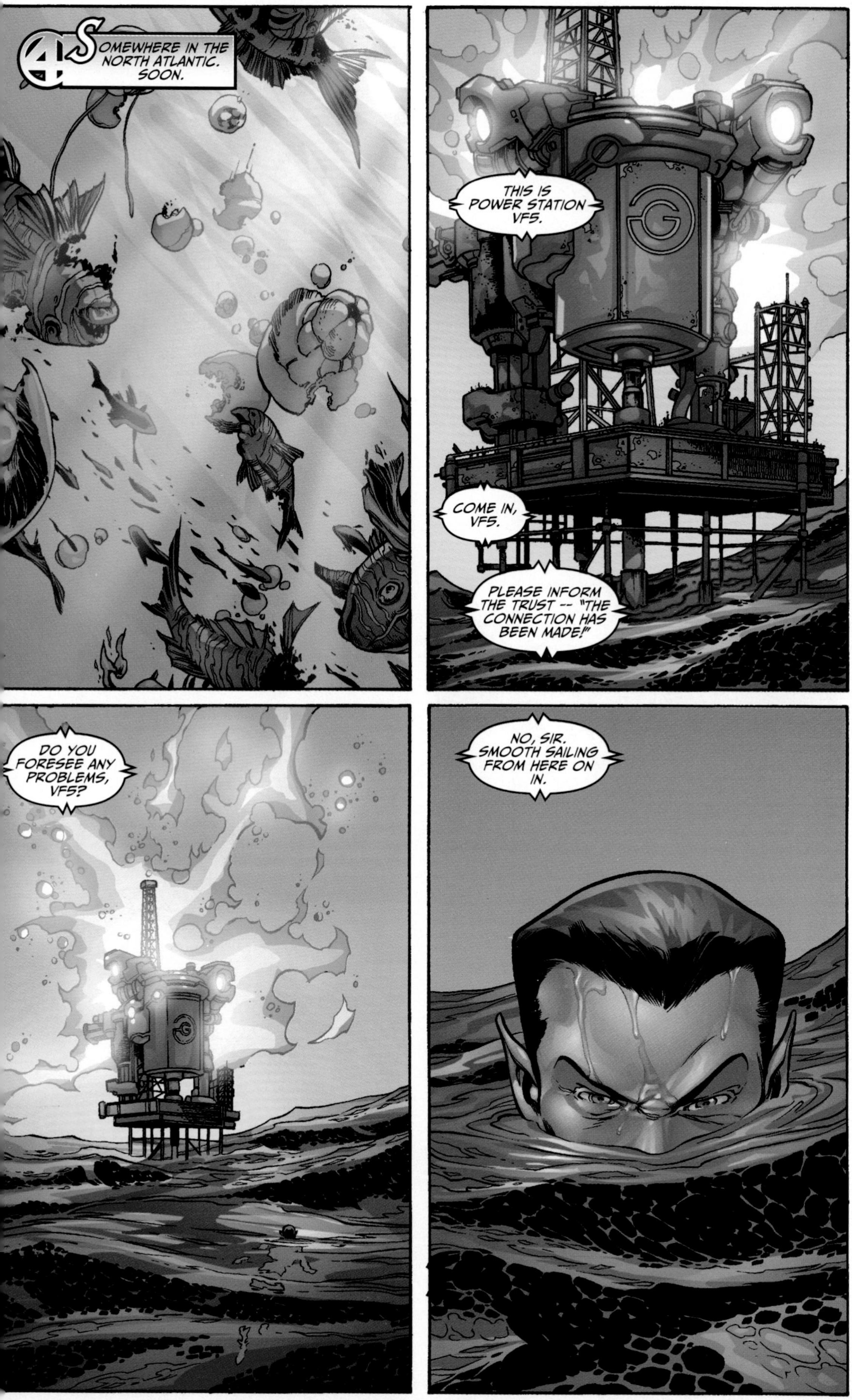
SOMEWHERE IN THE NORTH ATLANTIC. SOON.
THIS IS POWER STATION VF5.
COME IN, VF5.
PLEASE INFORM THE TRUST -- "THE CONNECTION HAS BEEN MADE!"
DO YOU FORESEE ANY PROBLEMS, VF5?
NO, SIR. SMOOTH SAILING FROM HERE ON IN.

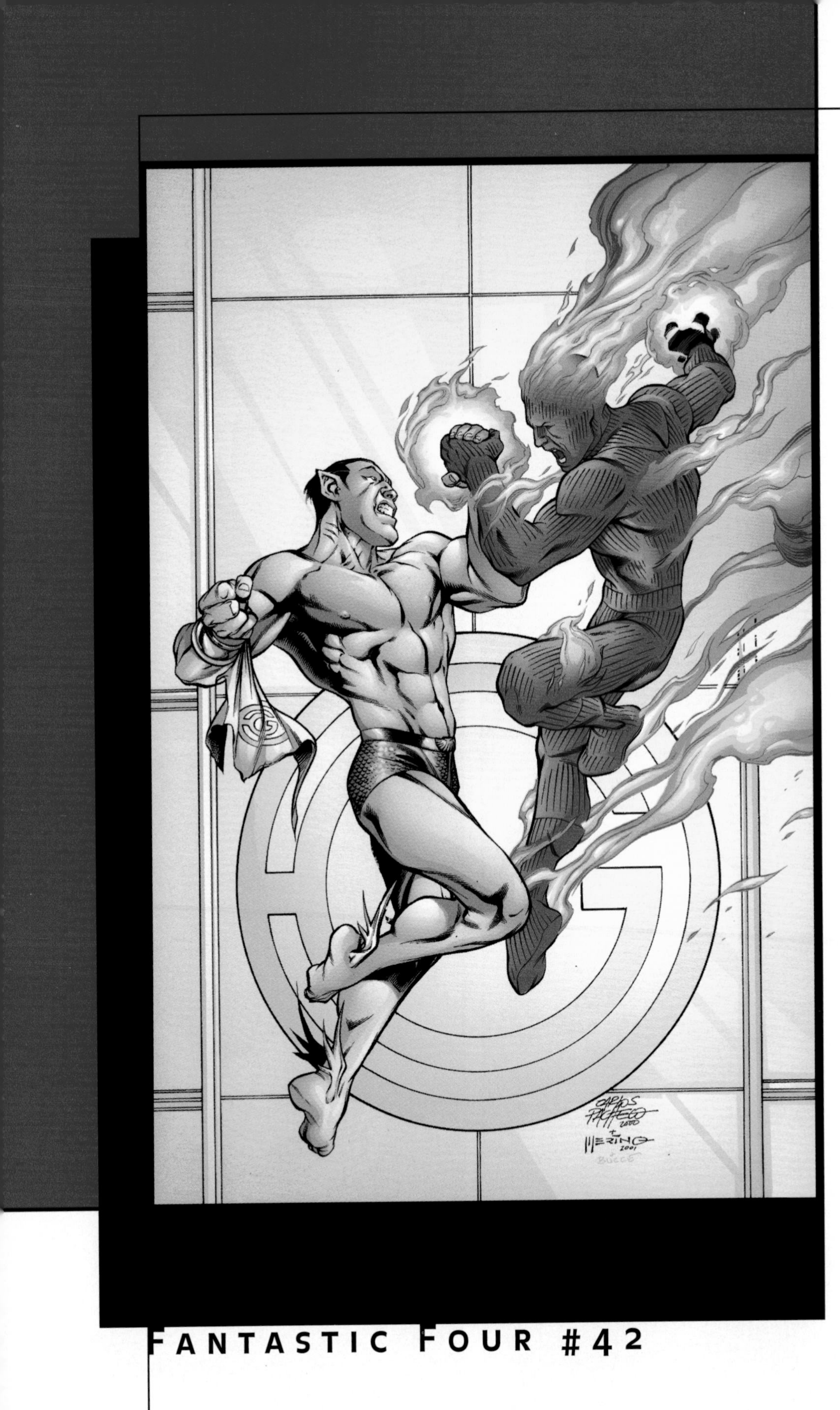
CARLOS PACHECO 2000
MERINO 2001

FANTASTIC FOUR #42

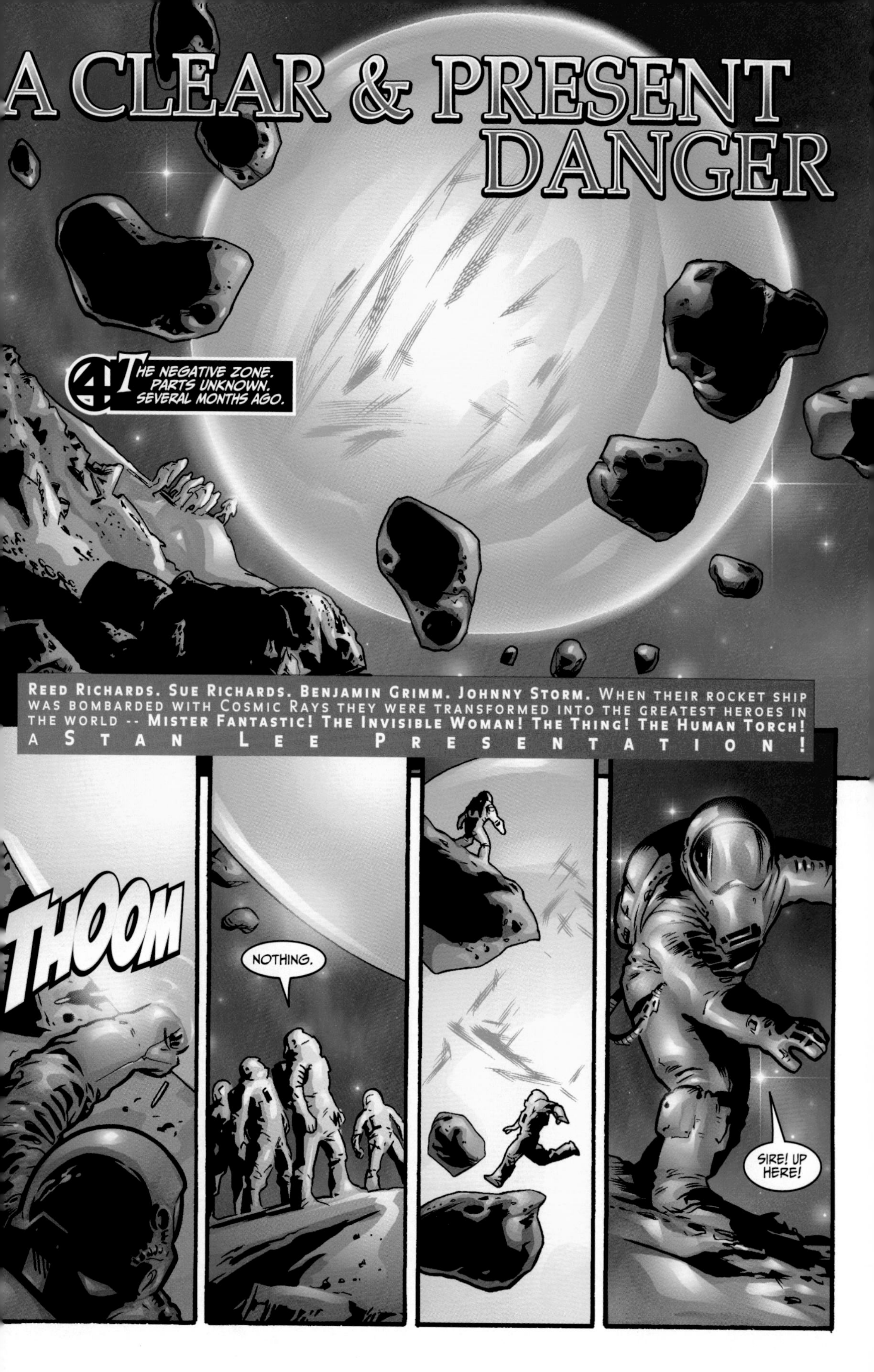
A CLEAR & PRESENT DANGER
THE NEGATIVE ZONE. PARTS UNKNOWN. SEVERAL MONTHS AGO.
REED RICHARDS. SUE RICHARDS. BENJAMIN GRIMM. JOHNNY STORM. WHEN THEIR ROCKET SHIP WAS BOMBARDED WITH COSMIC RAYS THEY WERE TRANSFORMED INTO THE GREATEST HEROES IN THE WORLD -- MISTER FANTASTIC! THE INVISIBLE WOMAN! THE THING! THE HUMAN TORCH!
A STAN LEE PRESENTATION!
THOOM
NOTHING.
SIRE! UP HERE!

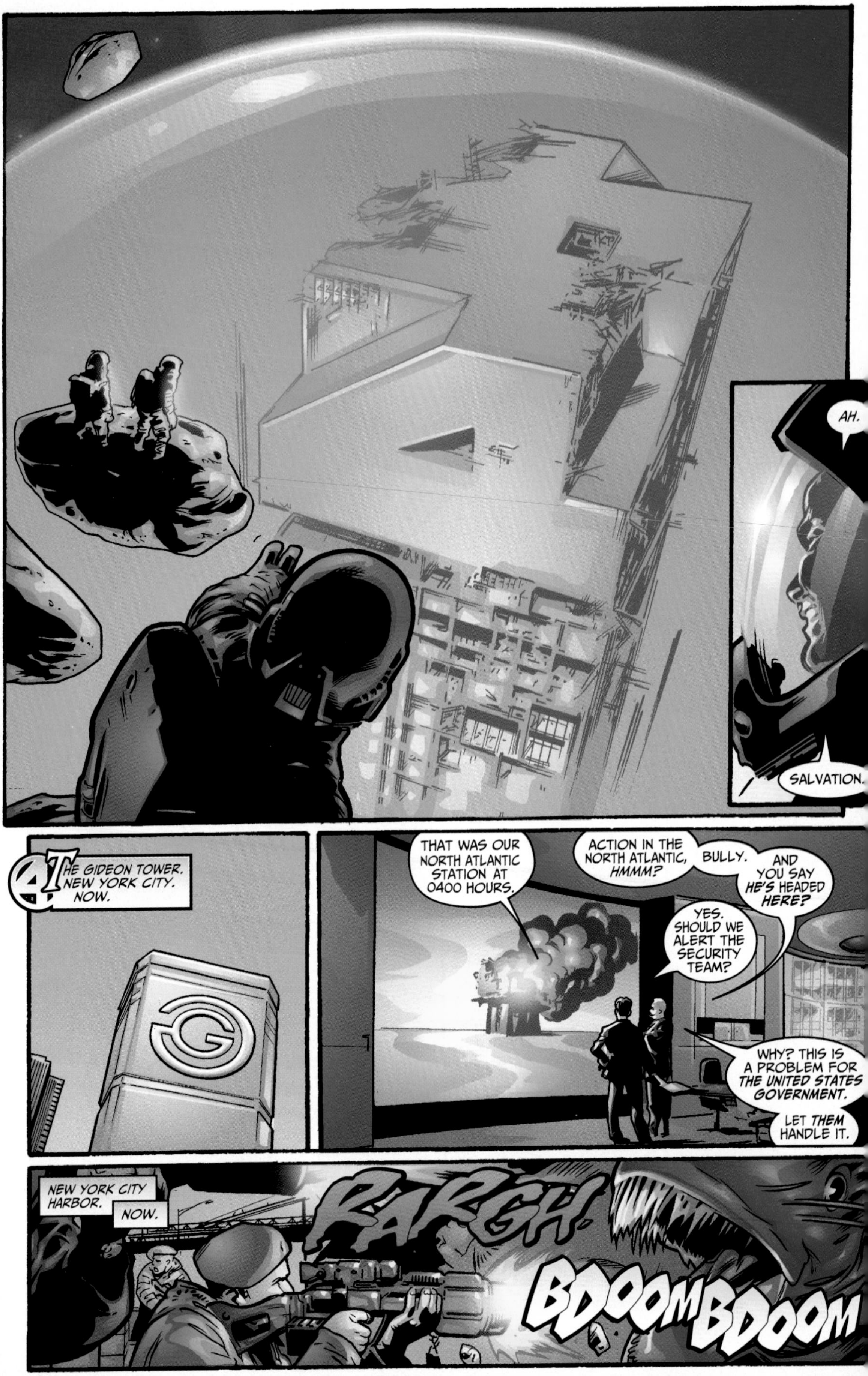
AH.
SALVATION.
THE GIDEON TOWER. NEW YORK CITY. NOW.
THAT WAS OUR NORTH ATLANTIC STATION AT 0400 HOURS.
ACTION IN THE NORTH ATLANTIC, HMMM?
BULLY.
AND YOU SAY HE'S HEADED HERE?
YES. SHOULD WE ALERT THE SECURITY TEAM?
WHY? THIS IS A PROBLEM FOR THE UNITED STATES GOVERNMENT.
LET THEM HANDLE IT.
NEW YORK CITY HARBOR.
NOW.
RARGH!
BDOOM BDOOM

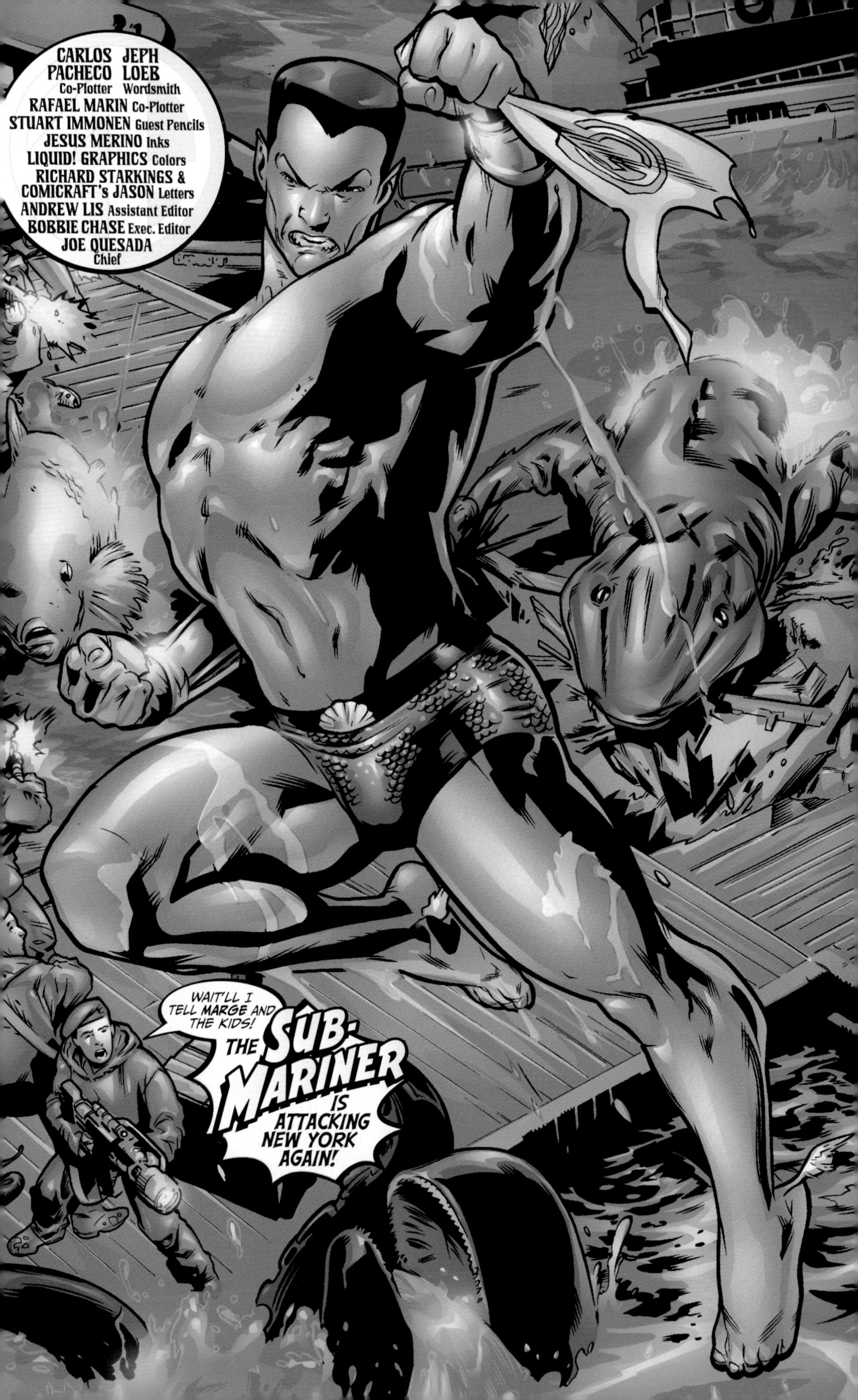
CARLOS PACHECO Co-Plotter
JEPH LOEB Wordsmith
RAFAEL MARIN Co-Plotter
STUART IMMONEN Guest Pencils
JESUS MERINO Inks
LIQUID! GRAPHICS Colors
RICHARD STARKINGS & COMICRAFT's JASON Letters
ANDREW LIS Assistant Editor
BOBBIE CHASE Exec. Editor
JOE QUESADA Chief
WAIT'LL I TELL MARGE AND THE KIDS! THE SUB-MARINER IS ATTACKING NEW YORK AGAIN!

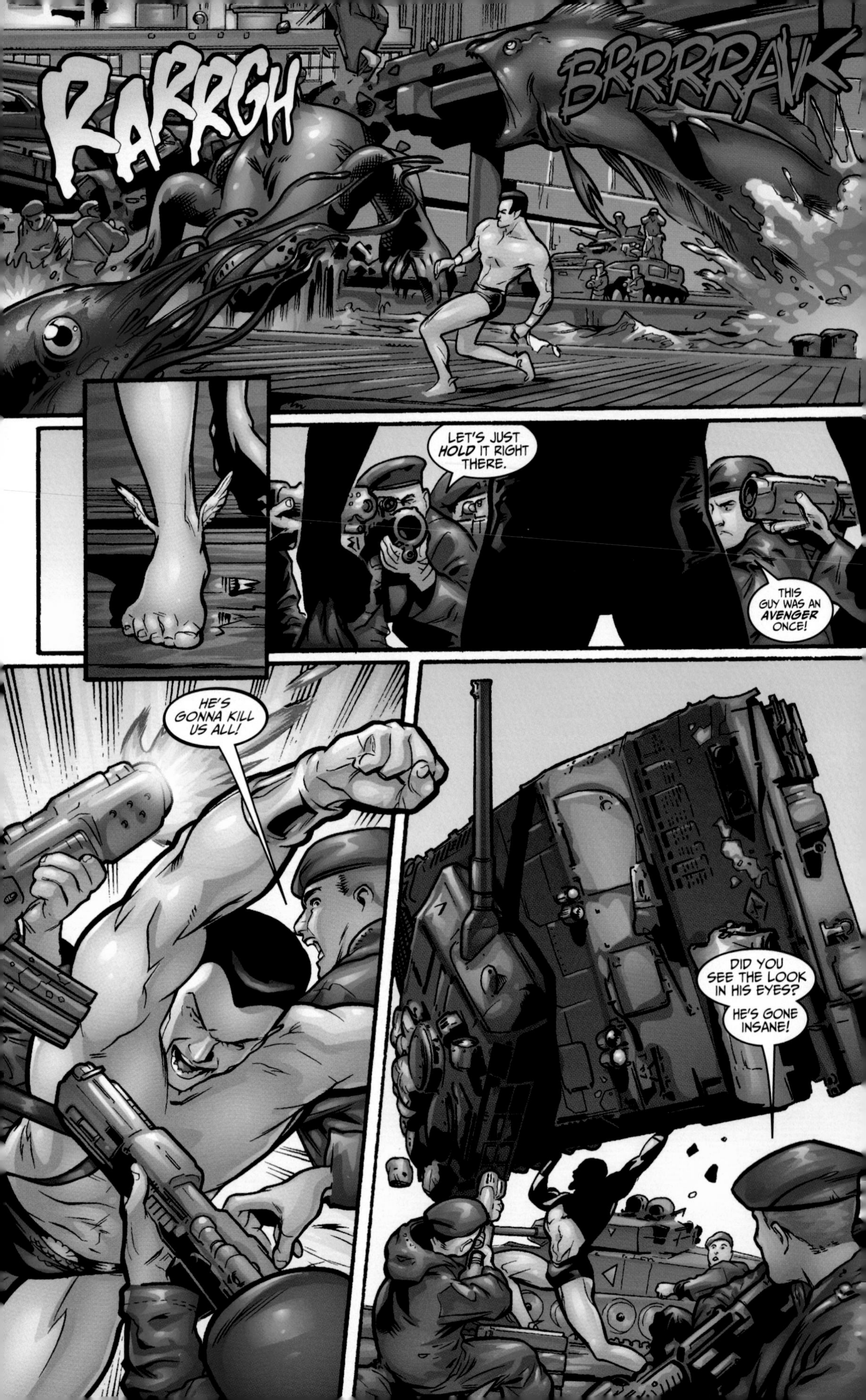
RARRGH
BRRRRRAK
LET'S JUST HOLD IT RIGHT THERE.
THIS GUY WAS AN AVENGER ONCE!
HE'S GONNA KILL US ALL!
DID YOU SEE THE LOOK IN HIS EYES?
HE'S GONE INSANE!

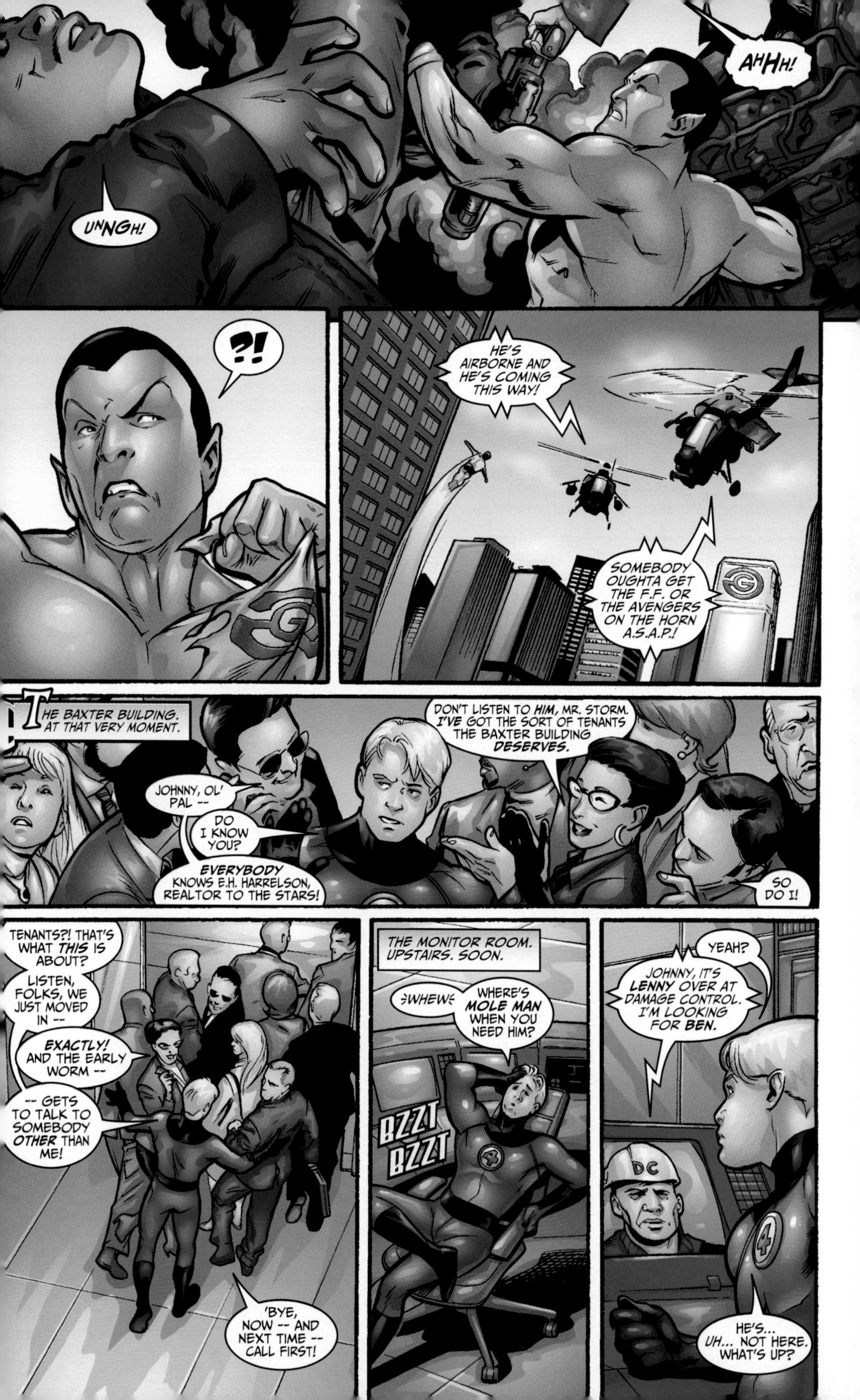
UNNGH!
AHHH!
?!
HE'S AIRBORNE AND HE'S COMING THIS WAY!
SOMEBODY OUGHTA GET THE F.F. OR THE AVENGERS ON THE HORN A.S.A.P.!
THE BAXTER BUILDING. AT THAT VERY MOMENT.
JOHNNY, OL' PAL --
DO I KNOW YOU?
EVERYBODY KNOWS E.H. HARRELSON, REALTOR TO THE STARS!
DON'T LISTEN TO HIM, MR. STORM. I'VE GOT THE SORT OF TENANTS THE BAXTER BUILDING DESERVES.
SO DO I!
TENANTS?! THAT'S WHAT THIS IS ABOUT?
LISTEN, FOLKS, WE JUST MOVED IN --
EXACTLY! AND THE EARLY WORM --
-- GETS TO TALK TO SOMEBODY OTHER THAN ME!
'BYE, NOW -- AND NEXT TIME -- CALL FIRST!
THE MONITOR ROOM. UPSTAIRS. SOON.
WHEW
WHERE'S MOLE MAN WHEN YOU NEED HIM?
BZZT BZZT
YEAH?
JOHNNY, IT'S LENNY OVER AT DAMAGE CONTROL. I'M LOOKING FOR BEN.
DC
HE'S... UH... NOT HERE. WHAT'S UP?

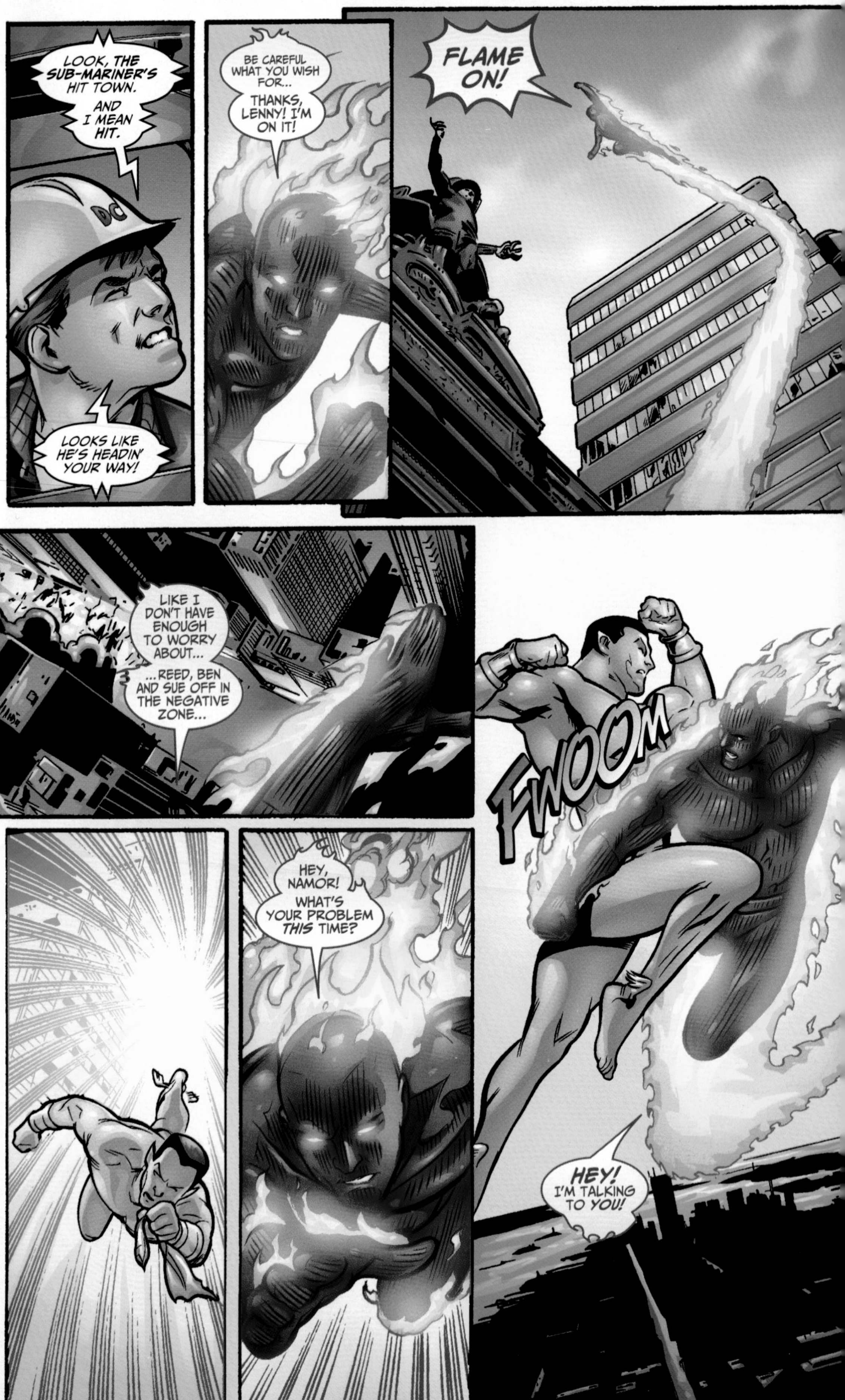
LOOK, THE SUB-MARINER'S HIT TOWN.
AND I MEAN HIT.
LOOKS LIKE HE'S HEADIN' YOUR WAY!
BE CAREFUL WHAT YOU WISH FOR...
THANKS, LENNY! I'M ON IT!
FLAME ON!
LIKE I DON'T HAVE ENOUGH TO WORRY ABOUT...
...REED, BEN AND SUE OFF IN THE NEGATIVE ZONE...
FWOOM
HEY, NAMOR! WHAT'S YOUR PROBLEM THIS TIME?
HEY! I'M TALKING TO YOU!

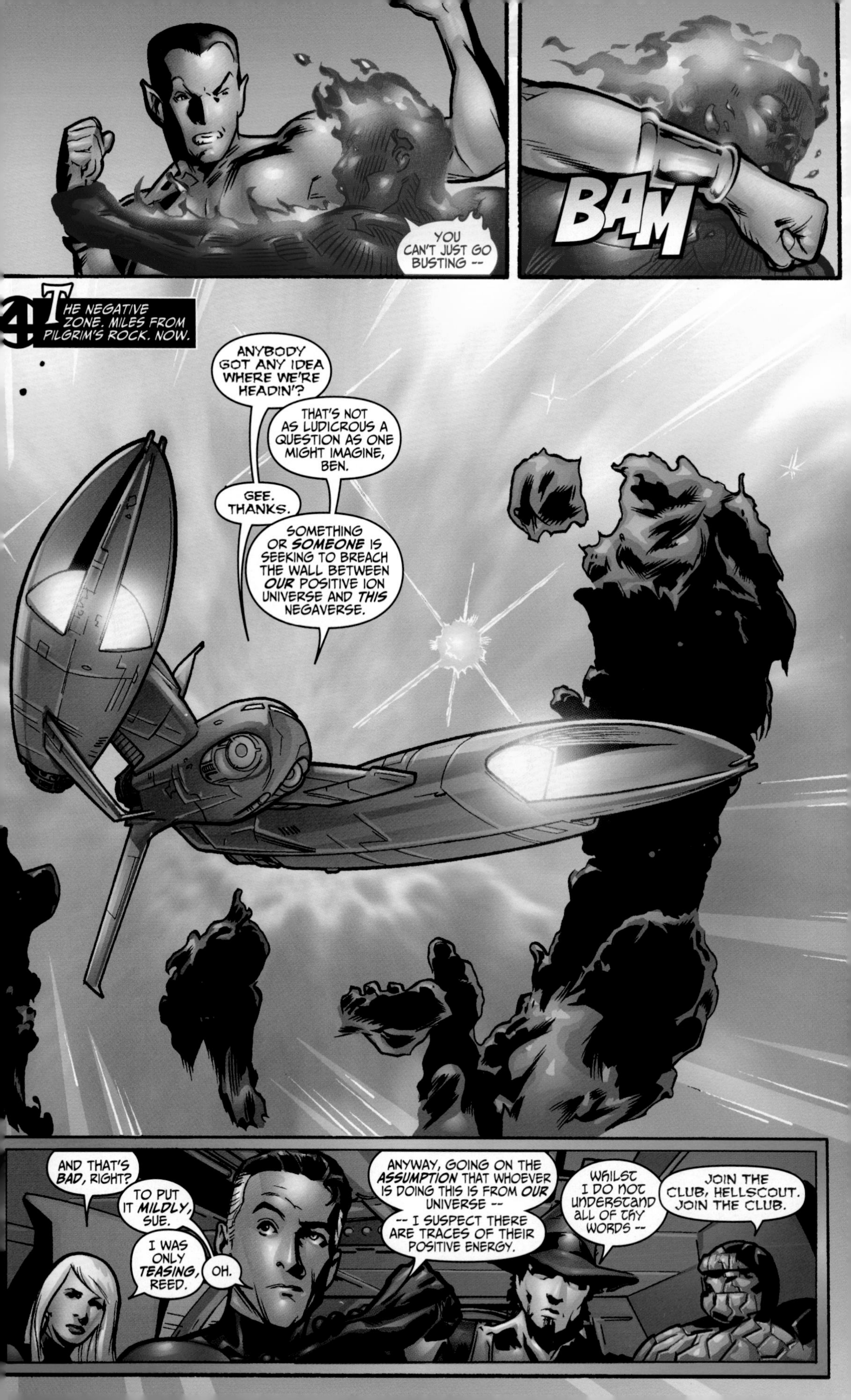

YOU CAN'T JUST GO BUSTING --
BAM
THE NEGATIVE ZONE. MILES FROM PILGRIM'S ROCK. NOW.
ANYBODY GOT ANY IDEA WHERE WE'RE HEADIN'?
THAT'S NOT AS LUDICROUS A QUESTION AS ONE MIGHT IMAGINE, BEN.
GEE. THANKS.
SOMETHING OR SOMEONE IS SEEKING TO BREACH THE WALL BETWEEN OUR POSITIVE ION UNIVERSE AND THIS NEGAVERSE.
AND THAT'S BAD, RIGHT?
TO PUT IT MILDLY, SUE.
I WAS ONLY TEASING, REED.
OH.
ANYWAY, GOING ON THE ASSUMPTION THAT WHOEVER IS DOING THIS IS FROM OUR UNIVERSE --
-- I SUSPECT THERE ARE TRACES OF THEIR POSITIVE ENERGY.
WHILST I DO NOT UNDERSTAND ALL OF THY WORDS --
JOIN THE CLUB, HELLSCOUT. JOIN THE CLUB.

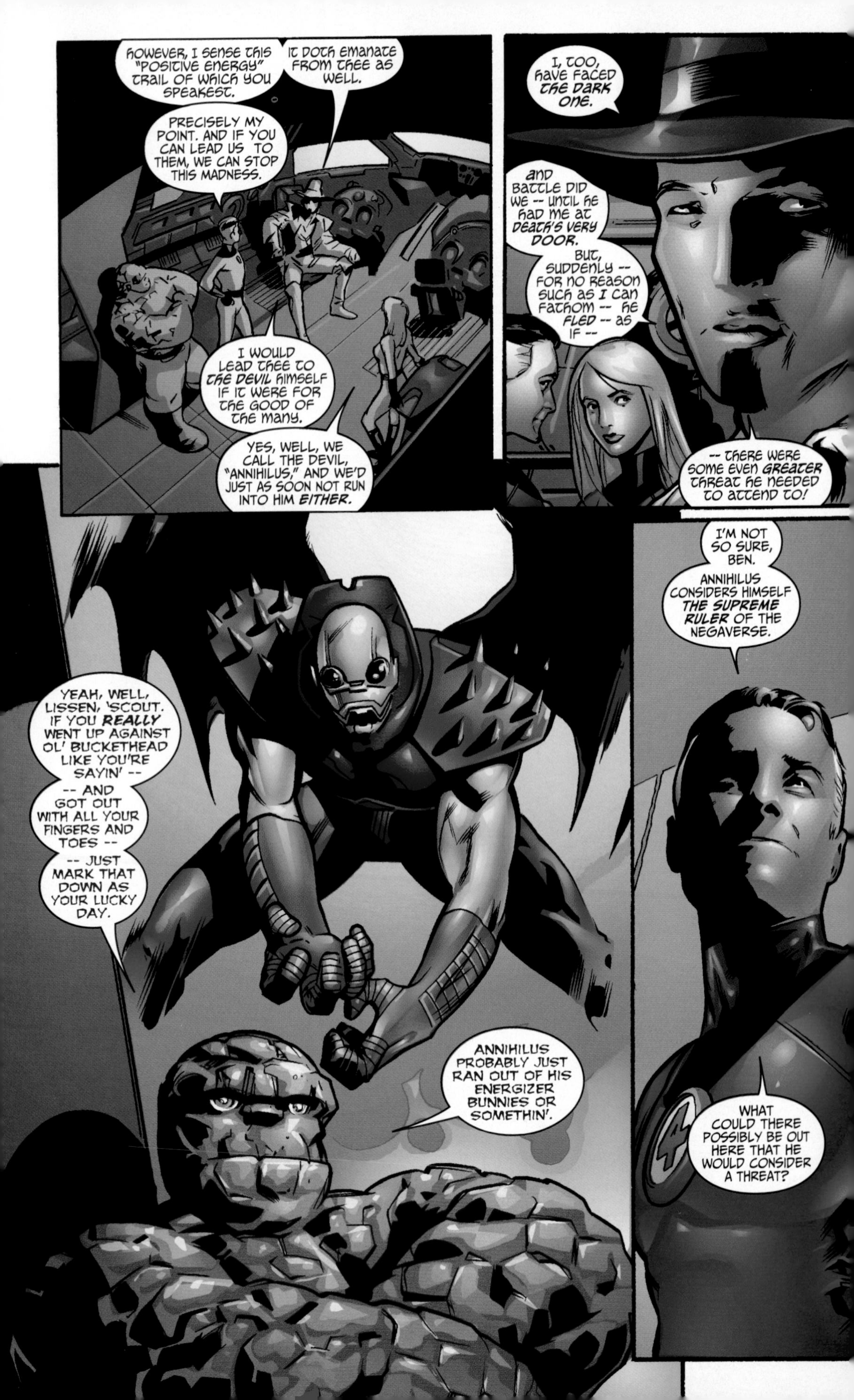
HOWEVER, I SENSE THIS "POSITIVE ENERGY" TRAIL OF WHICH YOU SPEAKEST.
IT DOTH EMANATE FROM THEE AS WELL.
PRECISELY MY POINT. AND IF YOU CAN LEAD US TO THEM, WE CAN STOP THIS MADNESS.
I WOULD LEAD THEE TO THE DEVIL HIMSELF IF IT WERE FOR THE GOOD OF THE MANY.
YES, WELL, WE CALL THE DEVIL, "ANNIHILUS," AND WE'D JUST AS SOON NOT RUN INTO HIM EITHER.
I, TOO, HAVE FACED THE DARK ONE.
AND BATTLE DID WE -- UNTIL HE HAD ME AT DEATH'S VERY DOOR.
BUT, SUDDENLY -- FOR NO REASON SUCH AS I CAN FATHOM -- HE FLED -- AS IF --
-- THERE WERE SOME EVEN GREATER THREAT HE NEEDED TO ATTEND TO!
YEAH, WELL, LISSEN, 'SCOUT. IF YOU REALLY WENT UP AGAINST OL' BUCKETHEAD LIKE YOU'RE SAYIN' --
-- AND GOT OUT WITH ALL YOUR FINGERS AND TOES --
-- JUST MARK THAT DOWN AS YOUR LUCKY DAY.
ANNIHILUS PROBABLY JUST RAN OUT OF HIS ENERGIZER BUNNIES OR SOMETHIN'.
I'M NOT SO SURE, BEN.
ANNIHILUS CONSIDERS HIMSELF THE SUPREME RULER OF THE NEGAVERSE.
WHAT COULD THERE POSSIBLY BE OUT HERE THAT HE WOULD CONSIDER A THREAT?

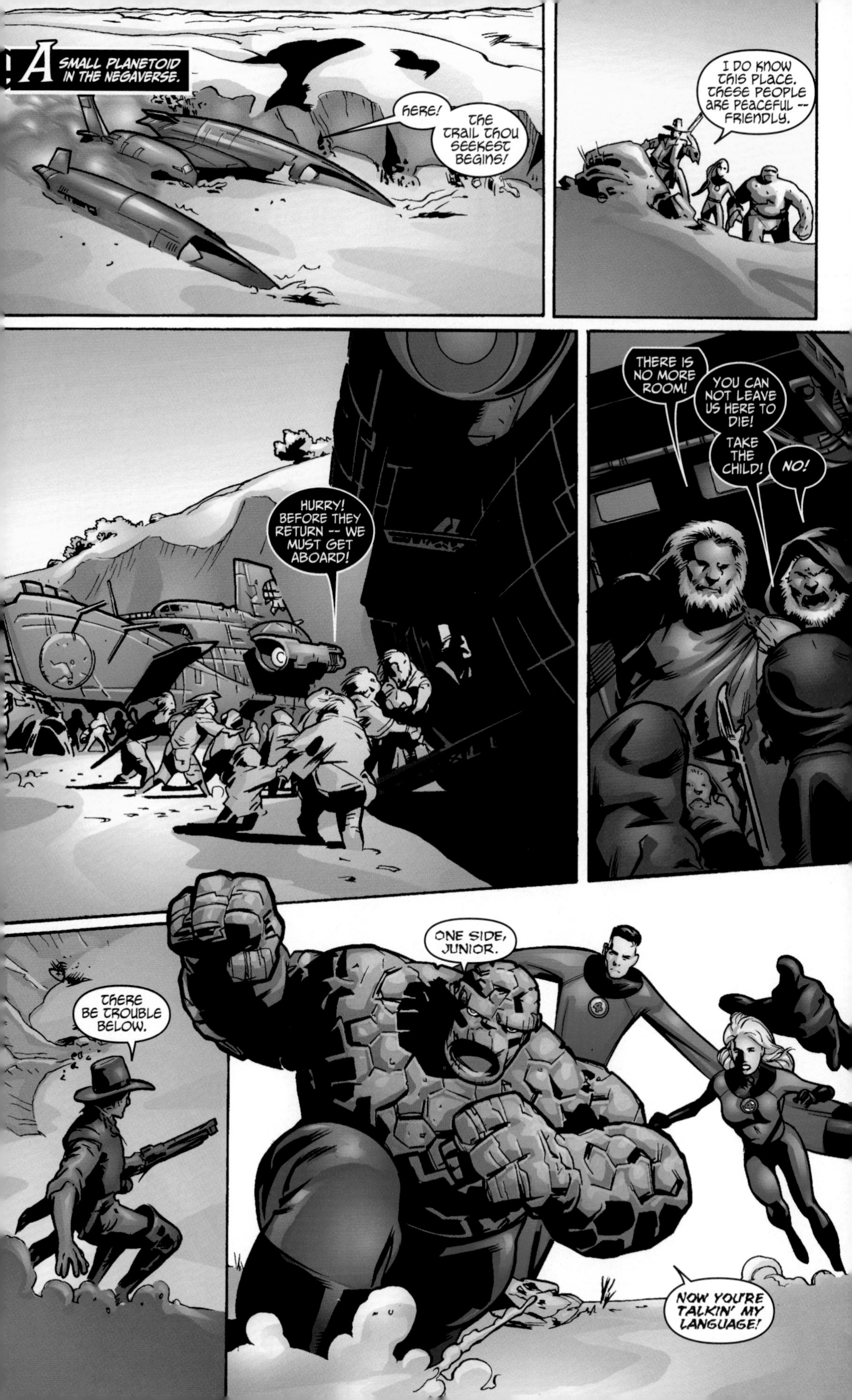
A SMALL PLANETOID IN THE NEGAVERSE.
HERE!
THE TRAIL THOU SEEKEST BEGINS!
I DO KNOW THIS PLACE. THESE PEOPLE ARE PEACEFUL -- FRIENDLY.
HURRY! BEFORE THEY RETURN -- WE MUST GET ABOARD!
THERE IS NO MORE ROOM!
YOU CAN NOT LEAVE US HERE TO DIE!
TAKE THE CHILD!
NO!
THERE BE TROUBLE BELOW.
ONE SIDE, JUNIOR.
NOW YOU'RE TALKIN' MY LANGUAGE!

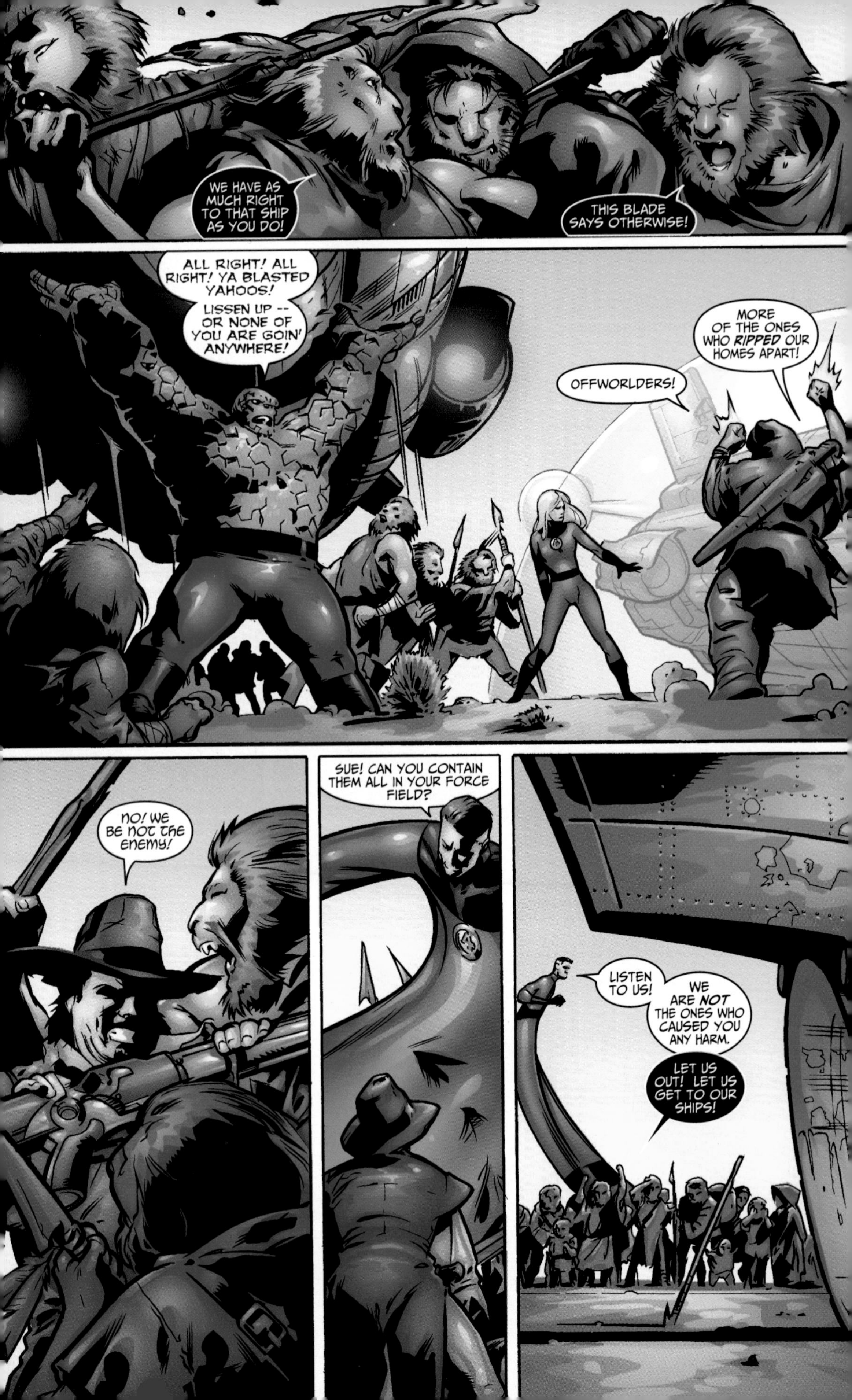
WE HAVE AS MUCH RIGHT TO THAT SHIP AS YOU DO!
THIS BLADE SAYS OTHERWISE!
ALL RIGHT! ALL RIGHT! YA BLASTED YAHOOS!
LISSEN UP -- OR NONE OF YOU ARE GOIN' ANYWHERE!
MORE OF THE ONES WHO RIPPED OUR HOMES APART!
OFFWORLDERS!
NO! WE BE NOT THE ENEMY!
SUE! CAN YOU CONTAIN THEM ALL IN YOUR FORCE FIELD?
LISTEN TO US!
WE ARE NOT THE ONES WHO CAUSED YOU ANY HARM.
LET US OUT! LET US GET TO OUR SHIPS!

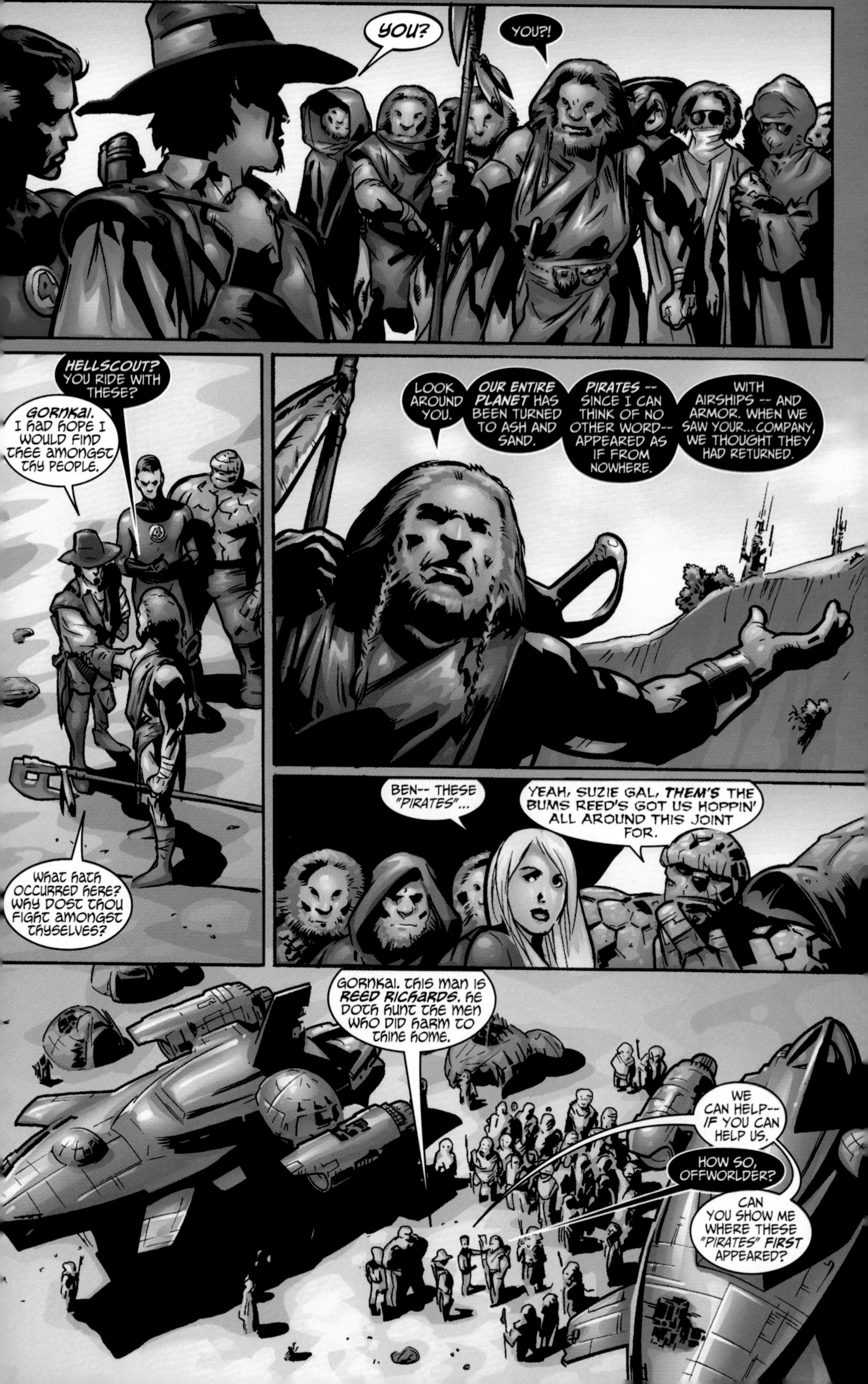
YOU?
YOU?!
HELLSCOUT? YOU RIDE WITH THESE?
GORNKAI. I HAD HOPE I WOULD FIND THEE AMONGST THY PEOPLE.
WHAT HATH OCCURRED HERE? WHY DOST THOU FIGHT AMONGST THYSELVES?
LOOK AROUND YOU.
OUR ENTIRE PLANET HAS BEEN TURNED TO ASH AND SAND.
PIRATES -- SINCE I CAN THINK OF NO OTHER WORD-- APPEARED AS IF FROM NOWHERE.
WITH AIRSHIPS -- AND ARMOR. WHEN WE SAW YOUR...COMPANY, WE THOUGHT THEY HAD RETURNED.
BEN-- THESE "PIRATES"...
YEAH, SUZIE GAL, THEM'S THE BUMS REED'S GOT US HOPPIN' ALL AROUND THIS JOINT FOR.
GORNKAI. THIS MAN IS REED RICHARDS. HE DOTH HUNT THE MEN WHO DID HARM TO THINE HOME.
WE CAN HELP-- IF YOU CAN HELP US.
HOW SO, OFFWORLDER?
CAN YOU SHOW ME WHERE THESE "PIRATES" FIRST APPEARED?

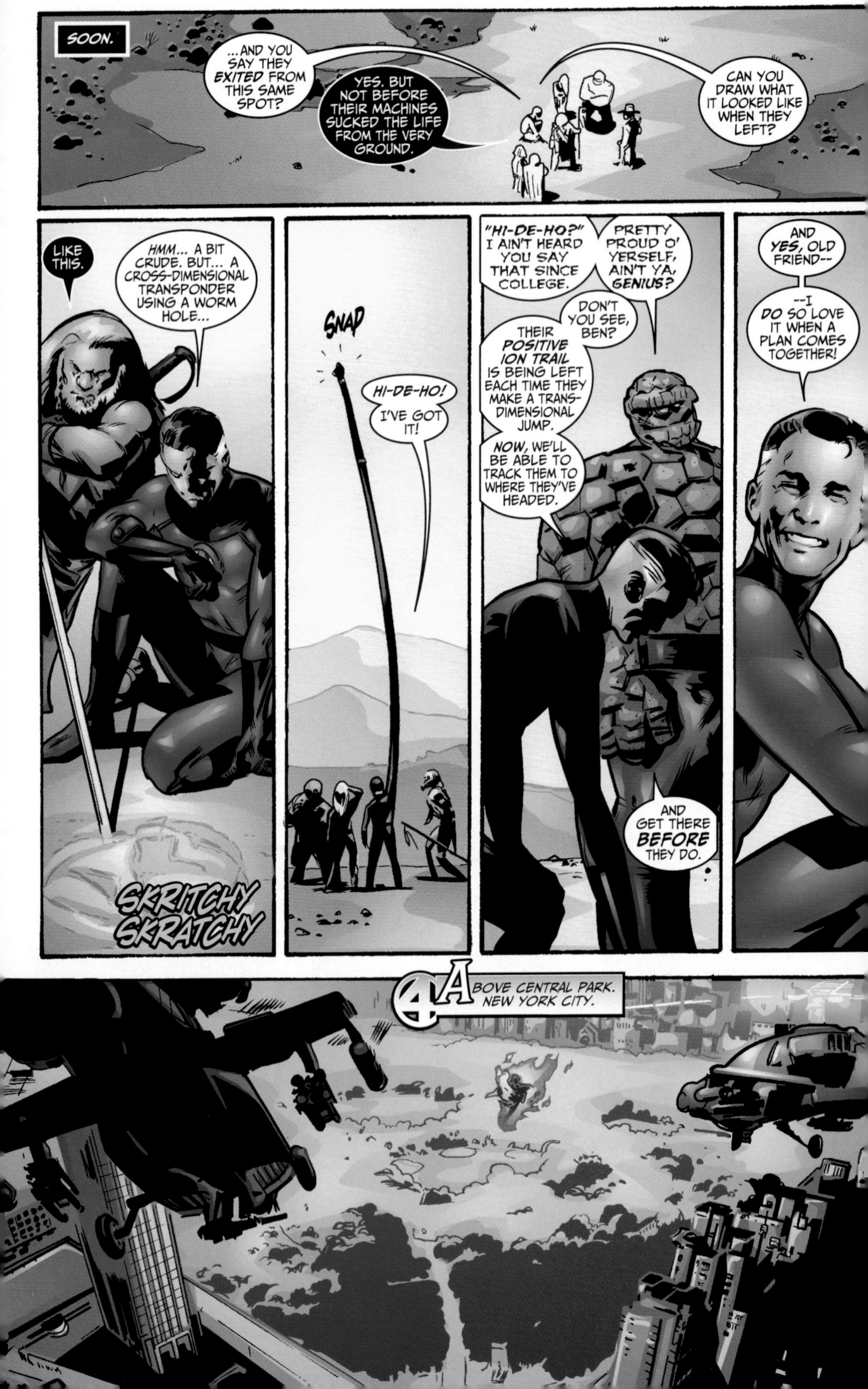
SOON.
...AND YOU SAY THEY EXITED FROM THIS SAME SPOT?
YES. BUT NOT BEFORE THEIR MACHINES SUCKED THE LIFE FROM THE VERY GROUND.
CAN YOU DRAW WHAT IT LOOKED LIKE WHEN THEY LEFT?
LIKE THIS.
HMM... A BIT CRUDE. BUT... A CROSS-DIMENSIONAL TRANSPONDER USING A WORM HOLE...
SKRITCHY SKRATCHY
SNAP
HI-DE-HO! I'VE GOT IT!
"HI-DE-HO?" I AIN'T HEARD YOU SAY THAT SINCE COLLEGE.
PRETTY PROUD O' YERSELF, AIN'T YA, GENIUS?
DON'T YOU SEE, BEN?
THEIR POSITIVE ION TRAIL IS BEING LEFT EACH TIME THEY MAKE A TRANS-DIMENSIONAL JUMP.
NOW, WE'LL BE ABLE TO TRACK THEM TO WHERE THEY'VE HEADED.
AND GET THERE BEFORE THEY DO.
AND YES, OLD FRIEND--
--I DO SO LOVE IT WHEN A PLAN COMES TOGETHER!
ABOVE CENTRAL PARK. NEW YORK CITY.

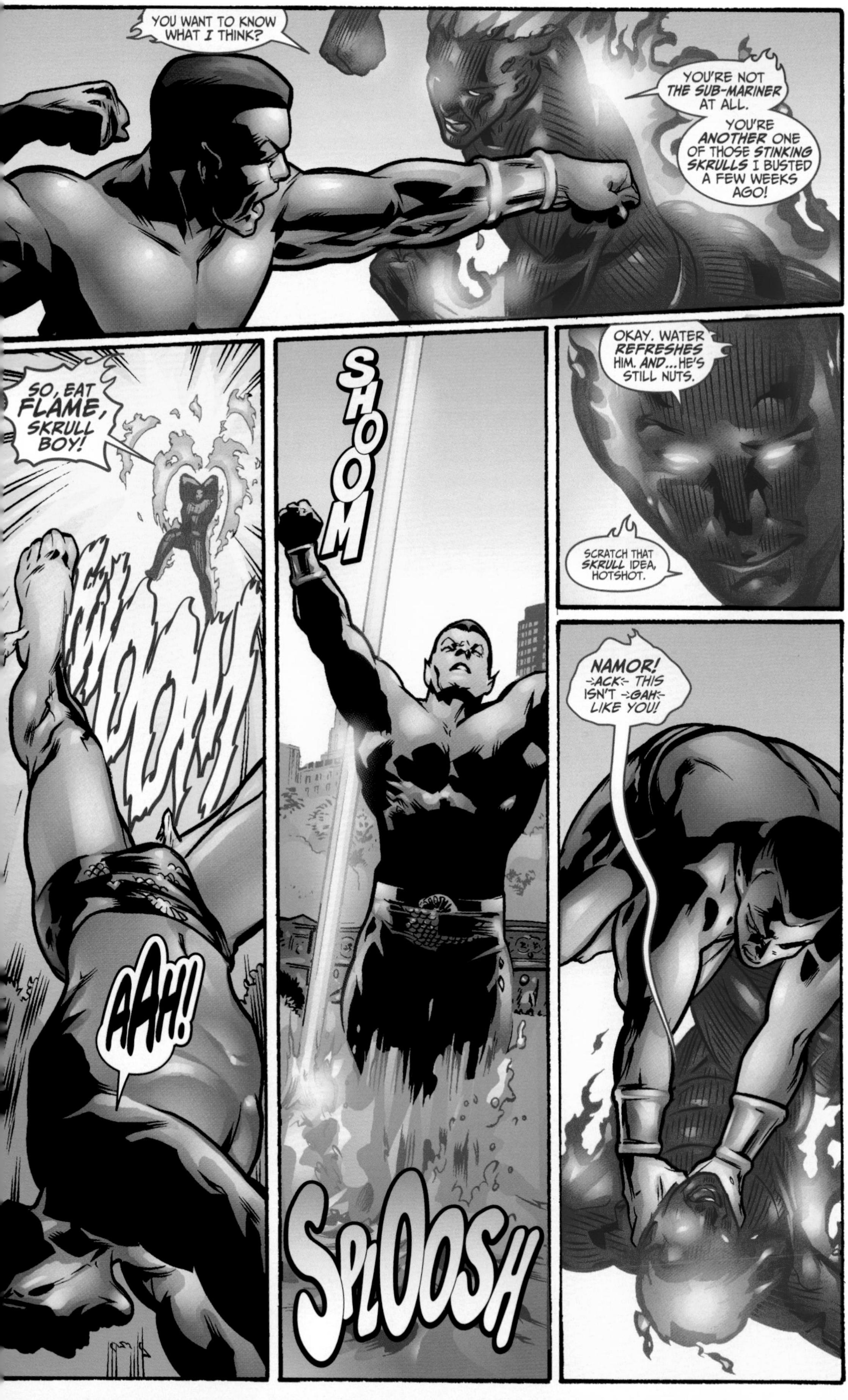

YOU WANT TO KNOW WHAT I THINK?
YOU'RE NOT THE SUB-MARINER AT ALL.
YOU'RE ANOTHER ONE OF THOSE STINKING SKRULLS I BUSTED A FEW WEEKS AGO!
SO, EAT FLAME, SKRULL BOY!
AAH!
SHOOM
SPLOOSH
OKAY. WATER REFRESHES HIM. AND... HE'S STILL NUTS.
SCRATCH THAT SKRULL IDEA, HOTSHOT.
NAMOR! ACK THIS ISN'T GAH LIKE YOU!

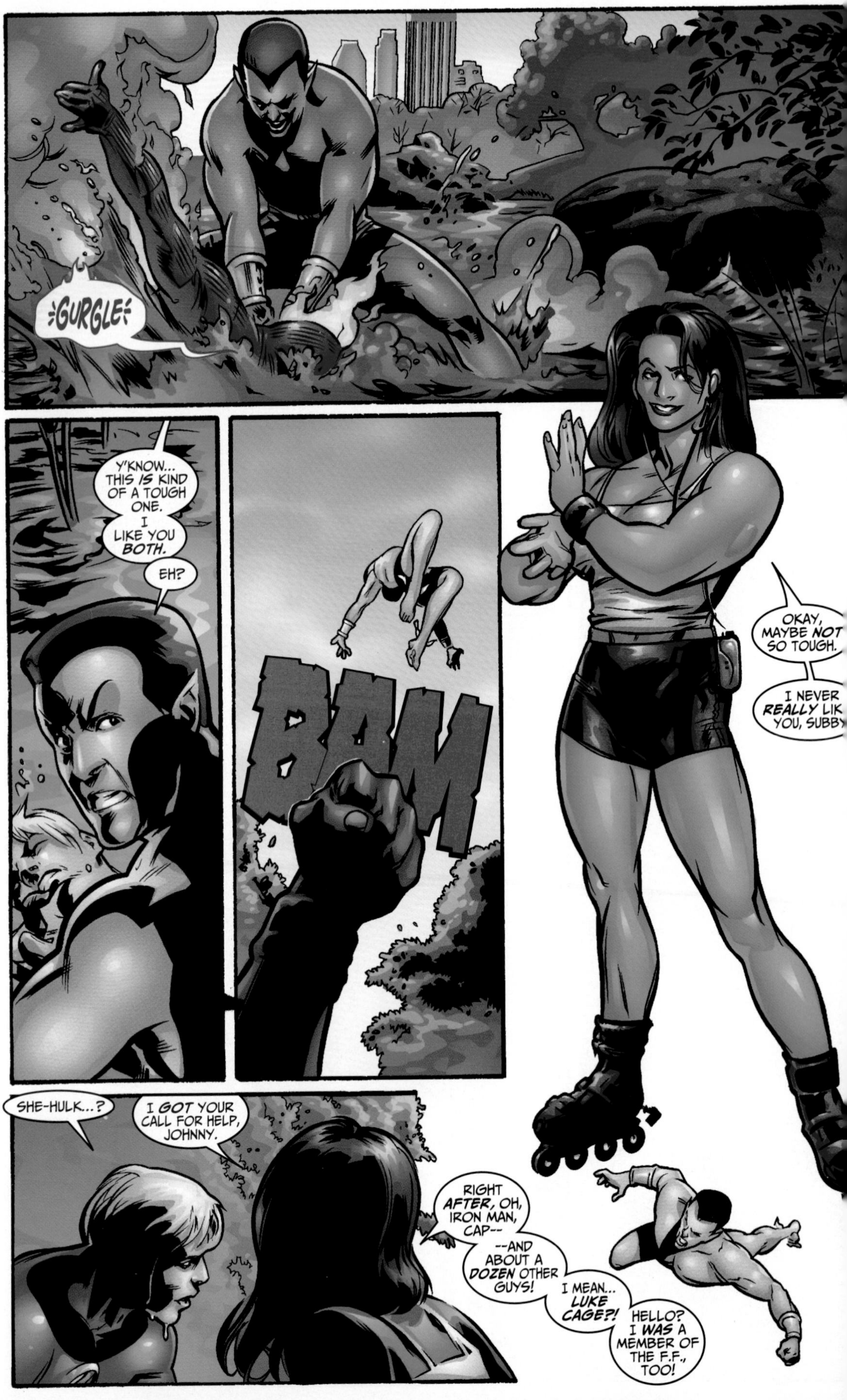
GURGLE
Y'KNOW... THIS IS KIND OF A TOUGH ONE. I LIKE YOU BOTH.
EH?
BAM
OKAY, MAYBE NOT SO TOUGH.
I NEVER REALLY LIK YOU, SUBBY
SHE-HULK...?
I GOT YOUR CALL FOR HELP, JOHNNY.
RIGHT AFTER, OH, IRON MAN, CAP--
--AND ABOUT A DOZEN OTHER GUYS!
I MEAN... LUKE CAGE?!
HELLO? I WAS A MEMBER OF THE F.F., TOO!

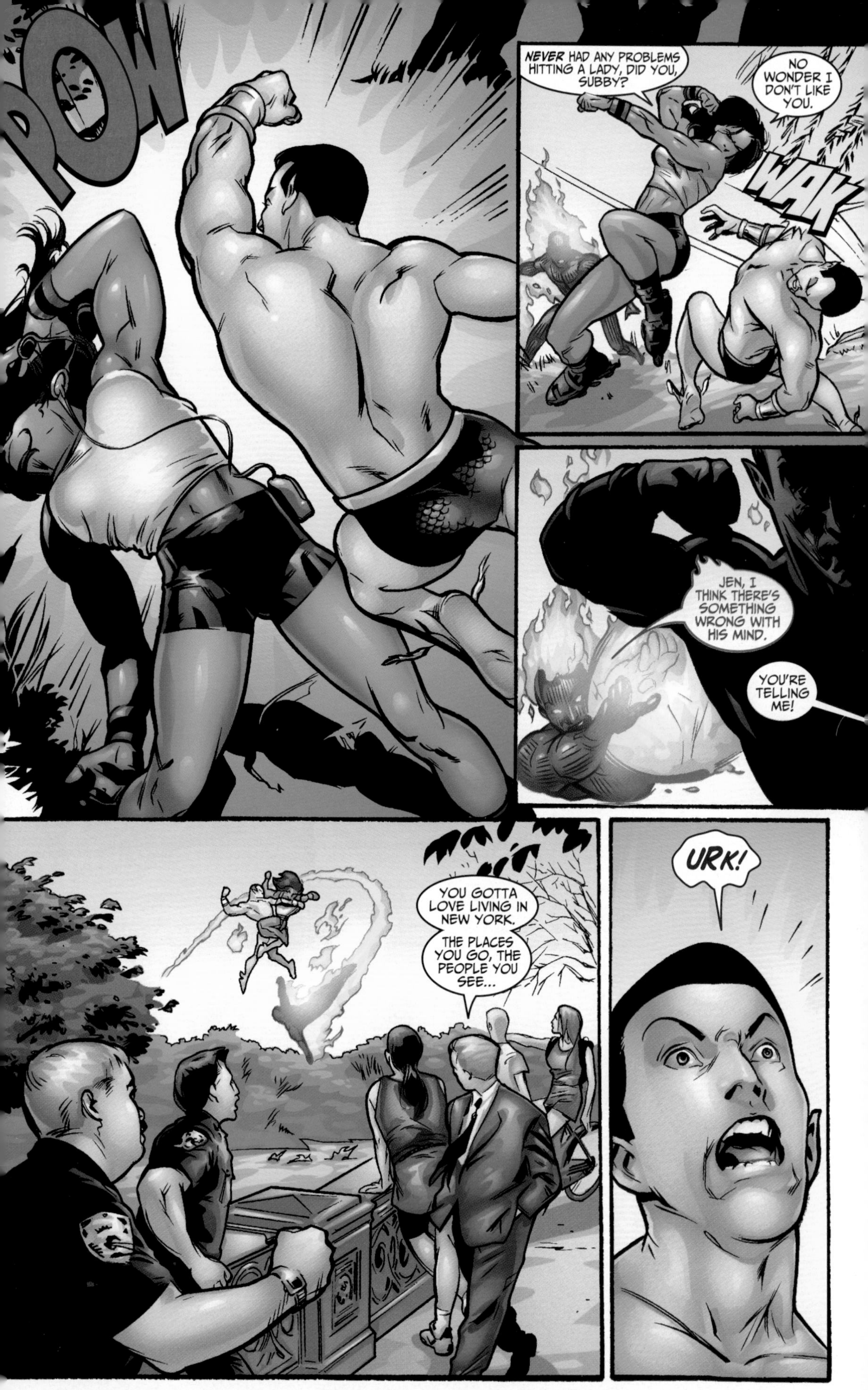
POW
NEVER HAD ANY PROBLEMS HITTING A LADY, DID YOU, SUBBY?
NO WONDER I DON'T LIKE YOU.
WAK
JEN, I THINK THERE'S SOMETHING WRONG WITH HIS MIND.
YOU'RE TELLING ME!
YOU GOTTA LOVE LIVING IN NEW YORK.
THE PLACES YOU GO, THE PEOPLE YOU SEE...
URK!

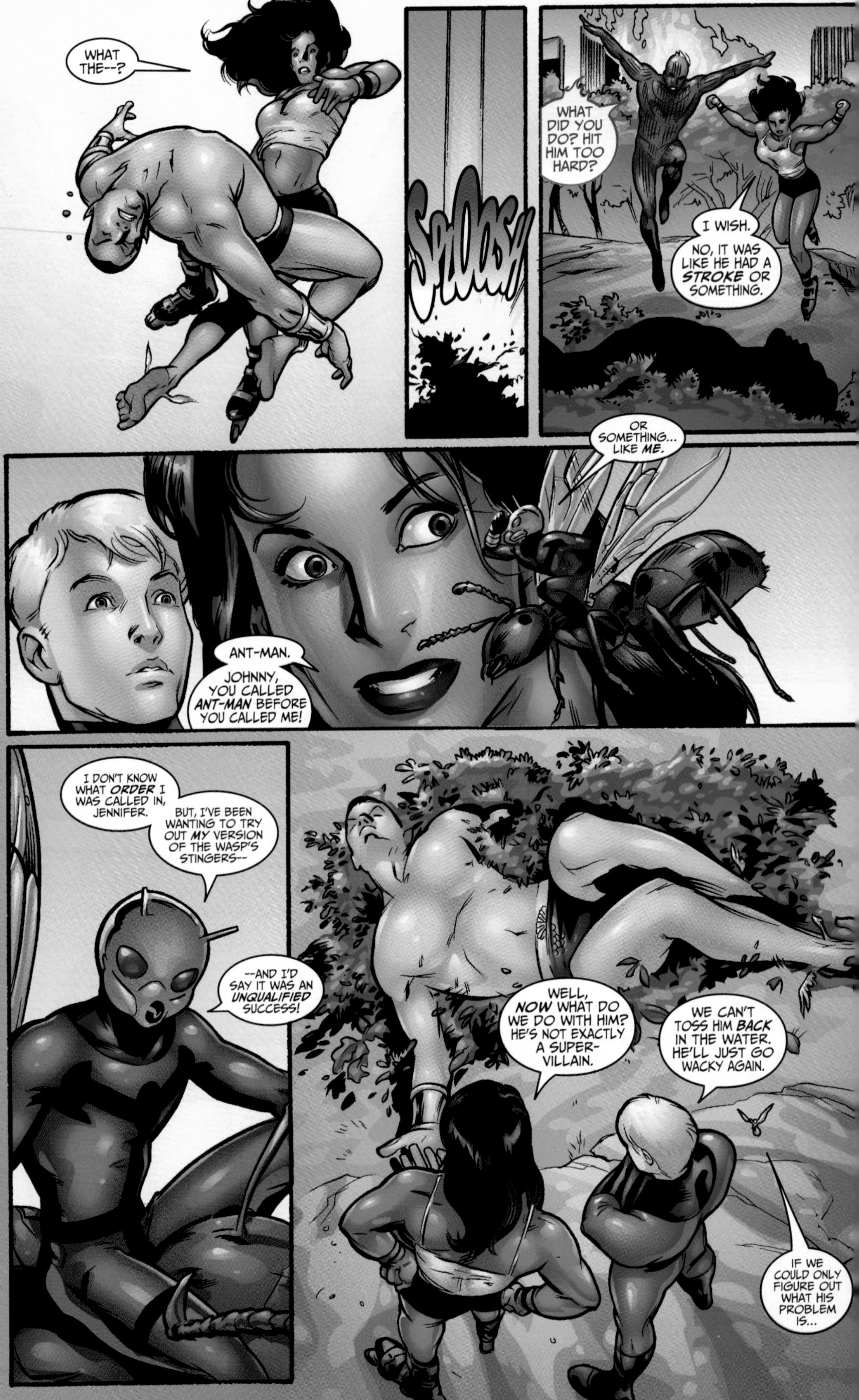

WHAT THE--?
SPLOOSH
WHAT DID YOU DO? HIT HIM TOO HARD?
I WISH.
NO, IT WAS LIKE HE HAD A STROKE OR SOMETHING.
OR SOMETHING... LIKE ME.
ANT-MAN.
JOHNNY, YOU CALLED ANT-MAN BEFORE YOU CALLED ME!
I DON'T KNOW WHAT ORDER I WAS CALLED IN, JENNIFER.
BUT, I'VE BEEN WANTING TO TRY OUT MY VERSION OF THE WASP'S STINGERS--
--AND I'D SAY IT WAS AN UNQUALIFIED SUCCESS!
WELL, NOW WHAT DO WE DO WITH HIM? HE'S NOT EXACTLY A SUPER-VILLAIN.
WE CAN'T TOSS HIM BACK IN THE WATER. HE'LL JUST GO WACKY AGAIN.
IF WE COULD ONLY FIGURE OUT WHAT HIS PROBLEM IS...

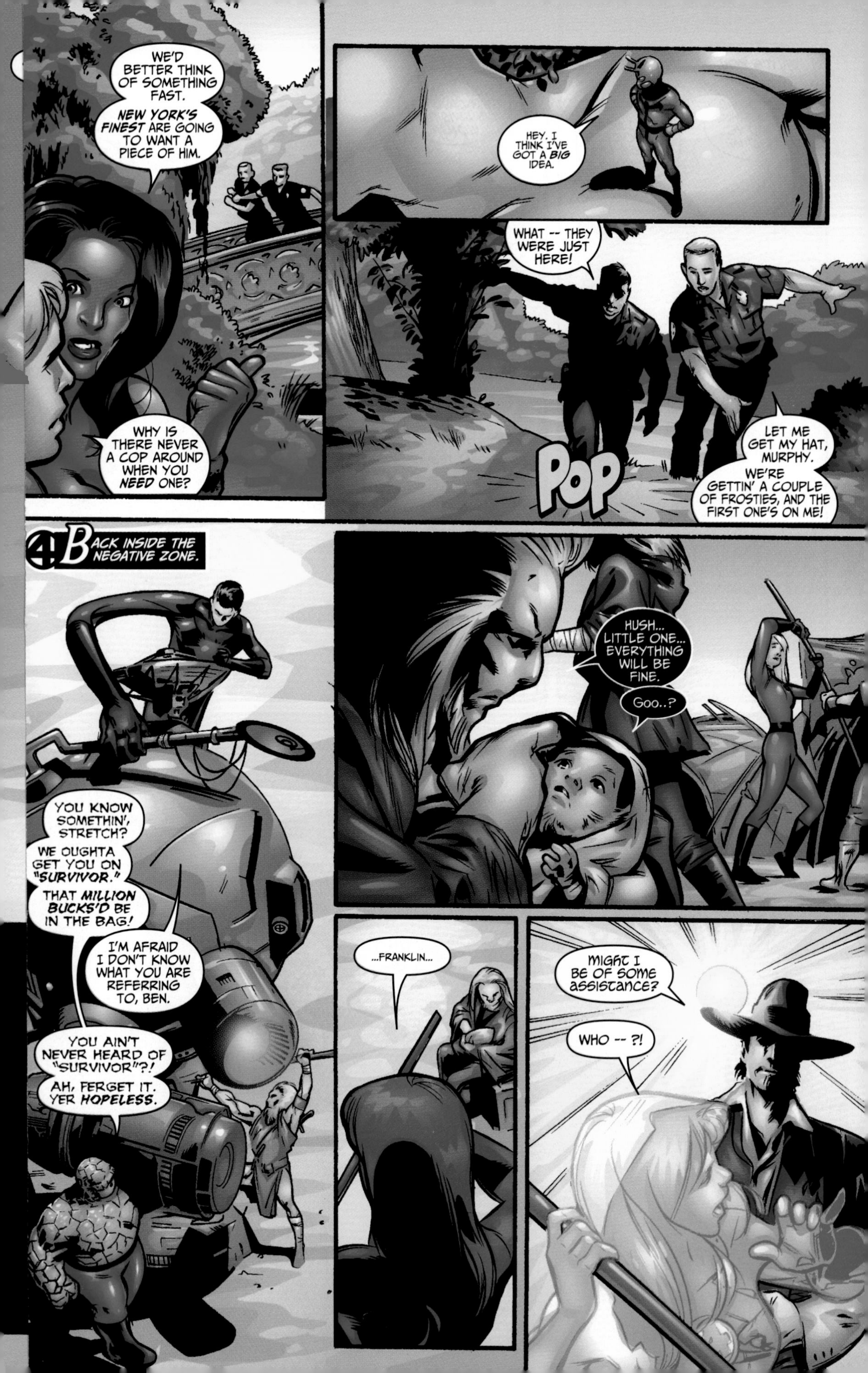

WE'D BETTER THINK OF SOMETHING FAST.
NEW YORK'S FINEST ARE GOING TO WANT A PIECE OF HIM.
WHY IS THERE NEVER A COP AROUND WHEN YOU NEED ONE?
HEY. I THINK I'VE GOT A BIG IDEA.
WHAT -- THEY WERE JUST HERE!
POP
LET ME GET MY HAT, MURPHY.
WE'RE GETTIN' A COUPLE OF FROSTIES, AND THE FIRST ONE'S ON ME!
BACK INSIDE THE NEGATIVE ZONE.
YOU KNOW SOMETHIN', STRETCH?
WE OUGHTA GET YOU ON "SURVIVOR."
THAT MILLION BUCKS'D BE IN THE BAG!
I'M AFRAID I DON'T KNOW WHAT YOU ARE REFERRING TO, BEN.
YOU AIN'T NEVER HEARD OF "SURVIVOR"?!
AH, FERGET IT. YER HOPELESS.
HUSH... LITTLE ONE... EVERYTHING WILL BE FINE.
GOO..?
...FRANKLIN...
MIGHT I BE OF SOME ASSISTANCE?
WHO -- ?!

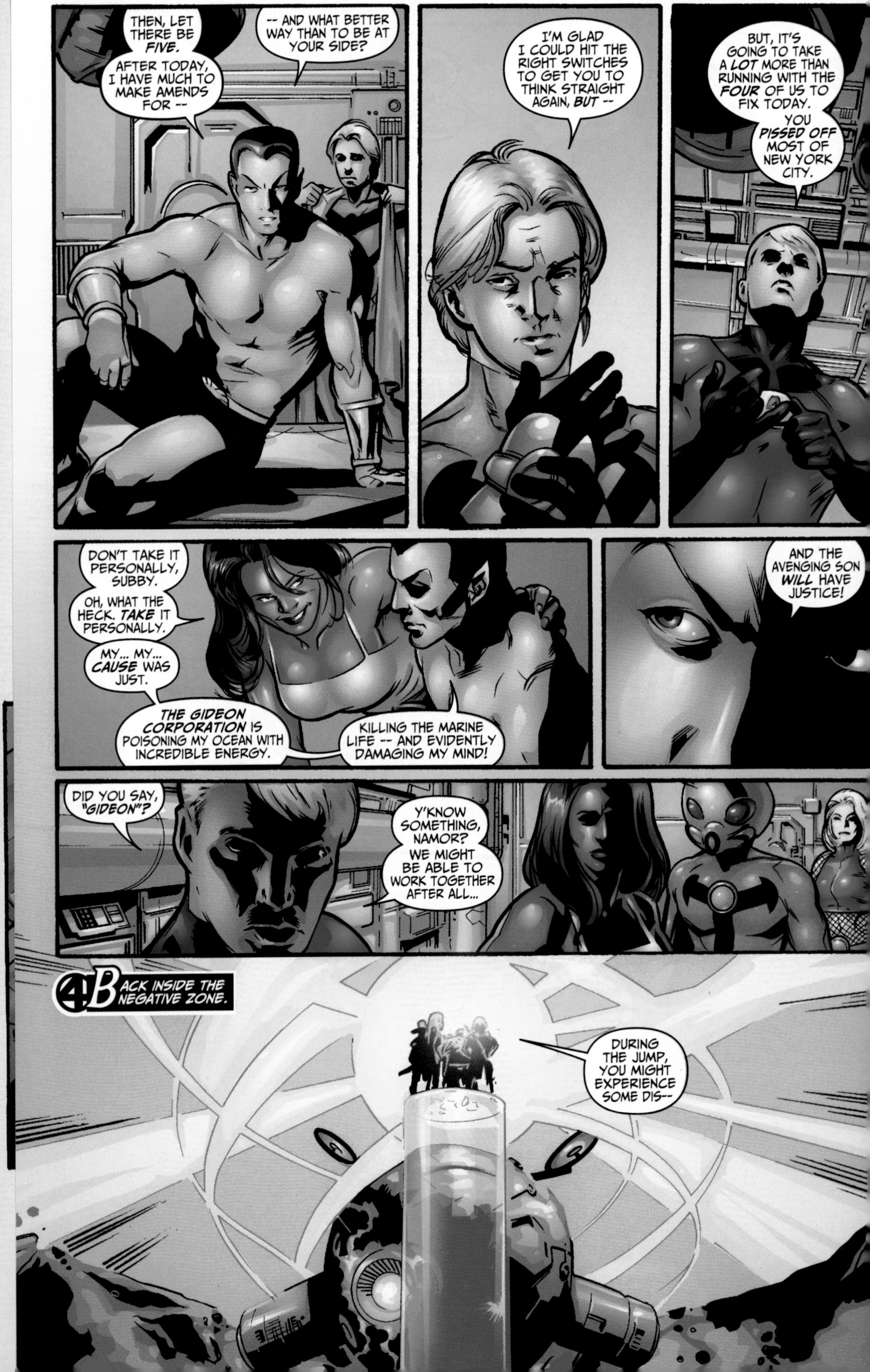

THEN, LET THERE BE *FIVE.*
AFTER TODAY, I HAVE MUCH TO MAKE AMENDS FOR --
-- AND WHAT BETTER WAY THAN TO BE AT YOUR SIDE?
I'M GLAD I COULD HIT THE RIGHT SWITCHES TO GET YOU TO THINK STRAIGHT AGAIN, *BUT* --
BUT, IT'S GOING TO TAKE A *LOT* MORE THAN RUNNING WITH THE *FOUR* OF US TO FIX TODAY.
YOU *PISSED OFF* MOST OF NEW YORK CITY.
DON'T TAKE IT PERSONALLY, SUBBY.
OH, WHAT THE HECK. *TAKE* IT PERSONALLY.
MY... MY... *CAUSE* WAS JUST.
THE GIDEON CORPORATION IS POISONING MY OCEAN WITH INCREDIBLE ENERGY.
KILLING THE MARINE LIFE -- AND EVIDENTLY DAMAGING MY MIND!
AND THE AVENGING SON *WILL* HAVE JUSTICE!
DID YOU SAY, *"GIDEON"?*
Y'KNOW SOMETHING, NAMOR? WE MIGHT BE ABLE TO WORK TOGETHER AFTER ALL...
BACK INSIDE THE NEGATIVE ZONE.
DURING THE JUMP, YOU MIGHT EXPERIENCE SOME DIS--

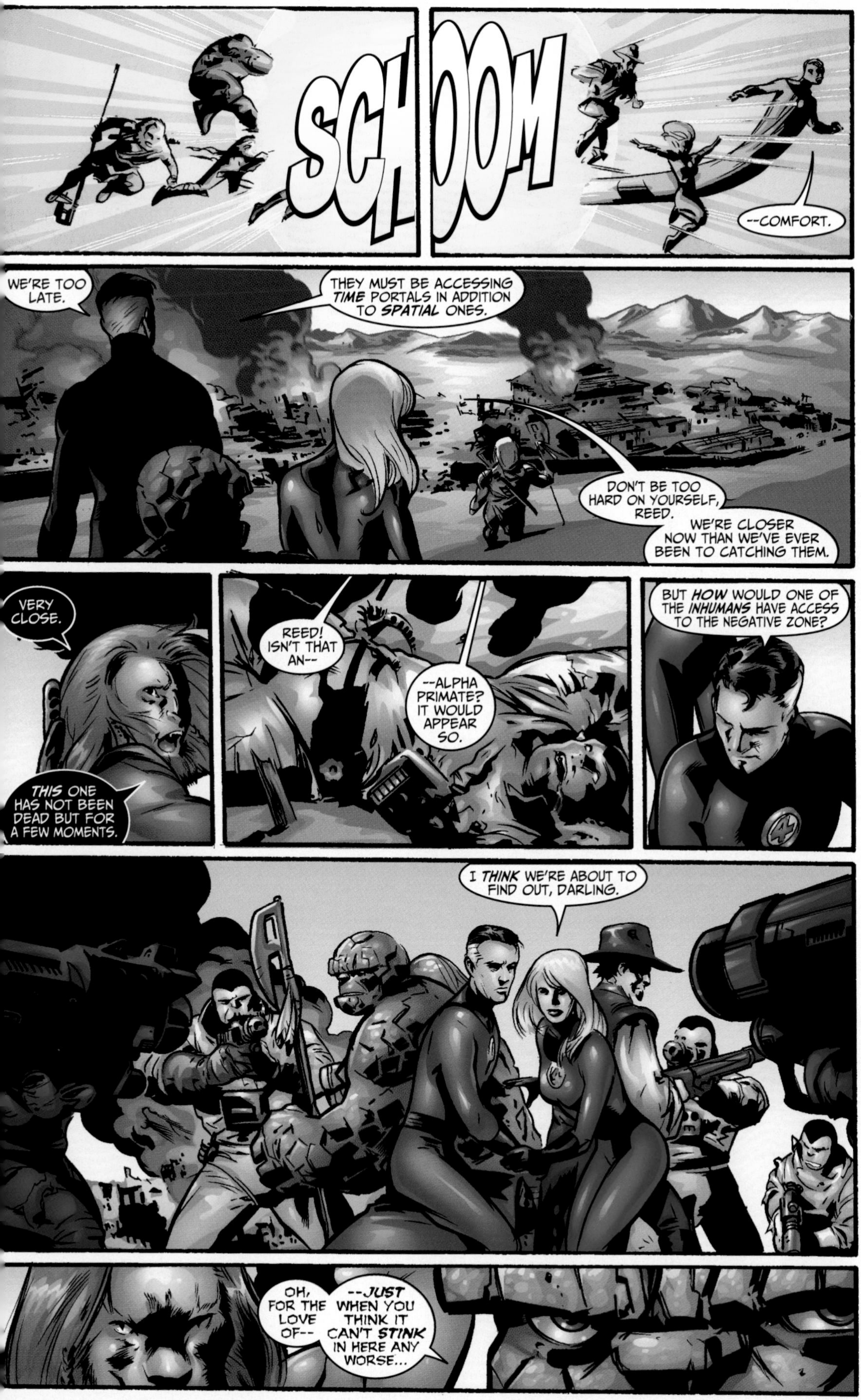
SCHOOM
--COMFORT.
WE'RE TOO LATE.
THEY MUST BE ACCESSING TIME PORTALS IN ADDITION TO SPATIAL ONES.
DON'T BE TOO HARD ON YOURSELF, REED.
WE'RE CLOSER NOW THAN WE'VE EVER BEEN TO CATCHING THEM.
VERY CLOSE.
THIS ONE HAS NOT BEEN DEAD BUT FOR A FEW MOMENTS.
REED! ISN'T THAT AN--
--ALPHA PRIMATE? IT WOULD APPEAR SO.
BUT HOW WOULD ONE OF THE INHUMANS HAVE ACCESS TO THE NEGATIVE ZONE?
I THINK WE'RE ABOUT TO FIND OUT, DARLING.
OH, FOR THE LOVE OF--
--JUST WHEN YOU THINK IT CAN'T STINK IN HERE ANY WORSE...

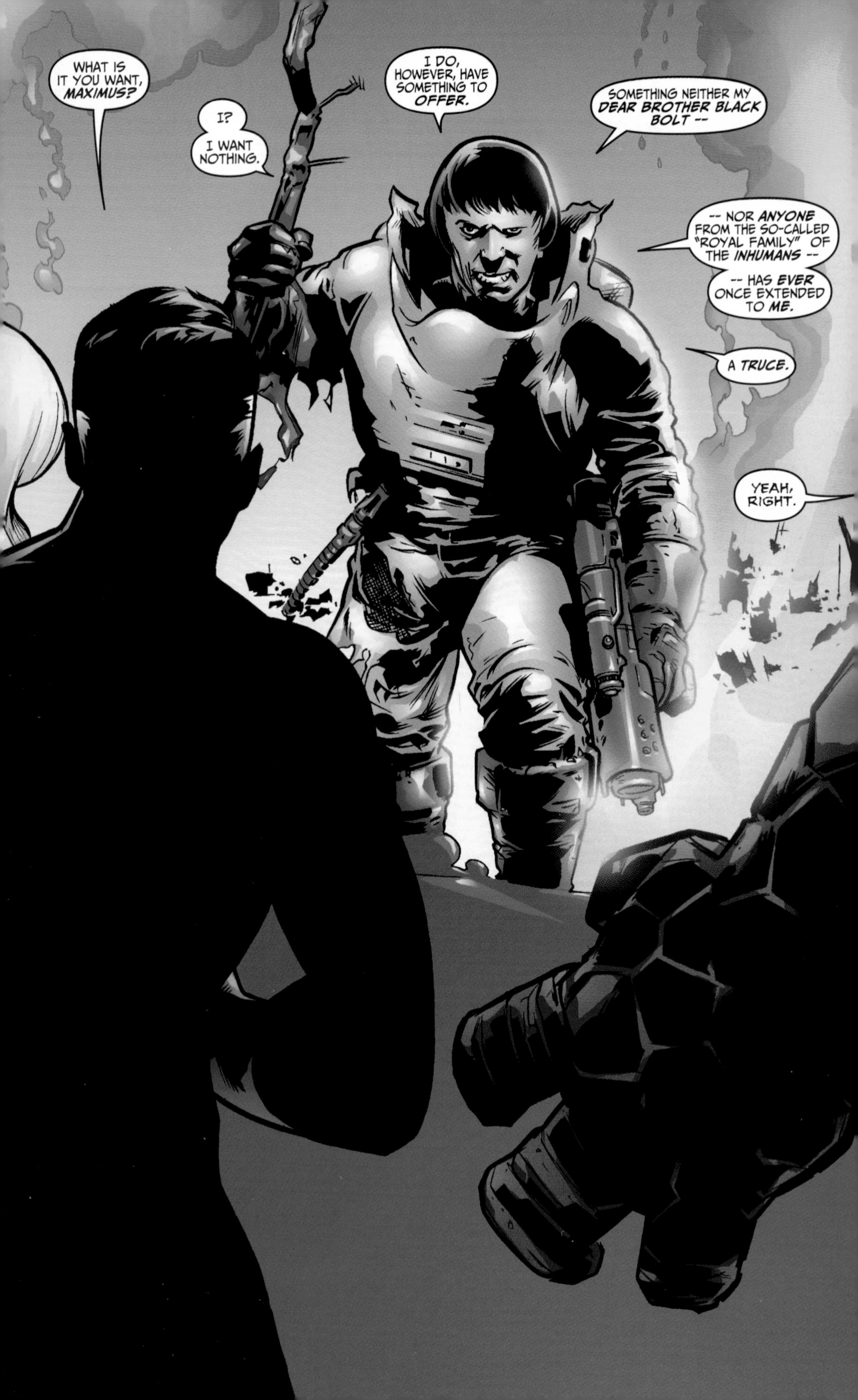

WHAT IS IT YOU WANT, MAXIMUS?
I? I WANT NOTHING.
I DO, HOWEVER, HAVE SOMETHING TO OFFER.
SOMETHING NEITHER MY DEAR BROTHER BLACK BOLT --
-- NOR ANYONE FROM THE SO-CALLED "ROYAL FAMILY" OF THE INHUMANS --
-- HAS EVER ONCE EXTENDED TO ME.
A TRUCE.
YEAH, RIGHT.

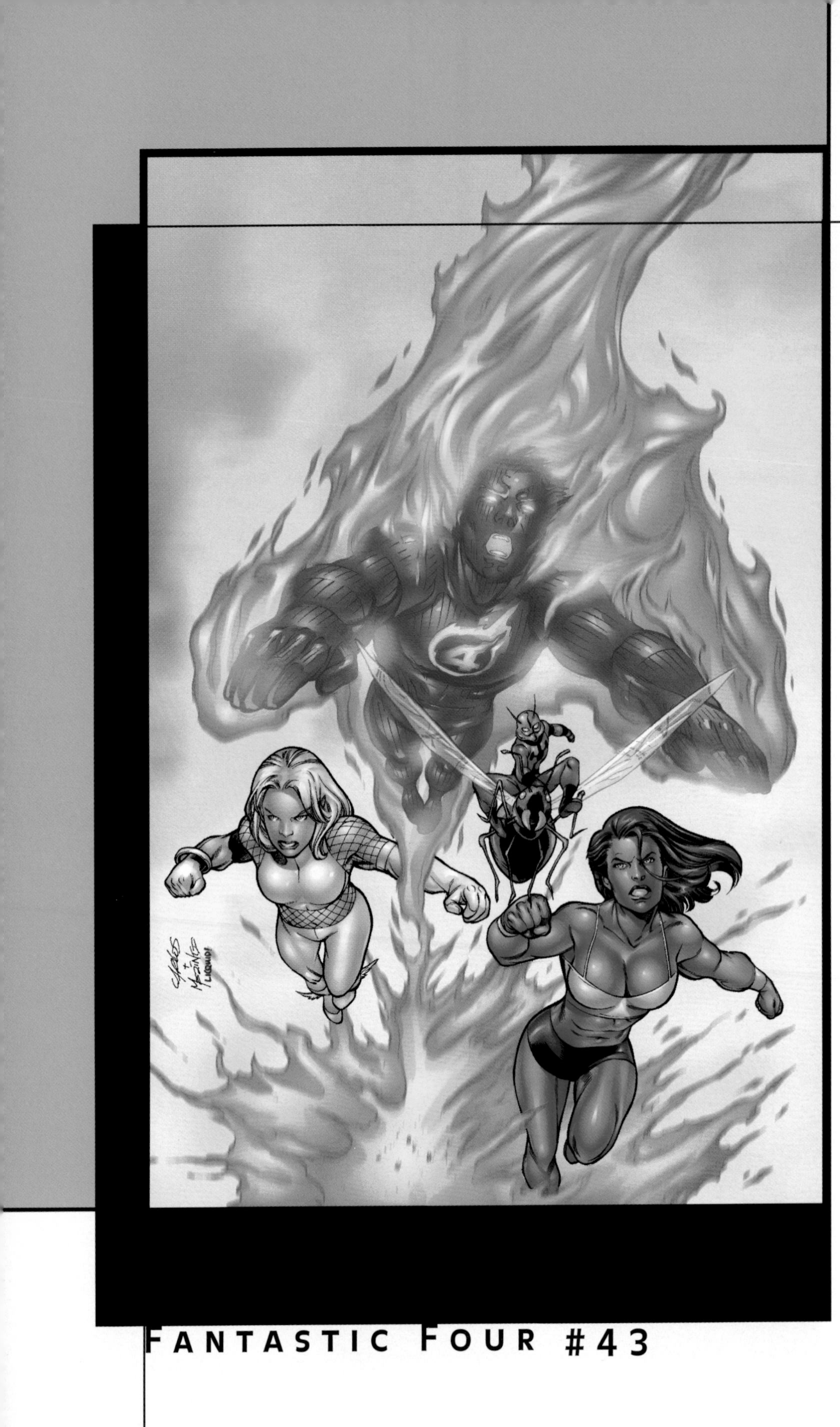

FANTASTIC FOUR #43

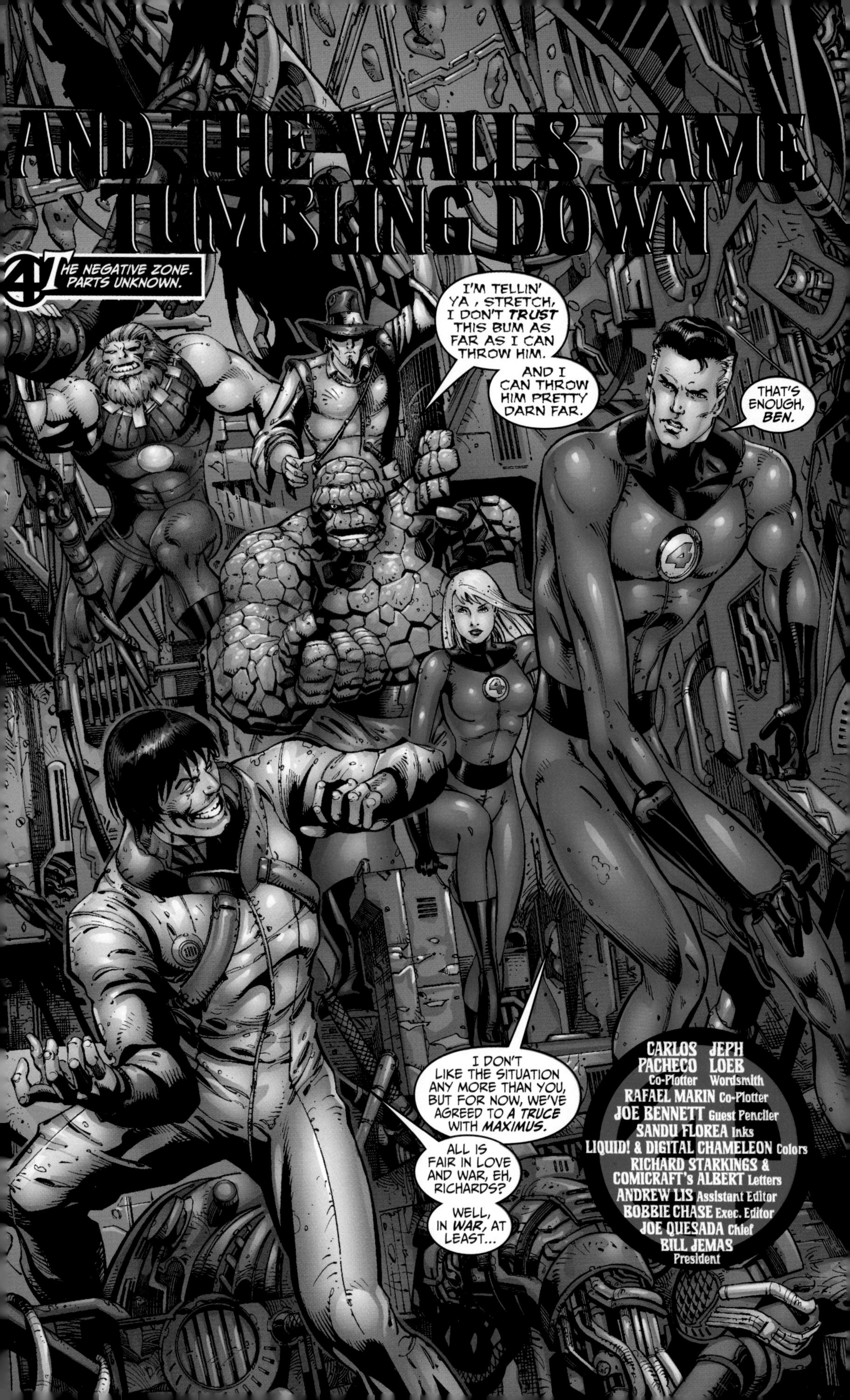
AND THE WALLS CAME TUMBLING DOWN
THE NEGATIVE ZONE. PARTS UNKNOWN.
I'M TELLIN' YA, STRETCH, I DON'T TRUST THIS BUM AS FAR AS I CAN THROW HIM.
AND I CAN THROW HIM PRETTY DARN FAR.
THAT'S ENOUGH, BEN.
I DON'T LIKE THE SITUATION ANY MORE THAN YOU, BUT FOR NOW, WE'VE AGREED TO A TRUCE WITH MAXIMUS.
ALL IS FAIR IN LOVE AND WAR, EH, RICHARDS?
WELL, IN WAR, AT LEAST...
CARLOS PACHECO Co-Plotter JEPH LOEB Wordsmith
RAFAEL MARIN Co-Plotter
JOE BENNETT Guest Penciler
SANDU FLOREA Inks
LIQUID! & DIGITAL CHAMELEON Colors
RICHARD STARKINGS & COMICRAFT's ALBERT Letters
ANDREW LIS Assistant Editor
BOBBIE CHASE Exec. Editor
JOE QUESADA Chief
BILL JEMAS President

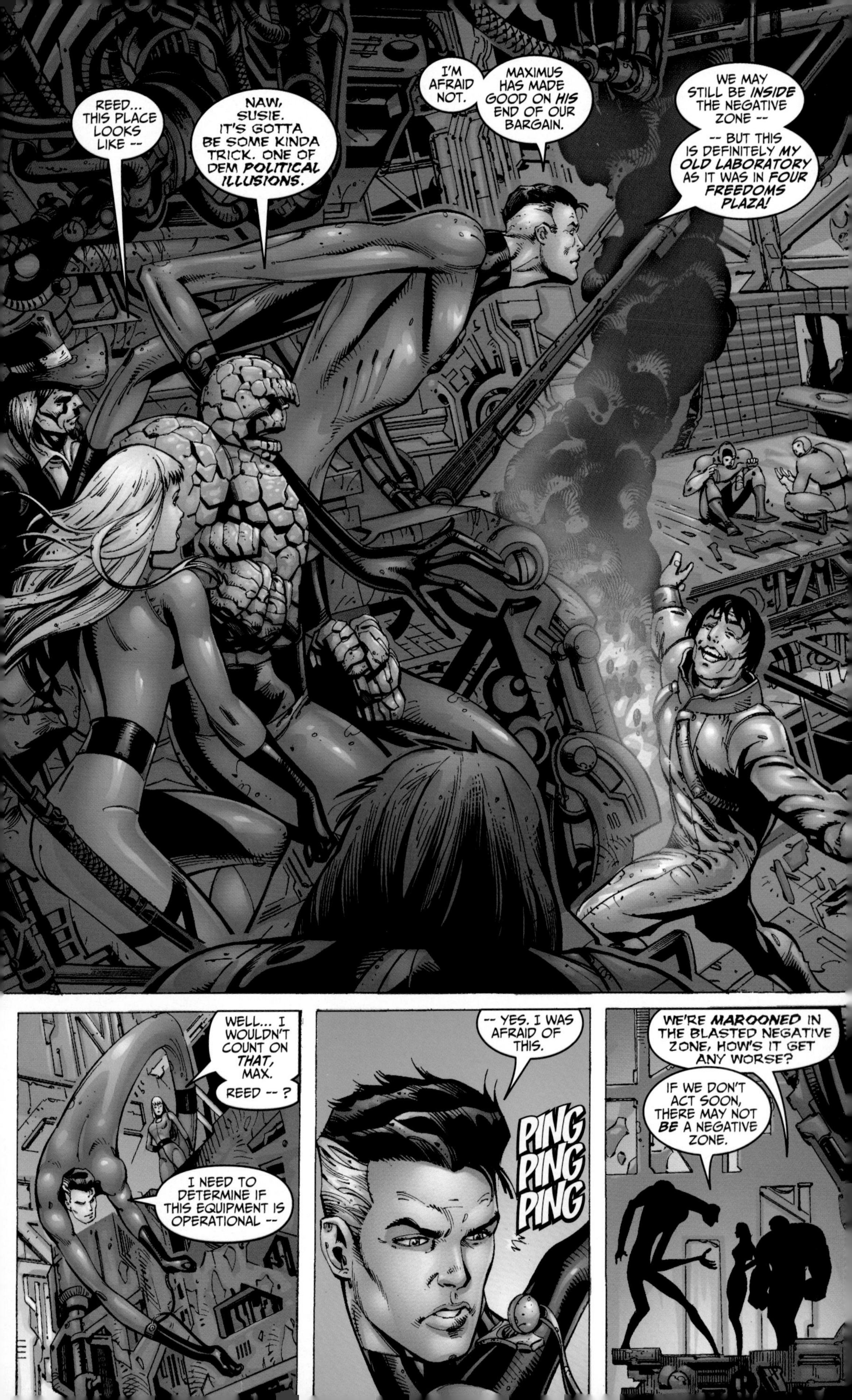

REED... THIS PLACE LOOKS LIKE --
NAW, SUSIE. IT'S GOTTA BE SOME KINDA TRICK. ONE OF DEM POLITICAL ILLUSIONS.
I'M AFRAID NOT.
MAXIMUS HAS MADE GOOD ON HIS END OF OUR BARGAIN.
WE MAY STILL BE INSIDE THE NEGATIVE ZONE --
-- BUT THIS IS DEFINITELY MY OLD LABORATORY AS IT WAS IN FOUR FREEDOMS PLAZA!
WELL... I WOULDN'T COUNT ON THAT, MAX.
REED -- ?
I NEED TO DETERMINE IF THIS EQUIPMENT IS OPERATIONAL --
-- YES. I WAS AFRAID OF THIS.
PING PING PING
WE'RE MAROONED IN THE BLASTED NEGATIVE ZONE, HOW'S IT GET ANY WORSE?
IF WE DON'T ACT SOON, THERE MAY NOT BE A NEGATIVE ZONE.

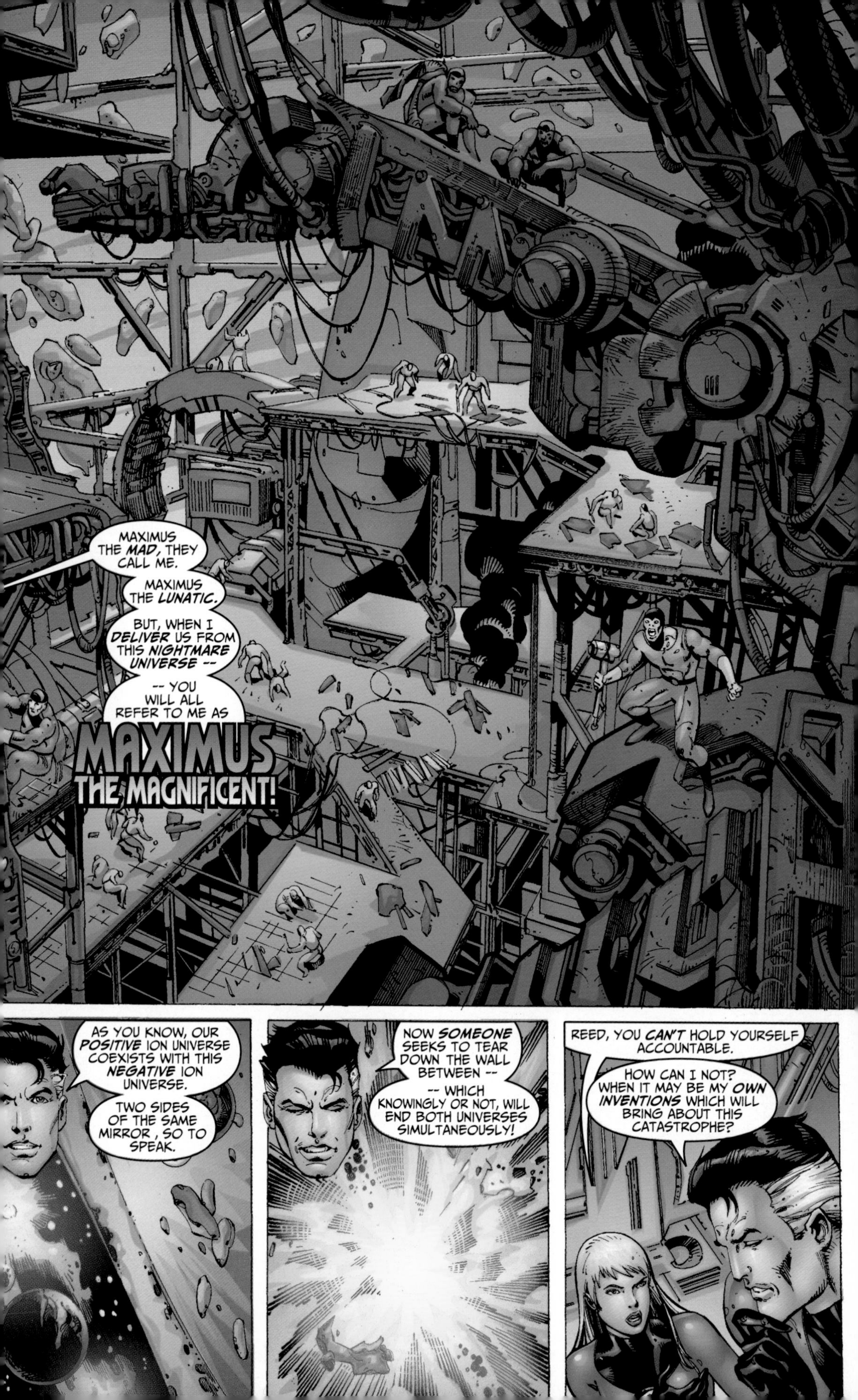
MAXIMUS THE MAD, THEY CALL ME.
MAXIMUS THE LUNATIC.
BUT, WHEN I DELIVER US FROM THIS NIGHTMARE UNIVERSE --
-- YOU WILL ALL REFER TO ME AS
MAXIMUS THE MAGNIFICENT!
AS YOU KNOW, OUR POSITIVE ION UNIVERSE COEXISTS WITH THIS NEGATIVE ION UNIVERSE.
TWO SIDES OF THE SAME MIRROR , SO TO SPEAK.
NOW SOMEONE SEEKS TO TEAR DOWN THE WALL BETWEEN --
-- WHICH KNOWINGLY OR NOT, WILL END BOTH UNIVERSES SIMULTANEOUSLY!
REED, YOU CAN'T HOLD YOURSELF ACCOUNTABLE.
HOW CAN I NOT? WHEN IT MAY BE MY OWN INVENTIONS WHICH WILL BRING ABOUT THIS CATASTROPHE?

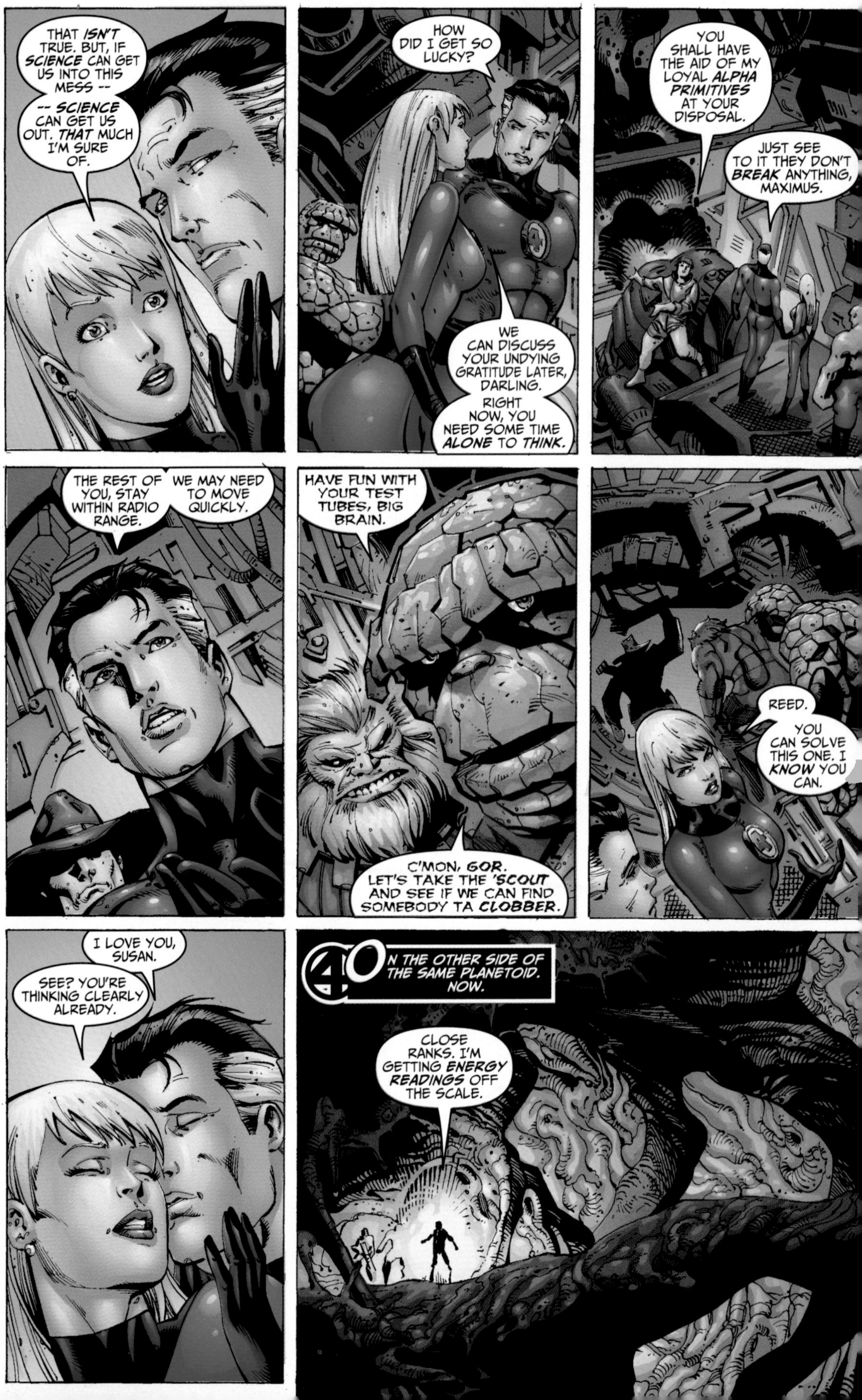
THAT ISN'T TRUE. BUT, IF SCIENCE CAN GET US INTO THIS MESS --
-- SCIENCE CAN GET US OUT. THAT MUCH I'M SURE OF.
HOW DID I GET SO LUCKY?
WE CAN DISCUSS YOUR UNDYING GRATITUDE LATER, DARLING.
RIGHT NOW, YOU NEED SOME TIME ALONE TO THINK.
YOU SHALL HAVE THE AID OF MY LOYAL ALPHA PRIMITIVES AT YOUR DISPOSAL.
JUST SEE TO IT THEY DON'T BREAK ANYTHING, MAXIMUS.
THE REST OF YOU, STAY WITHIN RADIO RANGE.
WE MAY NEED TO MOVE QUICKLY.
HAVE FUN WITH YOUR TEST TUBES, BIG BRAIN.
C'MON, GOR. LET'S TAKE THE 'SCOUT AND SEE IF WE CAN FIND SOMEBODY TA CLOBBER.
REED.
YOU CAN SOLVE THIS ONE. I KNOW YOU CAN.
I LOVE YOU, SUSAN.
SEE? YOU'RE THINKING CLEARLY ALREADY.
ON THE OTHER SIDE OF THE SAME PLANETOID. NOW.
CLOSE RANKS. I'M GETTING ENERGY READINGS OFF THE SCALE.

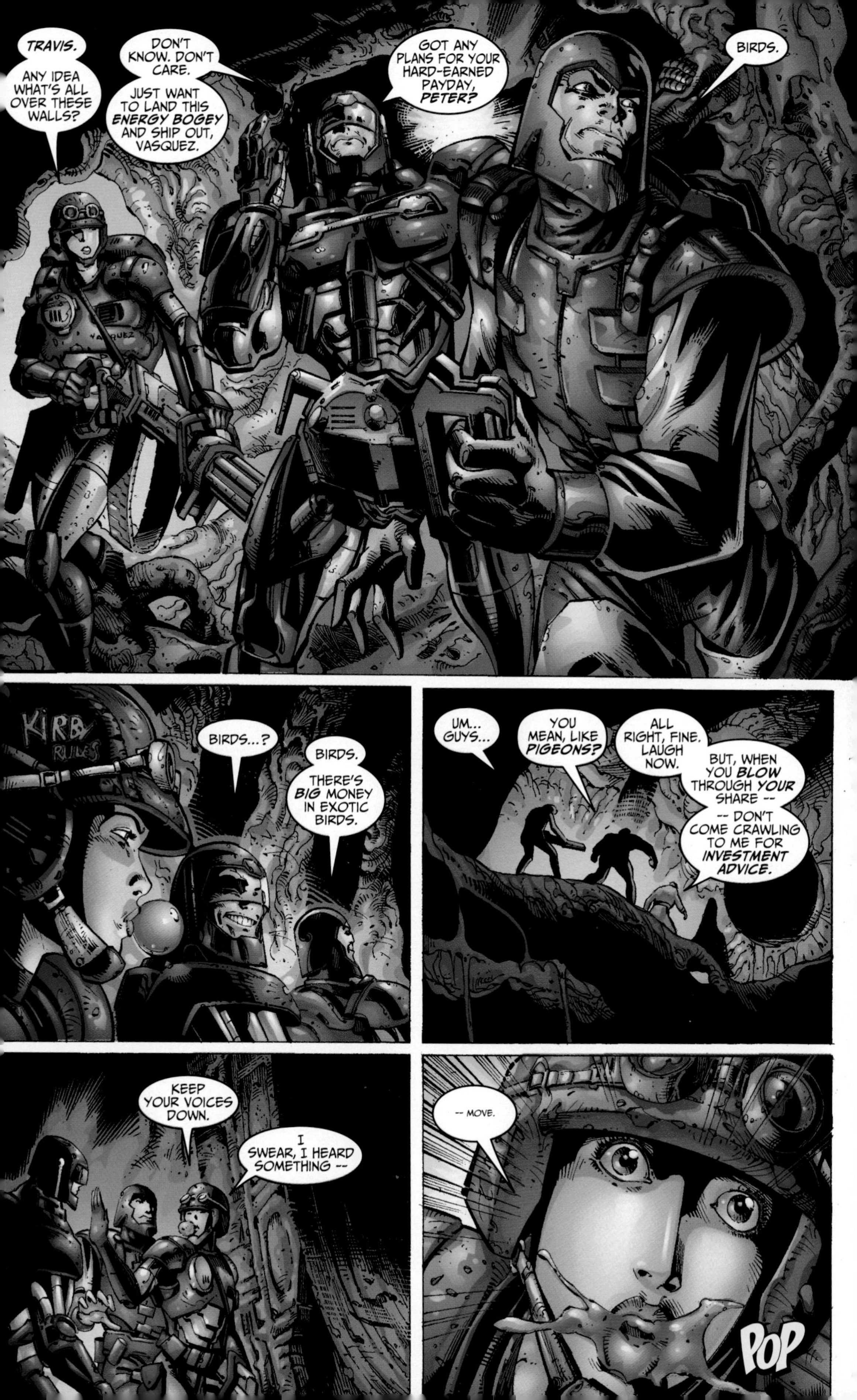
TRAVIS.
ANY IDEA WHAT'S ALL OVER THESE WALLS?
DON'T KNOW. DON'T CARE.
JUST WANT TO LAND THIS ENERGY BOGEY AND SHIP OUT, VASQUEZ.
GOT ANY PLANS FOR YOUR HARD-EARNED PAYDAY, PETER?
BIRDS.
KIRBY RULES
BIRDS...?
BIRDS.
THERE'S BIG MONEY IN EXOTIC BIRDS.
UM... GUYS...
YOU MEAN, LIKE PIGEONS?
ALL RIGHT, FINE. LAUGH NOW.
BUT, WHEN YOU BLOW THROUGH YOUR SHARE --
-- DON'T COME CRAWLING TO ME FOR INVESTMENT ADVICE.
KEEP YOUR VOICES DOWN.
I SWEAR, I HEARD SOMETHING --
-- MOVE.
POP

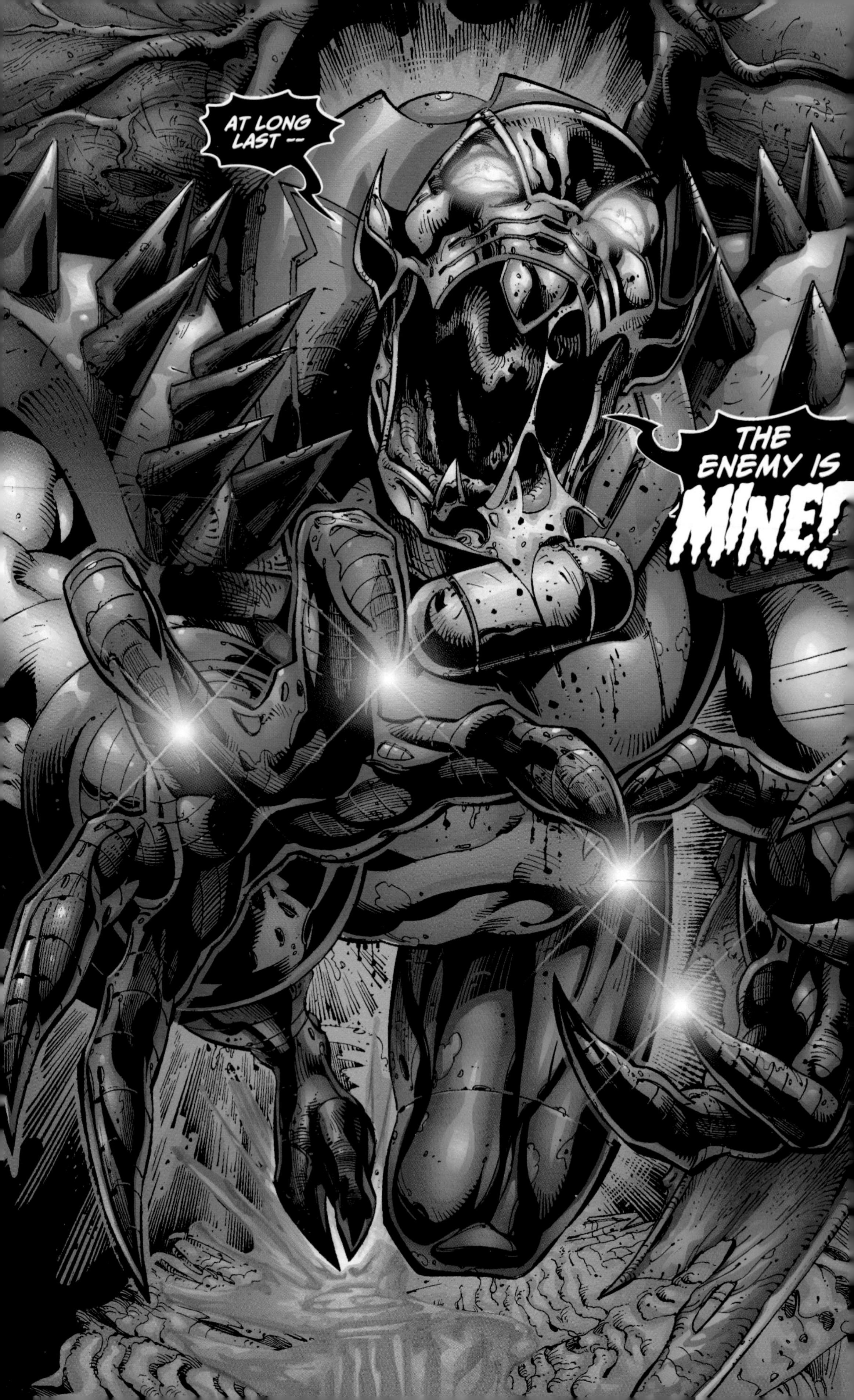
AT LONG LAST --
THE ENEMY IS MINE!

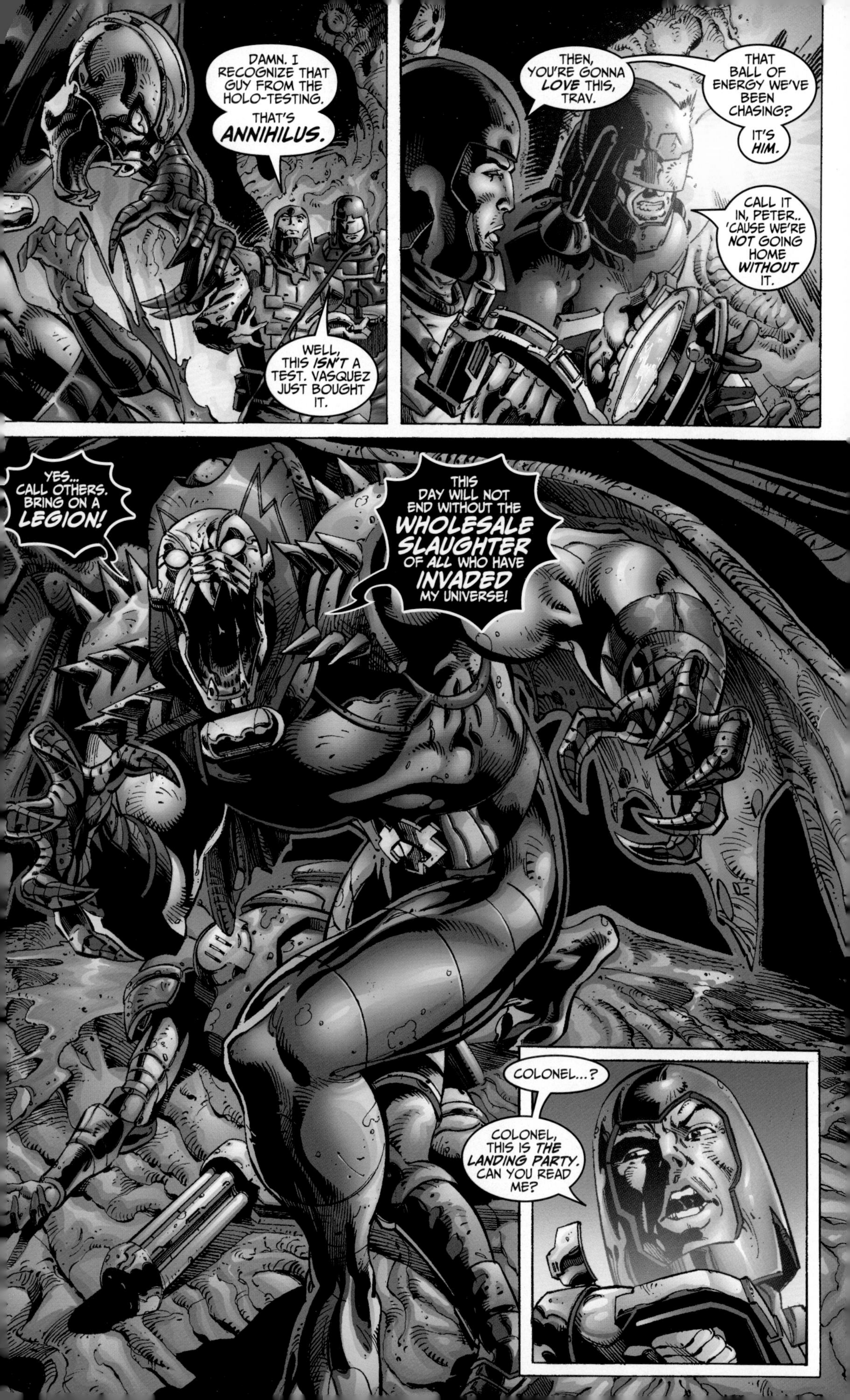
DAMN. I RECOGNIZE THAT GUY FROM THE HOLO-TESTING.
THAT'S ANNIHILUS.
WELL, THIS ISN'T A TEST. VASQUEZ JUST BOUGHT IT.
THEN, YOU'RE GONNA LOVE THIS, TRAV.
THAT BALL OF ENERGY WE'VE BEEN CHASING?
IT'S HIM.
CALL IT IN, PETER.. 'CAUSE WE'RE NOT GOING HOME WITHOUT IT.
YES... CALL OTHERS. BRING ON A LEGION!
THIS DAY WILL NOT END WITHOUT THE WHOLESALE SLAUGHTER OF ALL WHO HAVE INVADED MY UNIVERSE!
COLONEL...?
COLONEL, THIS IS THE LANDING PARTY. CAN YOU READ ME?

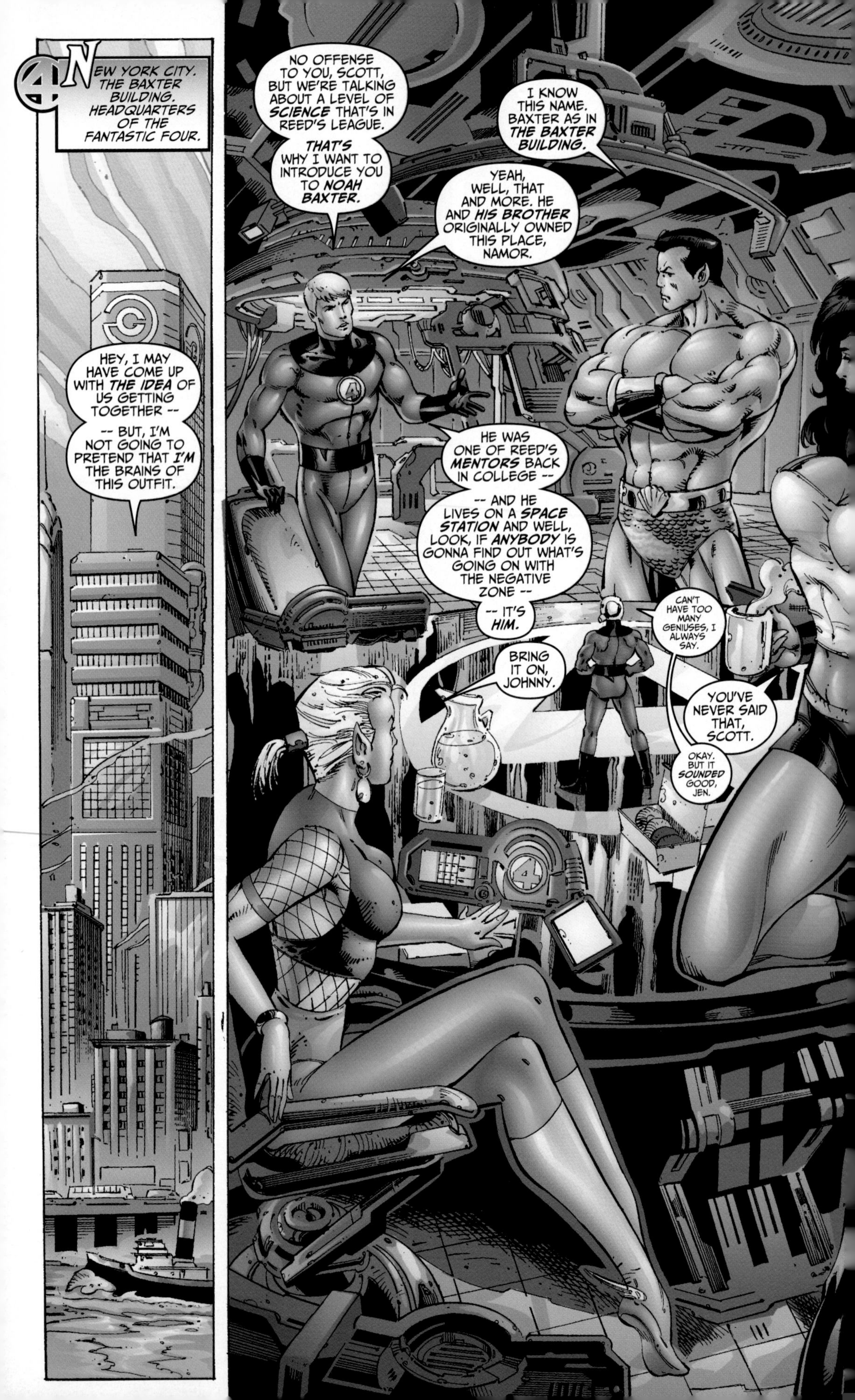
NEW YORK CITY. THE BAXTER BUILDING. HEADQUARTERS OF THE FANTASTIC FOUR.
NO OFFENSE TO YOU, SCOTT, BUT WE'RE TALKING ABOUT A LEVEL OF SCIENCE THAT'S IN REED'S LEAGUE.
THAT'S WHY I WANT TO INTRODUCE YOU TO NOAH BAXTER.
I KNOW THIS NAME. BAXTER AS IN THE BAXTER BUILDING.
YEAH, WELL, THAT AND MORE. HE AND HIS BROTHER ORIGINALLY OWNED THIS PLACE, NAMOR.
HEY, I MAY HAVE COME UP WITH THE IDEA OF US GETTING TOGETHER --
-- BUT, I'M NOT GOING TO PRETEND THAT I'M THE BRAINS OF THIS OUTFIT.
HE WAS ONE OF REED'S MENTORS BACK IN COLLEGE --
-- AND HE LIVES ON A SPACE STATION AND WELL, LOOK, IF ANYBODY IS GONNA FIND OUT WHAT'S GOING ON WITH THE NEGATIVE ZONE --
-- IT'S HIM.
CAN'T HAVE TOO MANY GENIUSES, I ALWAYS SAY.
BRING IT ON, JOHNNY.
YOU'VE NEVER SAID THAT, SCOTT.
OKAY. BUT IT SOUNDED GOOD, JEN.

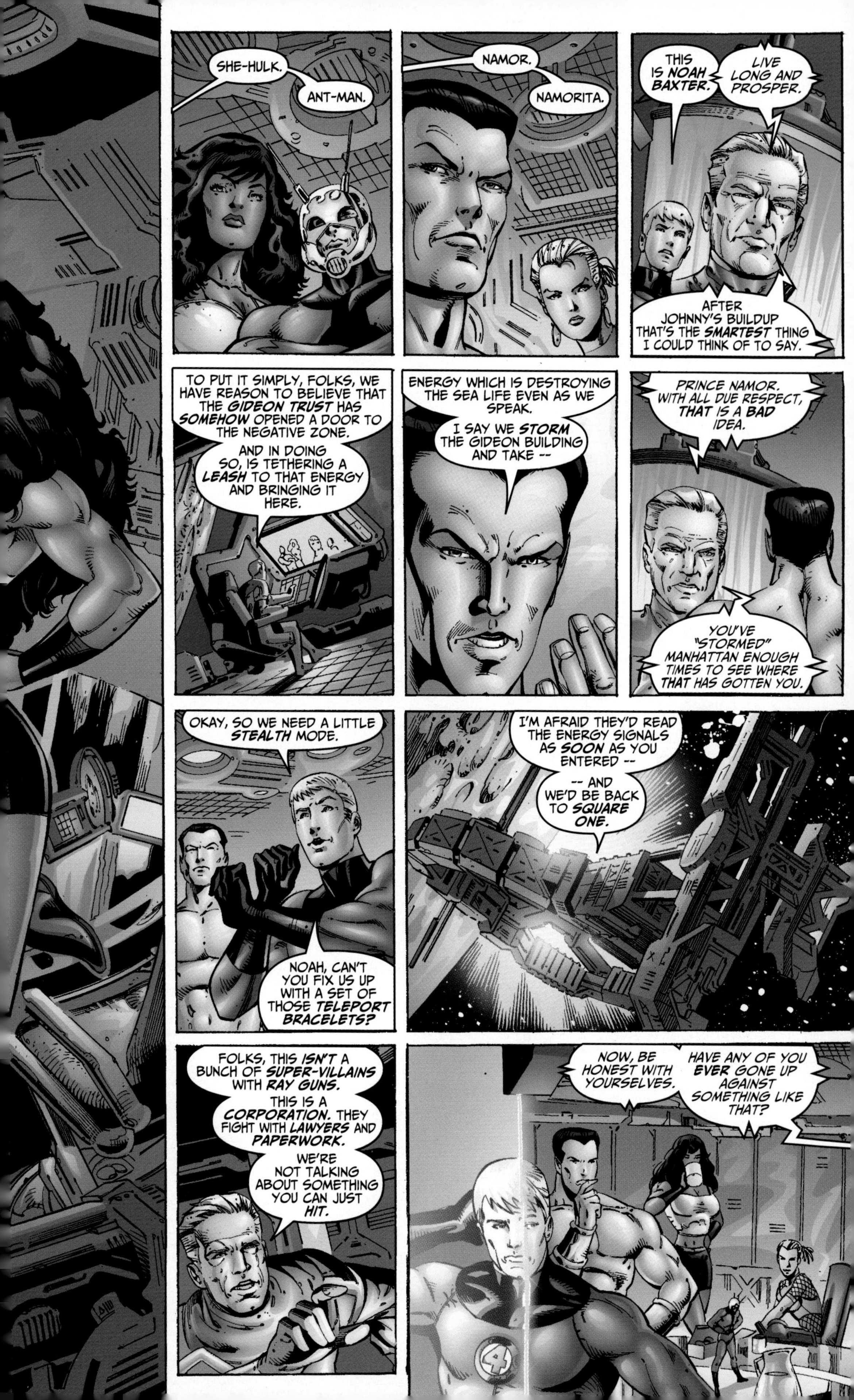

SHE-HULK.
ANT-MAN.
NAMOR.
NAMORITA.
THIS IS NOAH BAXTER.
LIVE LONG AND PROSPER.
AFTER JOHNNY'S BUILDUP THAT'S THE SMARTEST THING I COULD THINK OF TO SAY.
TO PUT IT SIMPLY, FOLKS, WE HAVE REASON TO BELIEVE THAT THE GIDEON TRUST HAS SOMEHOW OPENED A DOOR TO THE NEGATIVE ZONE.
AND IN DOING SO, IS TETHERING A LEASH TO THAT ENERGY AND BRINGING IT HERE.
ENERGY WHICH IS DESTROYING THE SEA LIFE EVEN AS WE SPEAK.
I SAY WE STORM THE GIDEON BUILDING AND TAKE --
PRINCE NAMOR. WITH ALL DUE RESPECT, THAT IS A BAD IDEA.
YOU'VE "STORMED" MANHATTAN ENOUGH TIMES TO SEE WHERE THAT HAS GOTTEN YOU.
OKAY, SO WE NEED A LITTLE STEALTH MODE.
NOAH, CAN'T YOU FIX US UP WITH A SET OF THOSE TELEPORT BRACELETS?
I'M AFRAID THEY'D READ THE ENERGY SIGNALS AS SOON AS YOU ENTERED --
-- AND WE'D BE BACK TO SQUARE ONE.
FOLKS, THIS ISN'T A BUNCH OF SUPER-VILLAINS WITH RAY GUNS.
THIS IS A CORPORATION. THEY FIGHT WITH LAWYERS AND PAPERWORK.
WE'RE NOT TALKING ABOUT SOMETHING YOU CAN JUST HIT.
NOW, BE HONEST WITH YOURSELVES.
HAVE ANY OF YOU EVER GONE UP AGAINST SOMETHING LIKE THAT?

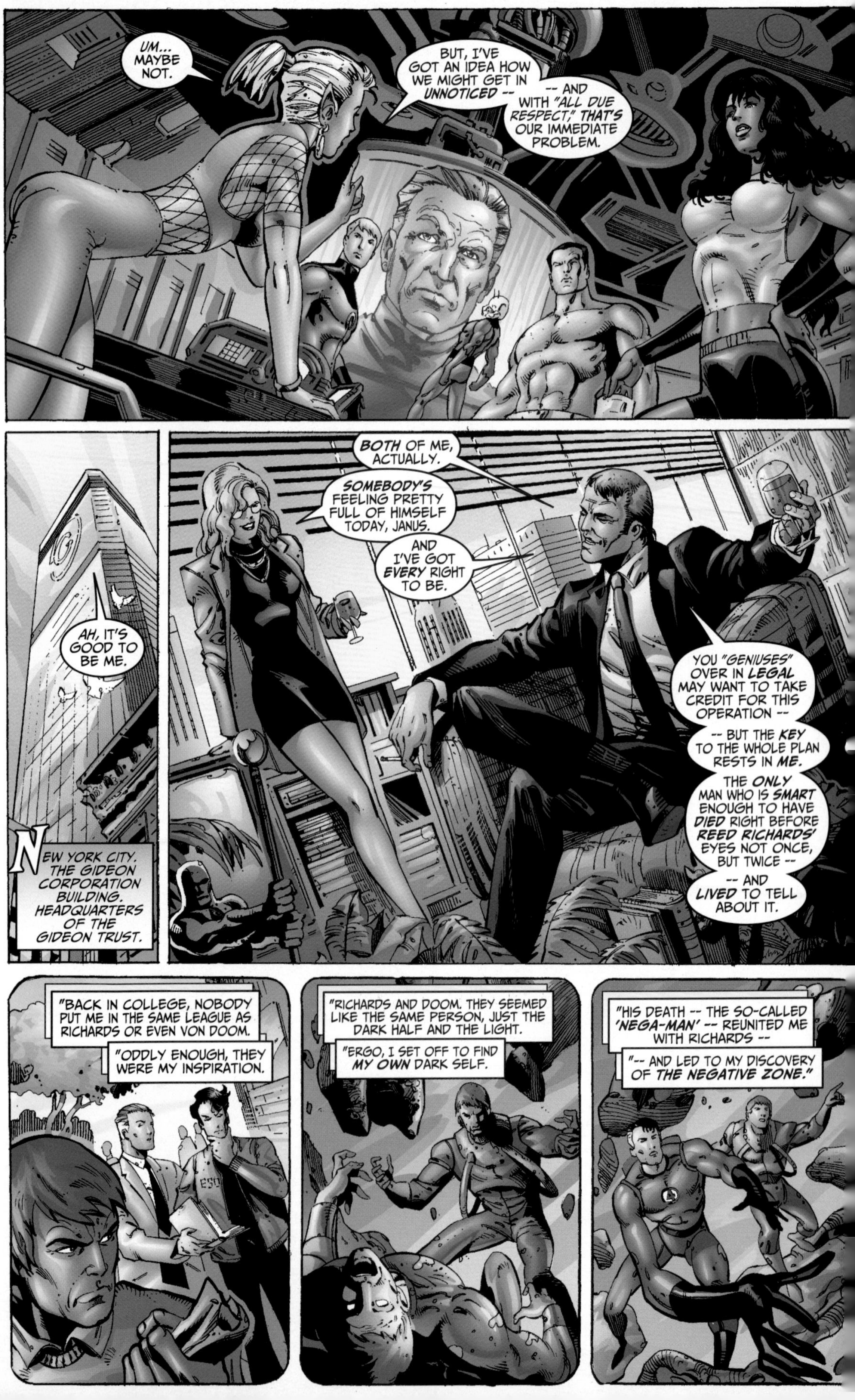
UM... MAYBE NOT.
BUT, I'VE GOT AN IDEA HOW WE MIGHT GET IN UNNOTICED --
-- AND WITH "ALL DUE RESPECT," THAT'S OUR IMMEDIATE PROBLEM.
NEW YORK CITY. THE GIDEON CORPORATION BUILDING. HEADQUARTERS OF THE GIDEON TRUST.
AH, IT'S GOOD TO BE ME.
SOMEBODY'S FEELING PRETTY FULL OF HIMSELF TODAY, JANUS.
BOTH OF ME, ACTUALLY.
AND I'VE GOT EVERY RIGHT TO BE.
YOU "GENIUSES" OVER IN LEGAL MAY WANT TO TAKE CREDIT FOR THIS OPERATION --
-- BUT THE KEY TO THE WHOLE PLAN RESTS IN ME.
THE ONLY MAN WHO IS SMART ENOUGH TO HAVE DIED RIGHT BEFORE REED RICHARDS' EYES NOT ONCE, BUT TWICE --
-- AND LIVED TO TELL ABOUT IT.
"BACK IN COLLEGE, NOBODY PUT ME IN THE SAME LEAGUE AS RICHARDS OR EVEN VON DOOM.
"ODDLY ENOUGH, THEY WERE MY INSPIRATION.
"RICHARDS AND DOOM. THEY SEEMED LIKE THE SAME PERSON, JUST THE DARK HALF AND THE LIGHT.
"ERGO, I SET OFF TO FIND MY OWN DARK SELF.
"HIS DEATH -- THE SO-CALLED 'NEGA-MAN' -- REUNITED ME WITH RICHARDS --
"-- AND LED TO MY DISCOVERY OF THE NEGATIVE ZONE."

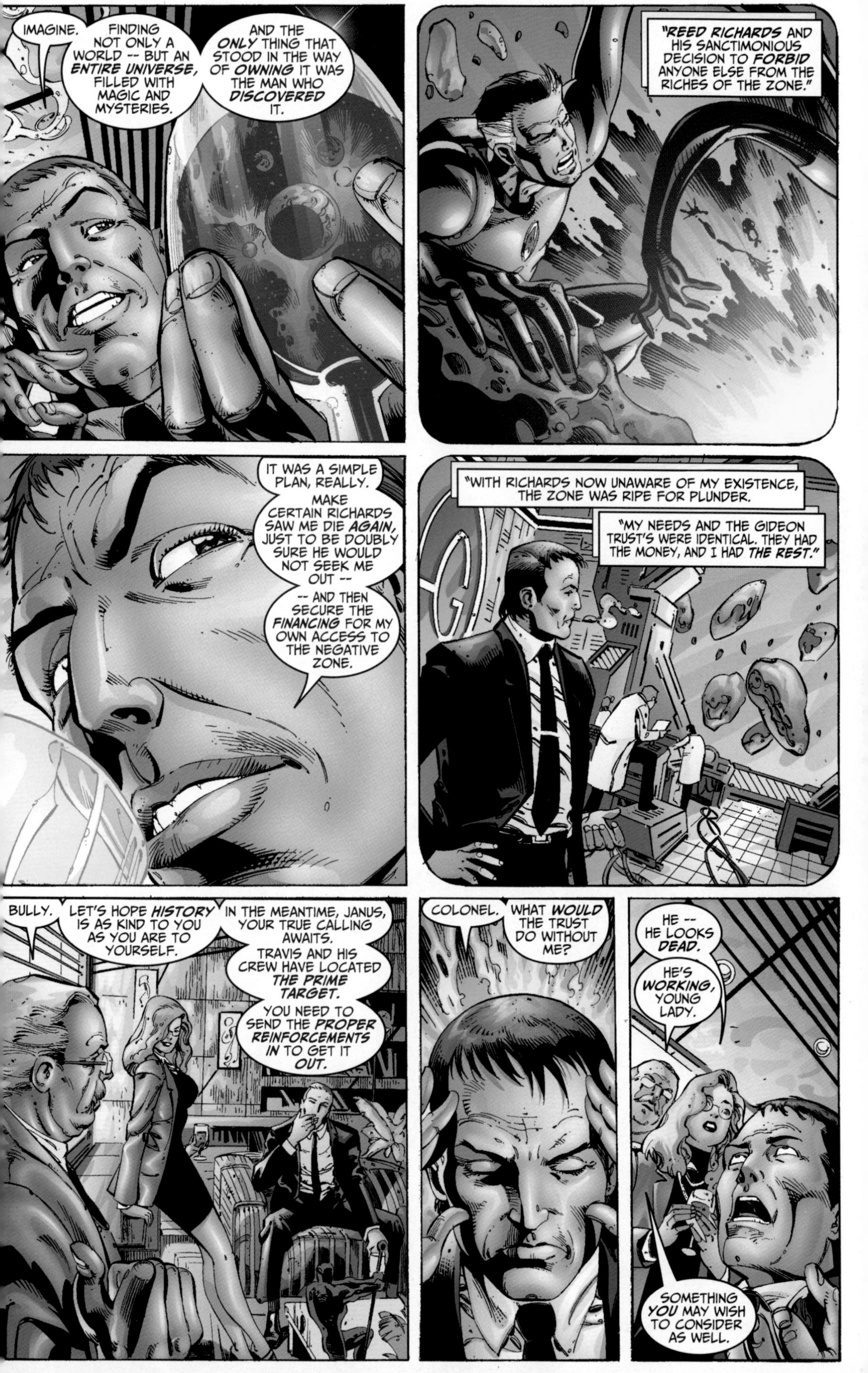
IMAGINE.
FINDING NOT ONLY A WORLD -- BUT AN ENTIRE UNIVERSE, FILLED WITH MAGIC AND MYSTERIES.
AND THE ONLY THING THAT STOOD IN THE WAY OF OWNING IT WAS THE MAN WHO DISCOVERED IT.
"REED RICHARDS AND HIS SANCTIMONIOUS DECISION TO FORBID ANYONE ELSE FROM THE RICHES OF THE ZONE."
IT WAS A SIMPLE PLAN, REALLY.
MAKE CERTAIN RICHARDS SAW ME DIE AGAIN, JUST TO BE DOUBLY SURE HE WOULD NOT SEEK ME OUT --
-- AND THEN SECURE THE FINANCING FOR MY OWN ACCESS TO THE NEGATIVE ZONE.
"WITH RICHARDS NOW UNAWARE OF MY EXISTENCE, THE ZONE WAS RIPE FOR PLUNDER.
"MY NEEDS AND THE GIDEON TRUST'S WERE IDENTICAL. THEY HAD THE MONEY, AND I HAD THE REST."
BULLY.
LET'S HOPE HISTORY IS AS KIND TO YOU AS YOU ARE TO YOURSELF.
IN THE MEANTIME, JANUS, YOUR TRUE CALLING AWAITS.
TRAVIS AND HIS CREW HAVE LOCATED THE PRIME TARGET.
YOU NEED TO SEND THE PROPER REINFORCEMENTS IN TO GET IT OUT.
COLONEL.
WHAT WOULD THE TRUST DO WITHOUT ME?
HE -- HE LOOKS DEAD.
HE'S WORKING, YOUNG LADY.
SOMETHING YOU MAY WISH TO CONSIDER AS WELL.

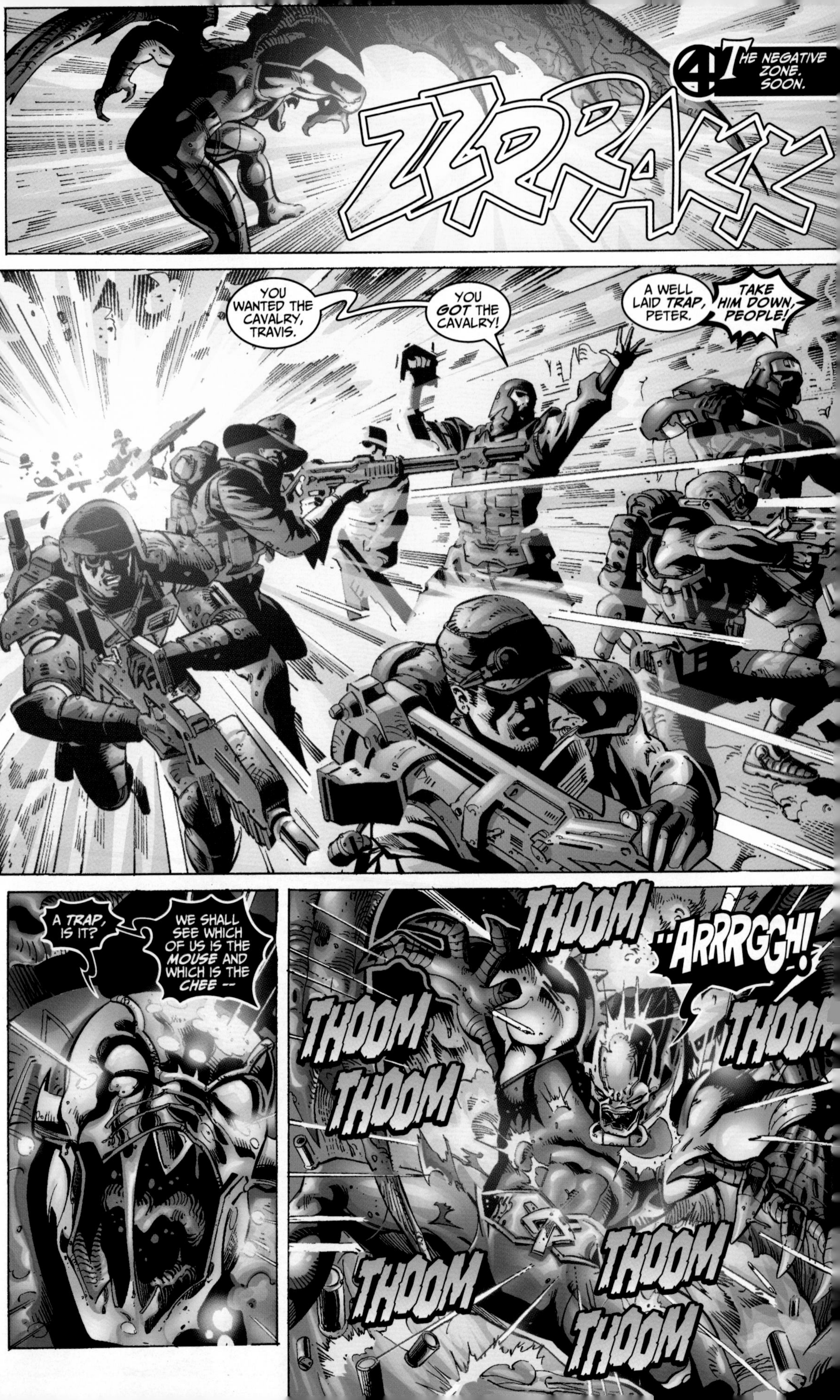

THE NEGATIVE ZONE. SOON.
ZZRRAKK
YOU WANTED THE CAVALRY, TRAVIS.
YOU GOT THE CAVALRY!
A WELL LAID TRAP, PETER.
TAKE HIM DOWN, PEOPLE!
A TRAP, IS IT?
WE SHALL SEE WHICH OF US IS THE MOUSE AND WHICH IS THE CHEE --
THOOM
--ARRRGGH!
THOOM
THOOM
THOOM
THOOM
THOOM
THOOM
THOOM

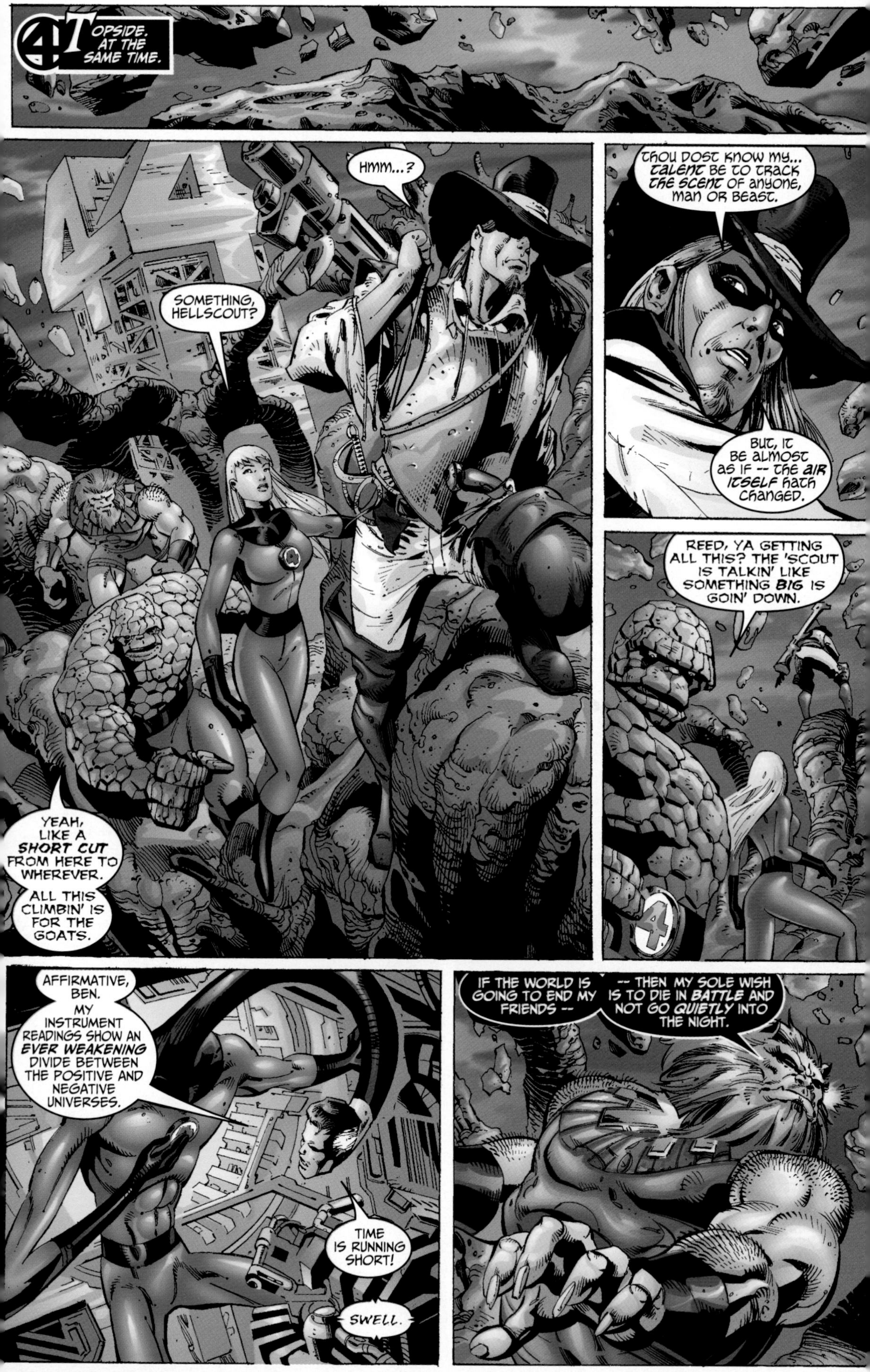
TOPSIDE. AT THE SAME TIME.
HMM...?
SOMETHING, HELLSCOUT?
THOU DOST KNOW MY... TALENT BE TO TRACK THE SCENT OF ANYONE, MAN OR BEAST.
BUT, IT BE ALMOST AS IF -- THE AIR ITSELF HATH CHANGED.
REED, YA GETTING ALL THIS? THE 'SCOUT IS TALKIN' LIKE SOMETHING BIG IS GOIN' DOWN.
YEAH, LIKE A SHORT CUT FROM HERE TO WHEREVER.
ALL THIS CLIMBIN' IS FOR THE GOATS.
AFFIRMATIVE, BEN.
MY INSTRUMENT READINGS SHOW AN EVER WEAKENING DIVIDE BETWEEN THE POSITIVE AND NEGATIVE UNIVERSES.
TIME IS RUNNING SHORT!
SWELL.
IF THE WORLD IS GOING TO END MY FRIENDS --
-- THEN MY SOLE WISH IS TO DIE IN BATTLE AND NOT GO QUIETLY INTO THE NIGHT.

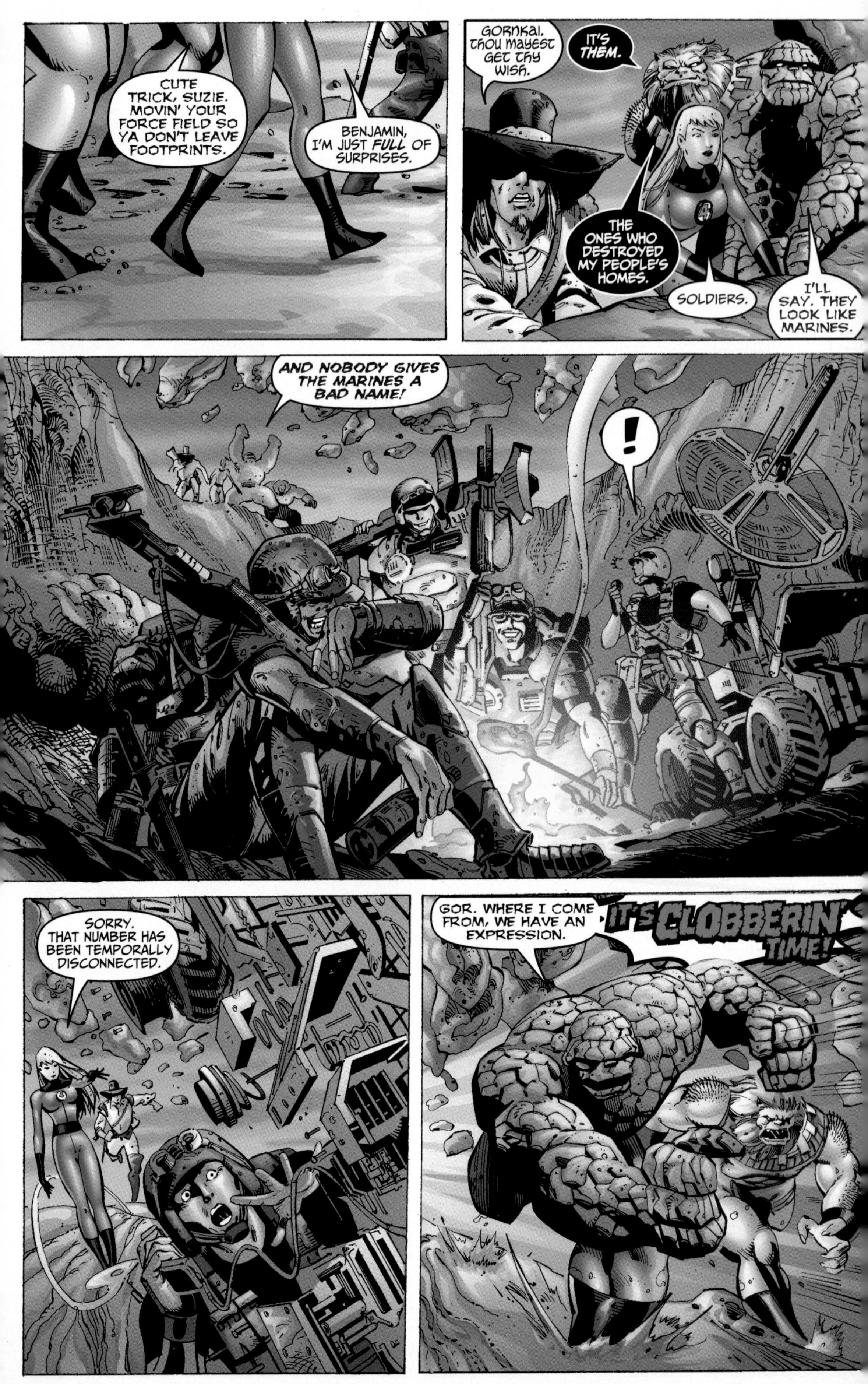
CUTE TRICK, SUZIE. MOVIN' YOUR FORCE FIELD SO YA DON'T LEAVE FOOTPRINTS.
BENJAMIN, I'M JUST FULL OF SURPRISES.
GORNKAI. THOU MAYEST GET THY WISH.
IT'S THEM.
THE ONES WHO DESTROYED MY PEOPLE'S HOMES.
SOLDIERS.
I'LL SAY. THEY LOOK LIKE MARINES.
AND NOBODY GIVES THE MARINES A BAD NAME!
!
SORRY. THAT NUMBER HAS BEEN TEMPORALLY DISCONNECTED.
GOR. WHERE I COME FROM, WE HAVE AN EXPRESSION.
IT'S CLOBBERIN' TIME!

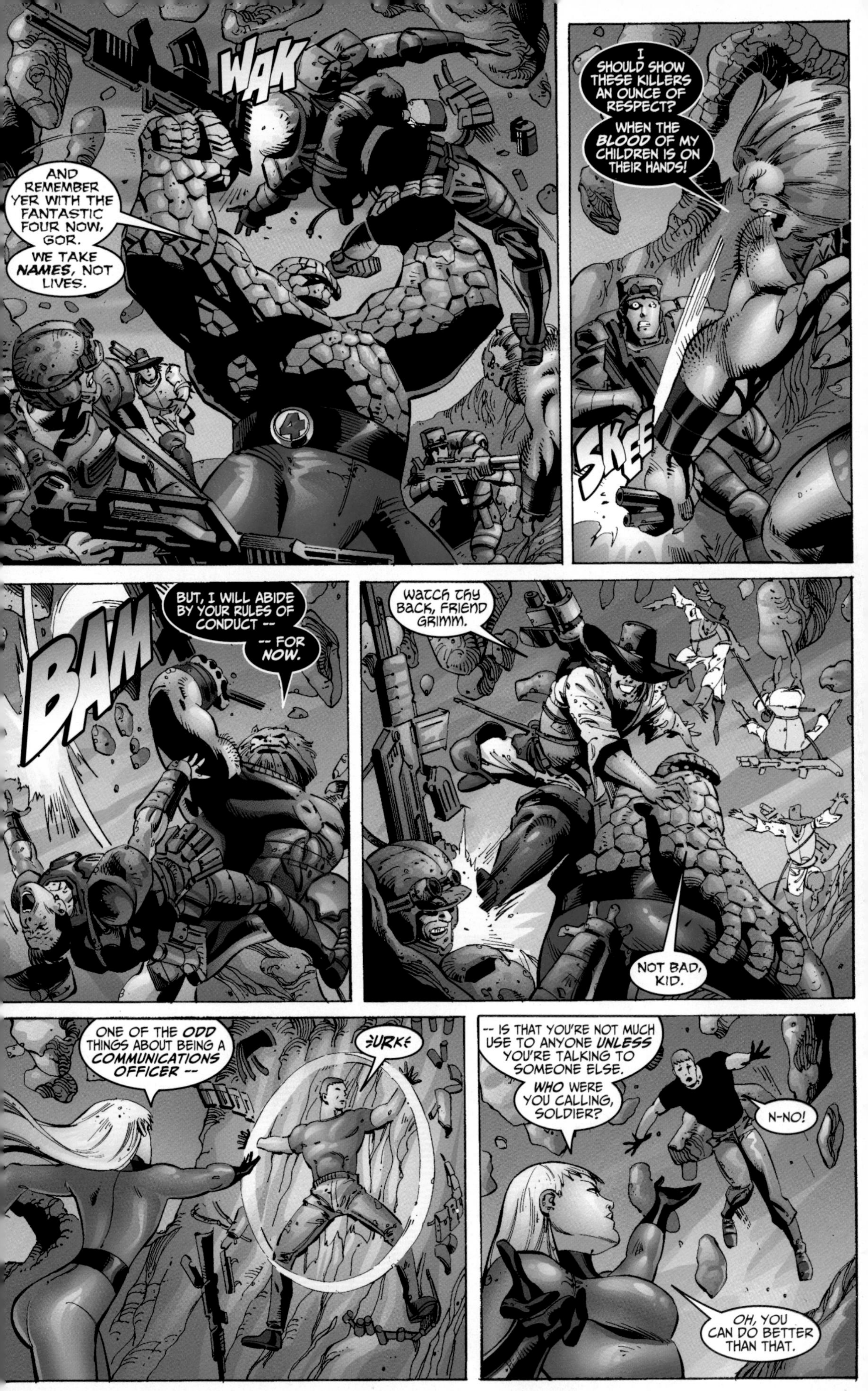
WAK
AND REMEMBER YER WITH THE FANTASTIC FOUR NOW, GOR.
WE TAKE NAMES, NOT LIVES.
I SHOULD SHOW THESE KILLERS AN OUNCE OF RESPECT?
WHEN THE BLOOD OF MY CHILDREN IS ON THEIR HANDS!
SKEE
BAM
BUT, I WILL ABIDE BY YOUR RULES OF CONDUCT --
-- FOR NOW.
WATCH THY BACK, FRIEND GRIMM.
NOT BAD, KID.
ONE OF THE ODD THINGS ABOUT BEING A COMMUNICATIONS OFFICER --
URK
-- IS THAT YOU'RE NOT MUCH USE TO ANYONE UNLESS YOU'RE TALKING TO SOMEONE ELSE.
WHO WERE YOU CALLING, SOLDIER?
N-NO!
OH, YOU CAN DO BETTER THAN THAT.

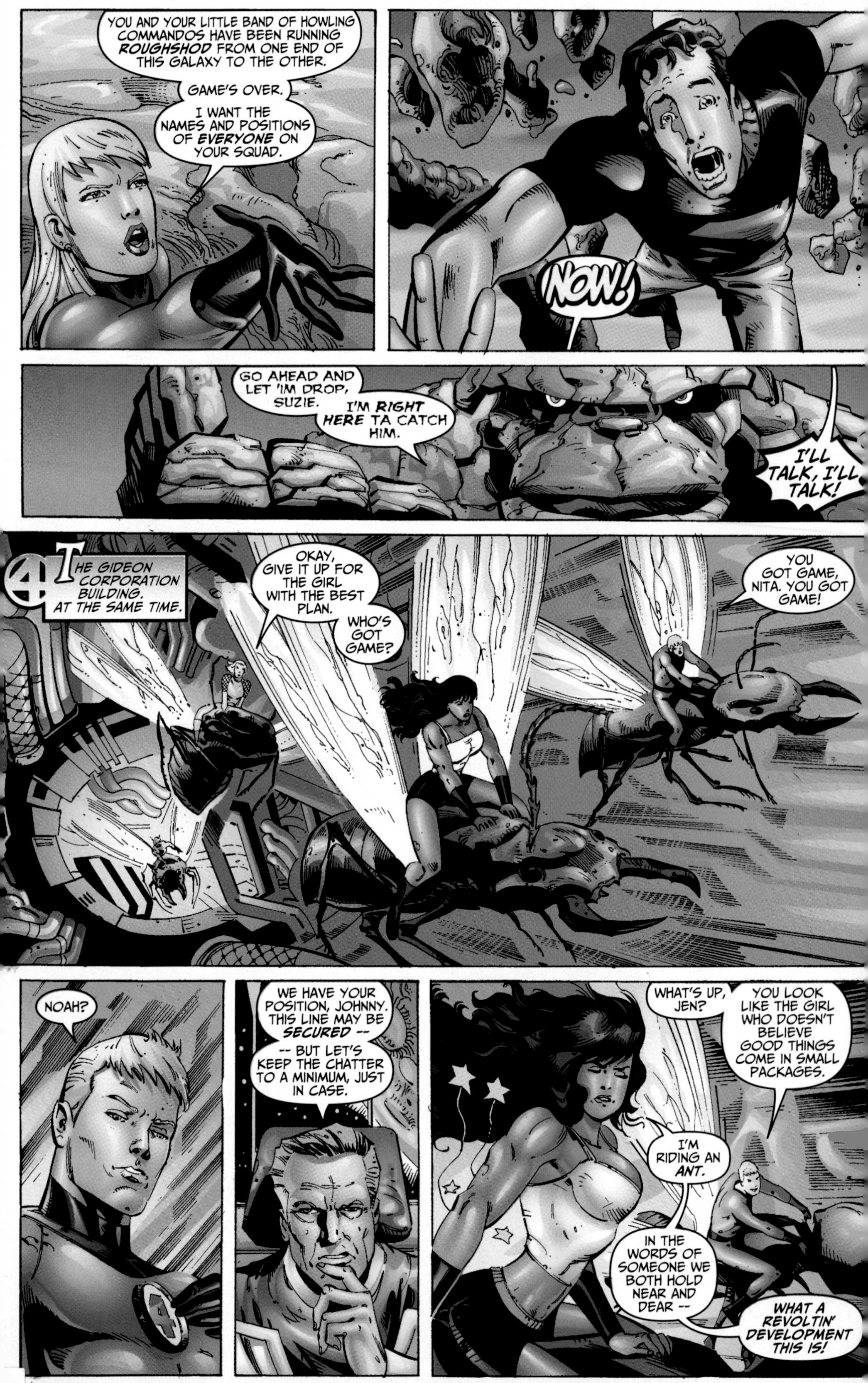

YOU AND YOUR LITTLE BAND OF HOWLING COMMANDOS HAVE BEEN RUNNING ROUGHSHOD FROM ONE END OF THIS GALAXY TO THE OTHER.
GAME'S OVER.
I WANT THE NAMES AND POSITIONS OF EVERYONE ON YOUR SQUAD.
NOW!
GO AHEAD AND LET 'IM DROP, SUZIE.
I'M RIGHT HERE TA CATCH HIM.
I'LL TALK, I'LL TALK!
THE GIDEON CORPORATION BUILDING. AT THE SAME TIME.
OKAY, GIVE IT UP FOR THE GIRL WITH THE BEST PLAN.
WHO'S GOT GAME?
YOU GOT GAME, NITA. YOU GOT GAME!
NOAH?
WE HAVE YOUR POSITION, JOHNNY. THIS LINE MAY BE SECURED --
-- BUT LET'S KEEP THE CHATTER TO A MINIMUM, JUST IN CASE.
WHAT'S UP, JEN?
YOU LOOK LIKE THE GIRL WHO DOESN'T BELIEVE GOOD THINGS COME IN SMALL PACKAGES.
I'M RIDING AN ANT.
IN THE WORDS OF SOMEONE WE BOTH HOLD NEAR AND DEAR --
WHAT A REVOLTIN' DEVELOPMENT THIS IS!

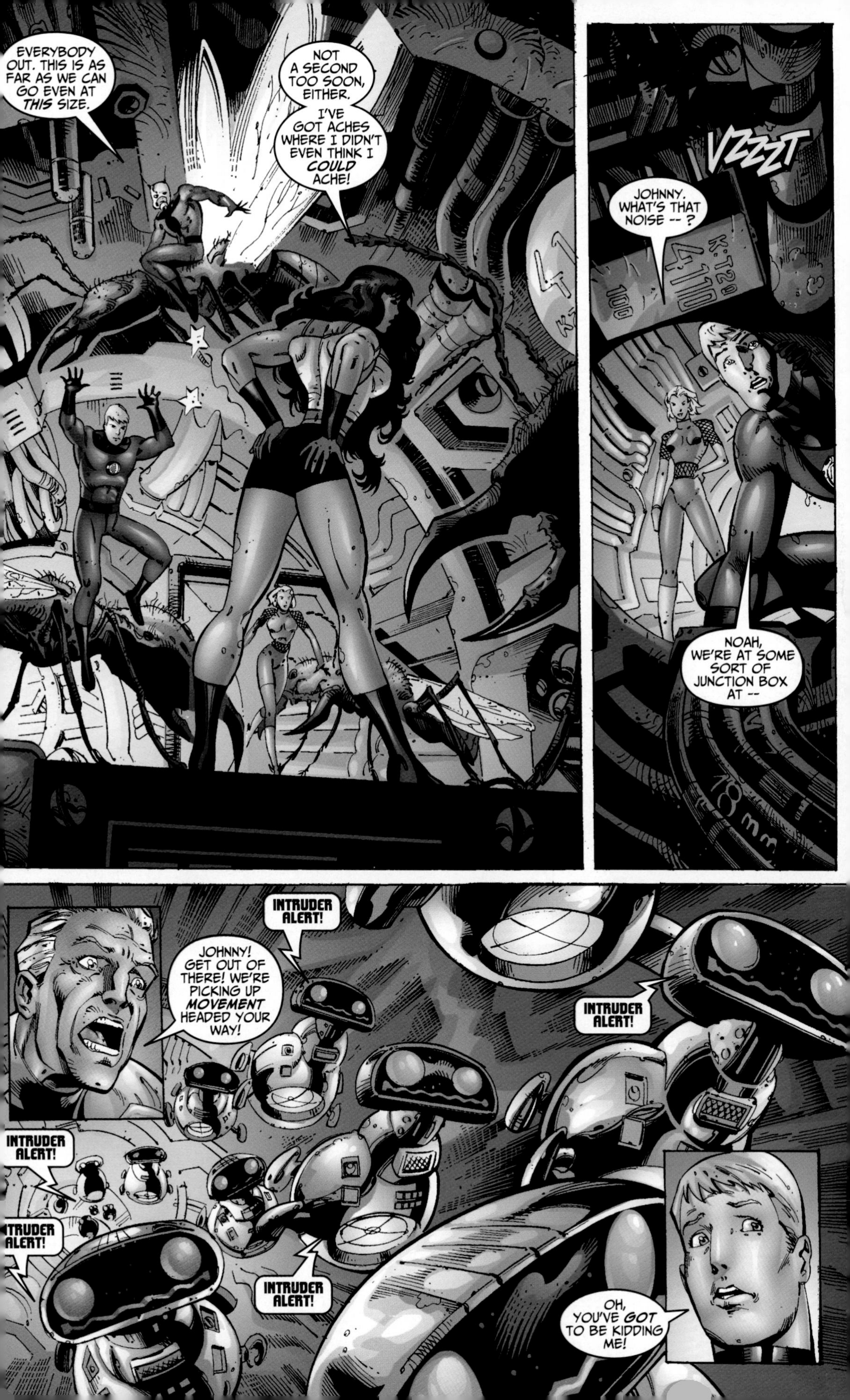
EVERYBODY OUT. THIS IS AS FAR AS WE CAN GO EVEN AT THIS SIZE.
NOT A SECOND TOO SOON, EITHER.
I'VE GOT ACHES WHERE I DIDN'T EVEN THINK I COULD ACHE!
VZZZT
JOHNNY. WHAT'S THAT NOISE -- ?
NOAH, WE'RE AT SOME SORT OF JUNCTION BOX AT --
INTRUDER ALERT!
JOHNNY! GET OUT OF THERE! WE'RE PICKING UP MOVEMENT HEADED YOUR WAY!
INTRUDER ALERT!
INTRUDER ALERT!
INTRUDER ALERT!
INTRUDER ALERT!
OH, YOU'VE GOT TO BE KIDDING ME!

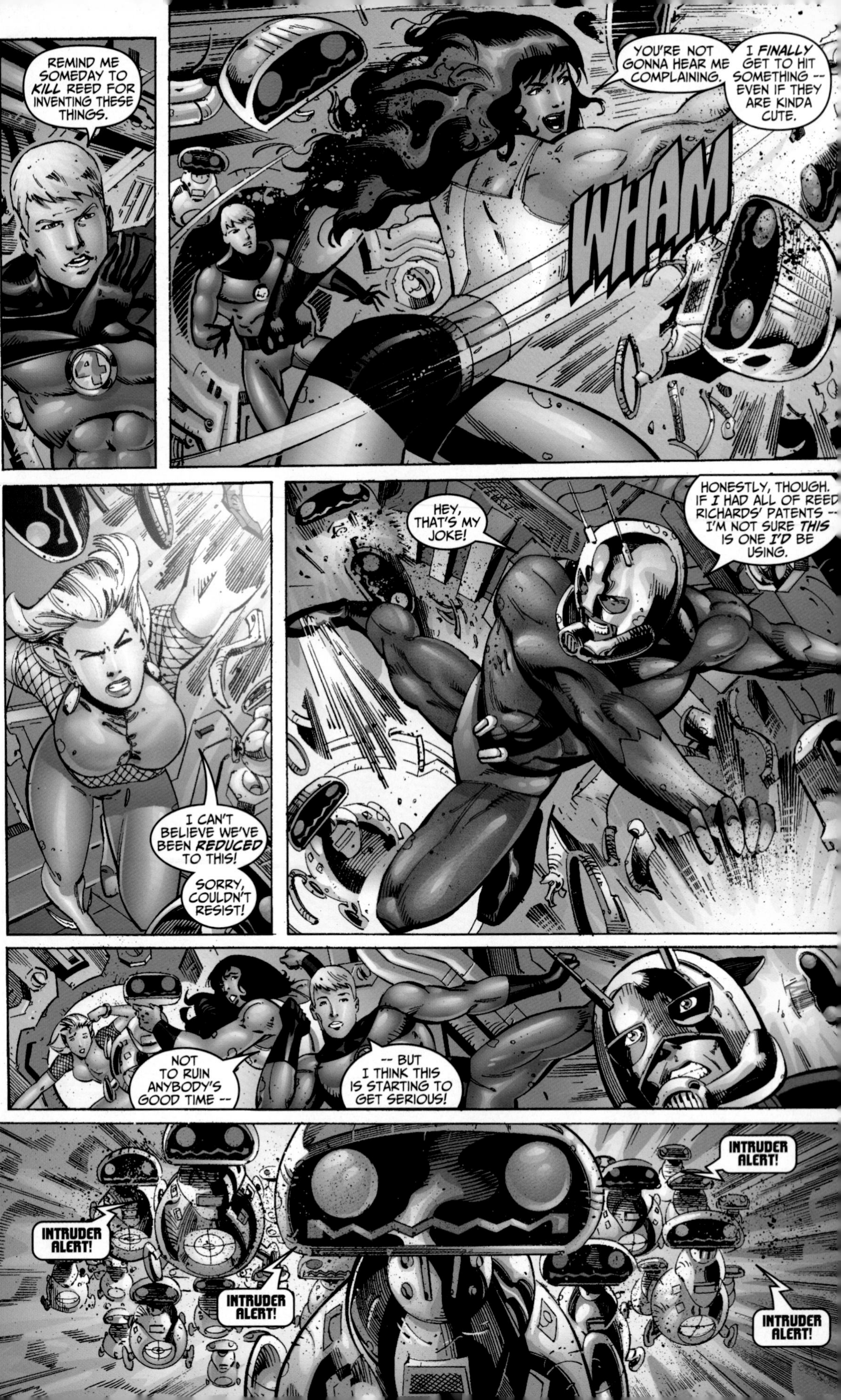
REMIND ME SOMEDAY TO KILL REED FOR INVENTING THESE THINGS.
YOU'RE NOT GONNA HEAR ME COMPLAINING.
I FINALLY GET TO HIT SOMETHING -- EVEN IF THEY ARE KINDA CUTE.
WHAM
HEY, THAT'S MY JOKE!
HONESTLY, THOUGH. IF I HAD ALL OF REED RICHARDS' PATENTS -- I'M NOT SURE THIS IS ONE I'D BE USING.
I CAN'T BELIEVE WE'VE BEEN REDUCED TO THIS!
SORRY, COULDN'T RESIST!
NOT TO RUIN ANYBODY'S GOOD TIME --
-- BUT I THINK THIS IS STARTING TO GET SERIOUS!
INTRUDER ALERT!
INTRUDER ALERT!
INTRUDER ALERT!
INTRUDER ALERT!

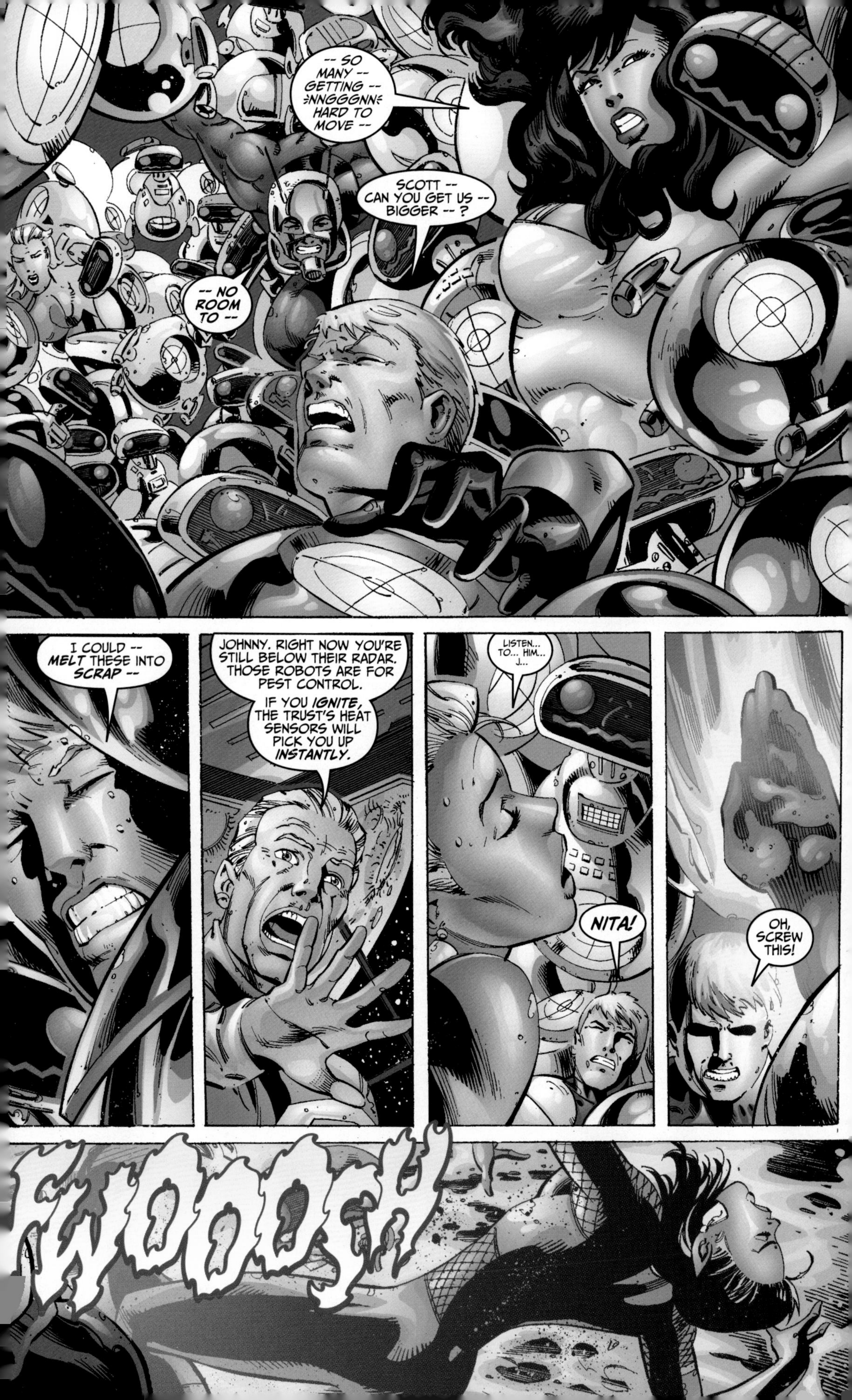
-- SO MANY -- GETTING -- =NNGGGNN= HARD TO MOVE --
SCOTT -- CAN YOU GET US -- BIGGER -- ?
-- NO ROOM TO --
I COULD -- MELT THESE INTO SCRAP --
JOHNNY. RIGHT NOW YOU'RE STILL BELOW THEIR RADAR. THOSE ROBOTS ARE FOR PEST CONTROL.
IF YOU IGNITE, THE TRUST'S HEAT SENSORS WILL PICK YOU UP INSTANTLY.
LISTEN... TO... HIM... J...
NITA!
OH, SCREW THIS!

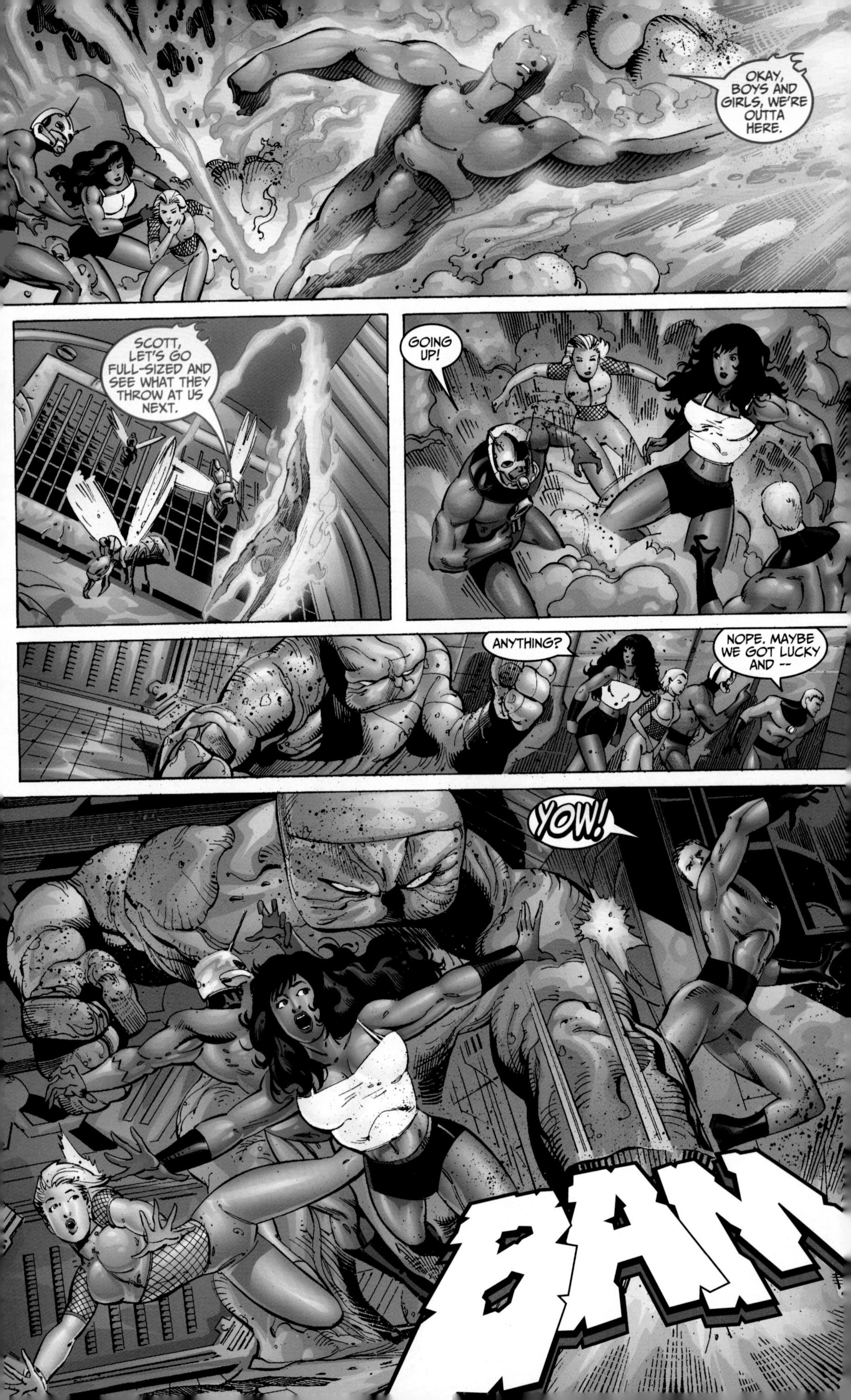
OKAY, BOYS AND GIRLS, WE'RE OUTTA HERE.
SCOTT, LET'S GO FULL-SIZED AND SEE WHAT THEY THROW AT US NEXT.
GOING UP!
ANYTHING?
NOPE. MAYBE WE GOT LUCKY AND --
YOW!
BAM

JEN! DAMMIT -- WE'RE IN REAL TROUBLE NOW!

THE NEGATIVE ZONE. NOW.

AAAAAAHH!

'TIS THE DEVIL HIMSELF!

SUZIE, I AIN'T GOT NO LOVE FER GREEN AND GRUESOME --

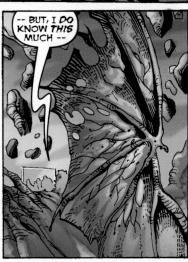

-- BUT, I DO KNOW THIS MUCH --

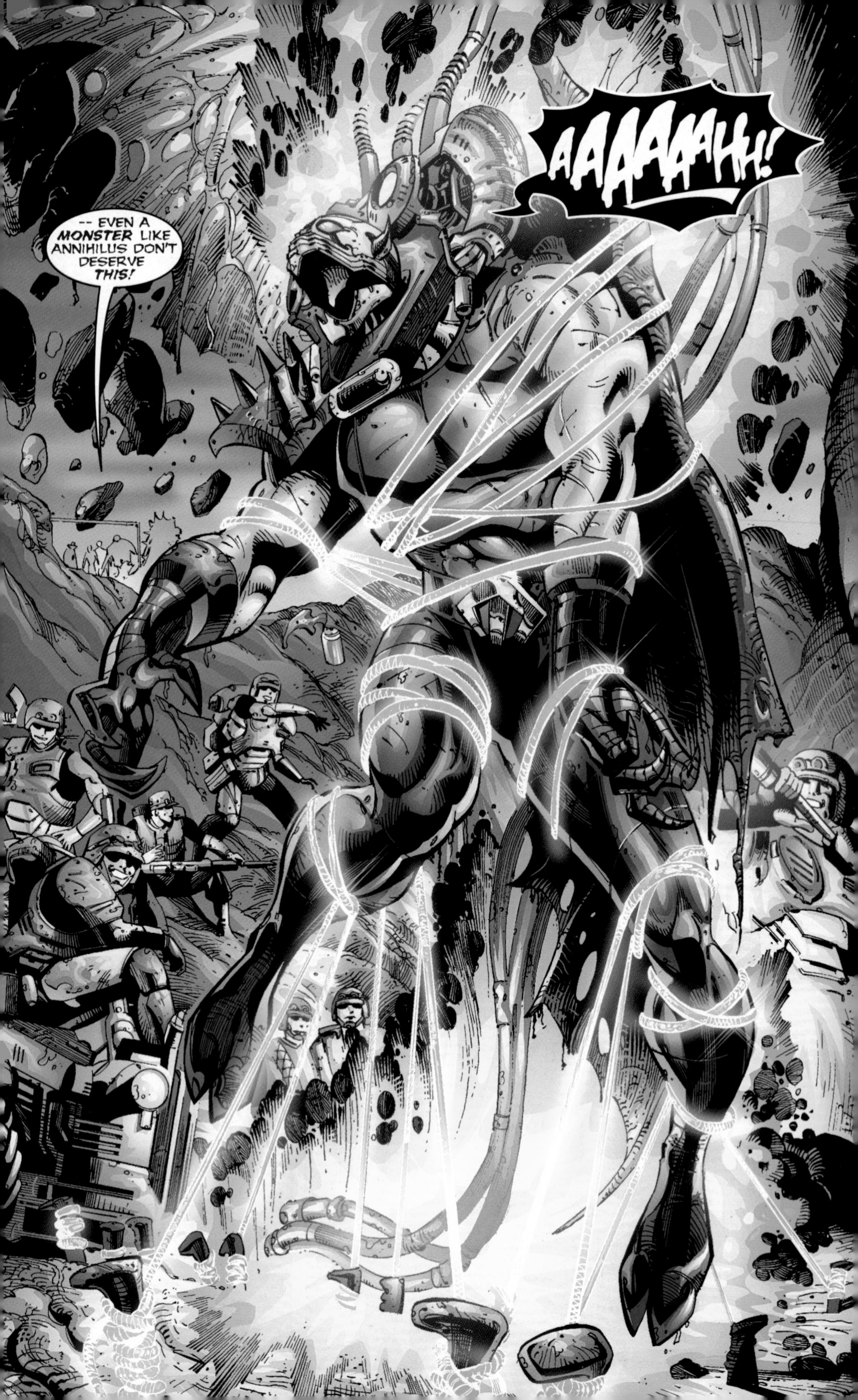
-- EVEN A MONSTER LIKE ANNIHILUS DON'T DESERVE THIS!
AAAAAAHH!

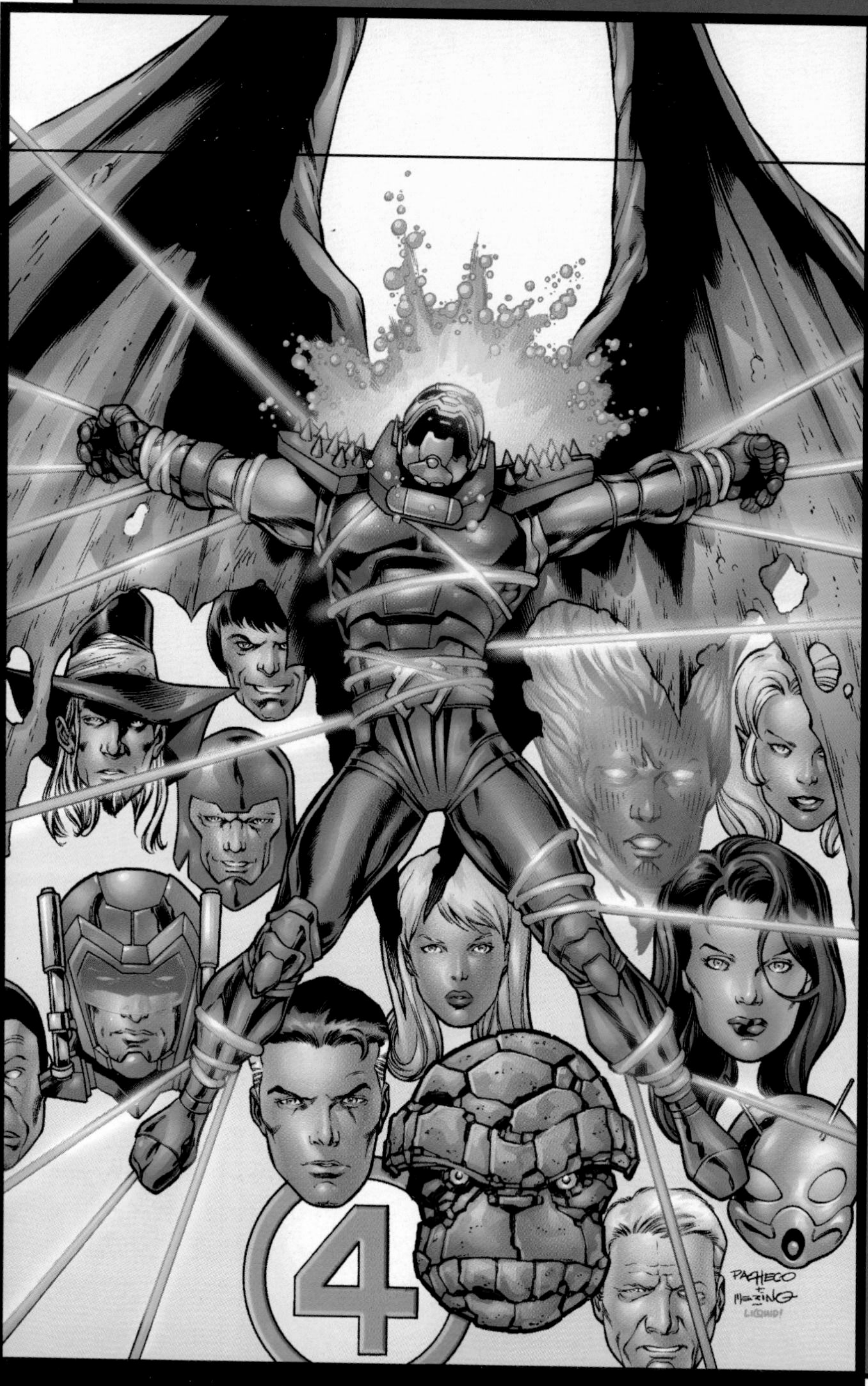
PACHECO

FANTASTIC FOUR #44

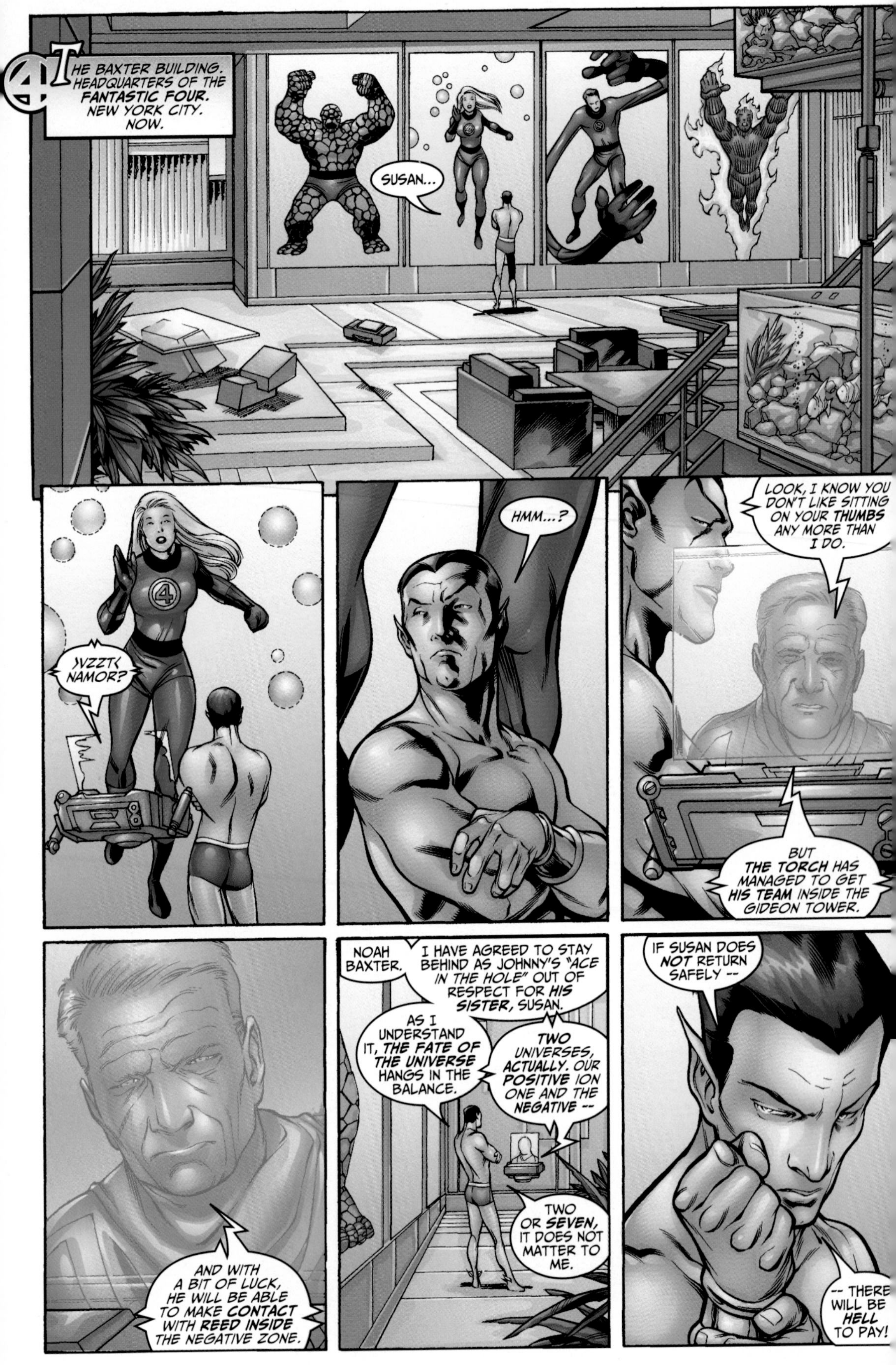
THE BAXTER BUILDING. HEADQUARTERS OF THE FANTASTIC FOUR. NEW YORK CITY. NOW.
SUSAN...
›VZZT‹ NAMOR?
HMM...?
LOOK, I KNOW YOU DON'T LIKE SITTING ON YOUR THUMBS ANY MORE THAN I DO.
BUT THE TORCH HAS MANAGED TO GET HIS TEAM INSIDE THE GIDEON TOWER.
AND WITH A BIT OF LUCK, HE WILL BE ABLE TO MAKE CONTACT WITH REED INSIDE THE NEGATIVE ZONE.
NOAH BAXTER.
I HAVE AGREED TO STAY BEHIND AS JOHNNY'S "ACE IN THE HOLE" OUT OF RESPECT FOR HIS SISTER, SUSAN.
AS I UNDERSTAND IT, THE FATE OF THE UNIVERSE HANGS IN THE BALANCE.
TWO UNIVERSES, ACTUALLY. OUR POSITIVE ION ONE AND THE NEGATIVE --
TWO OR SEVEN, IT DOES NOT MATTER TO ME.
IF SUSAN DOES NOT RETURN SAFELY --
-- THERE WILL BE HELL TO PAY!

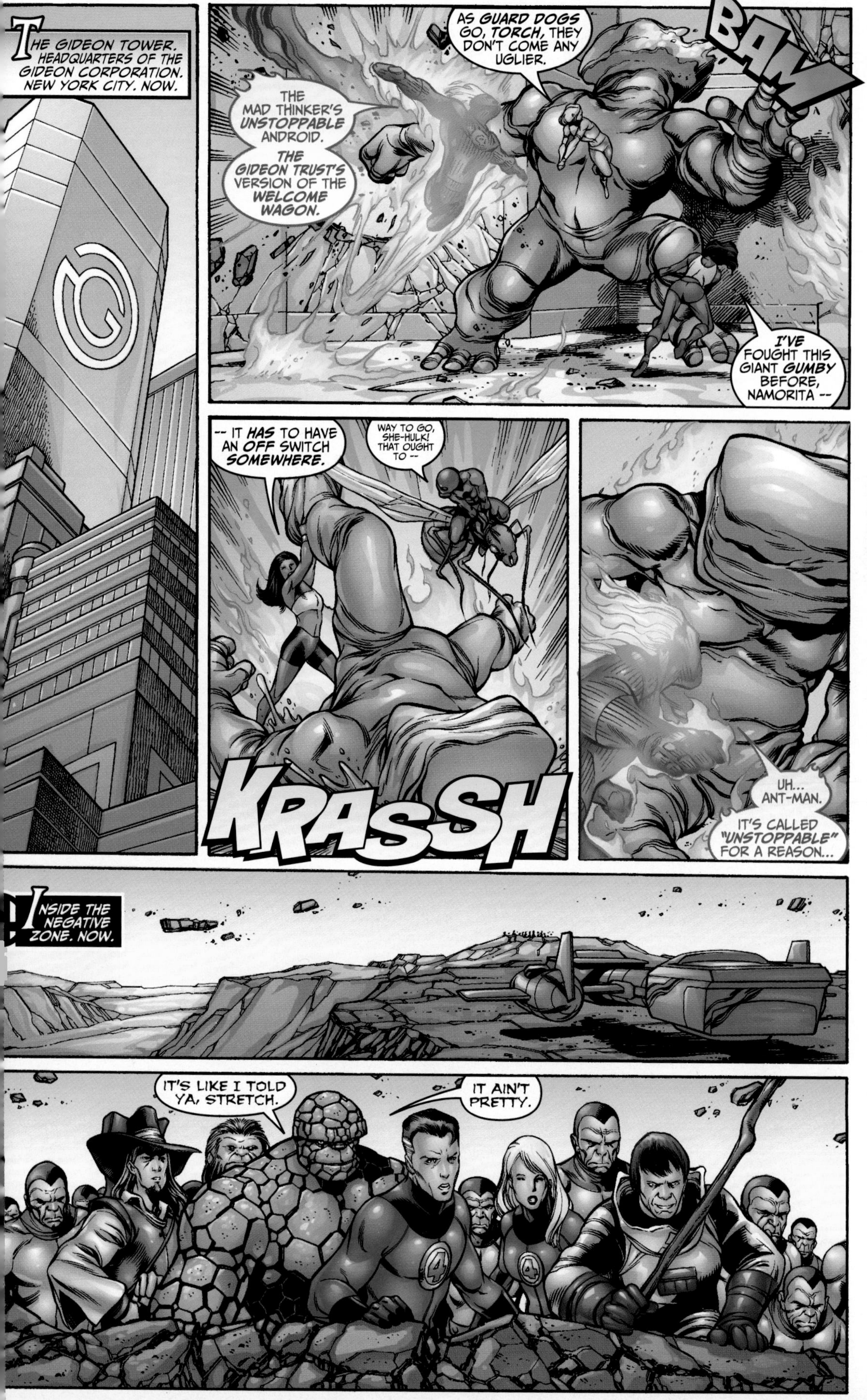
THE GIDEON TOWER. HEADQUARTERS OF THE GIDEON CORPORATION. NEW YORK CITY. NOW.
AS GUARD DOGS GO, TORCH, THEY DON'T COME ANY UGLIER.
BAM
THE MAD THINKER'S UNSTOPPABLE ANDROID.
THE GIDEON TRUST'S VERSION OF THE WELCOME WAGON.
I'VE FOUGHT THIS GIANT GUMBY BEFORE, NAMORITA --
-- IT HAS TO HAVE AN OFF SWITCH SOMEWHERE.
WAY TO GO, SHE-HULK! THAT OUGHT TO --
KRASSH
UH... ANT-MAN.
IT'S CALLED "UNSTOPPABLE" FOR A REASON...
INSIDE THE NEGATIVE ZONE. NOW.
IT'S LIKE I TOLD YA, STRETCH.
IT AIN'T PRETTY.

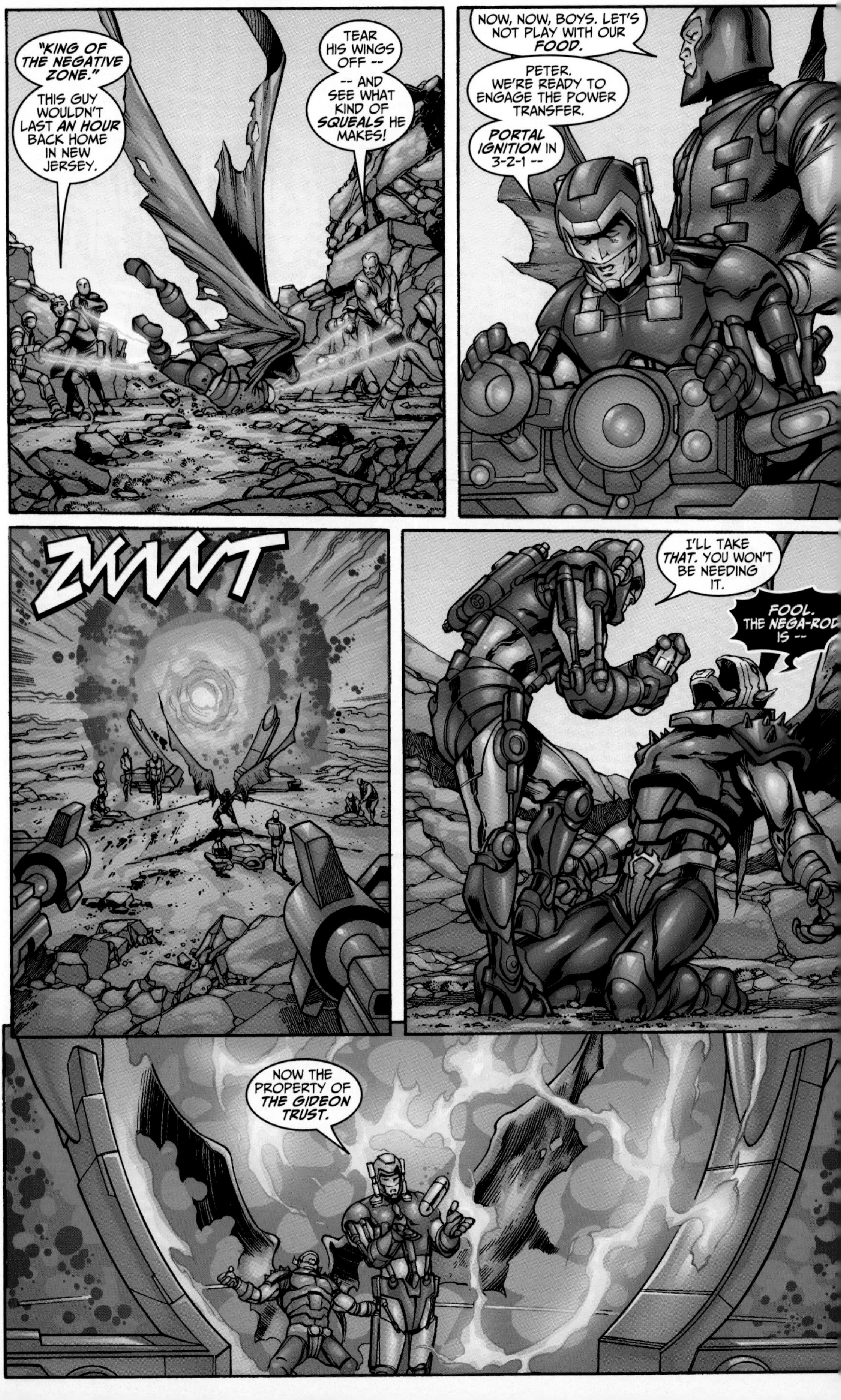
"KING OF THE NEGATIVE ZONE."
THIS GUY WOULDN'T LAST AN HOUR BACK HOME IN NEW JERSEY.
TEAR HIS WINGS OFF --
-- AND SEE WHAT KIND OF SQUEALS HE MAKES!
NOW, NOW, BOYS. LET'S NOT PLAY WITH OUR FOOD.
PETER. WE'RE READY TO ENGAGE THE POWER TRANSFER.
PORTAL IGNITION IN 3-2-1 --
ZWAAT
I'LL TAKE THAT. YOU WON'T BE NEEDING IT.
FOOL. THE NEGA-ROD IS --
NOW THE PROPERTY OF THE GIDEON TRUST.

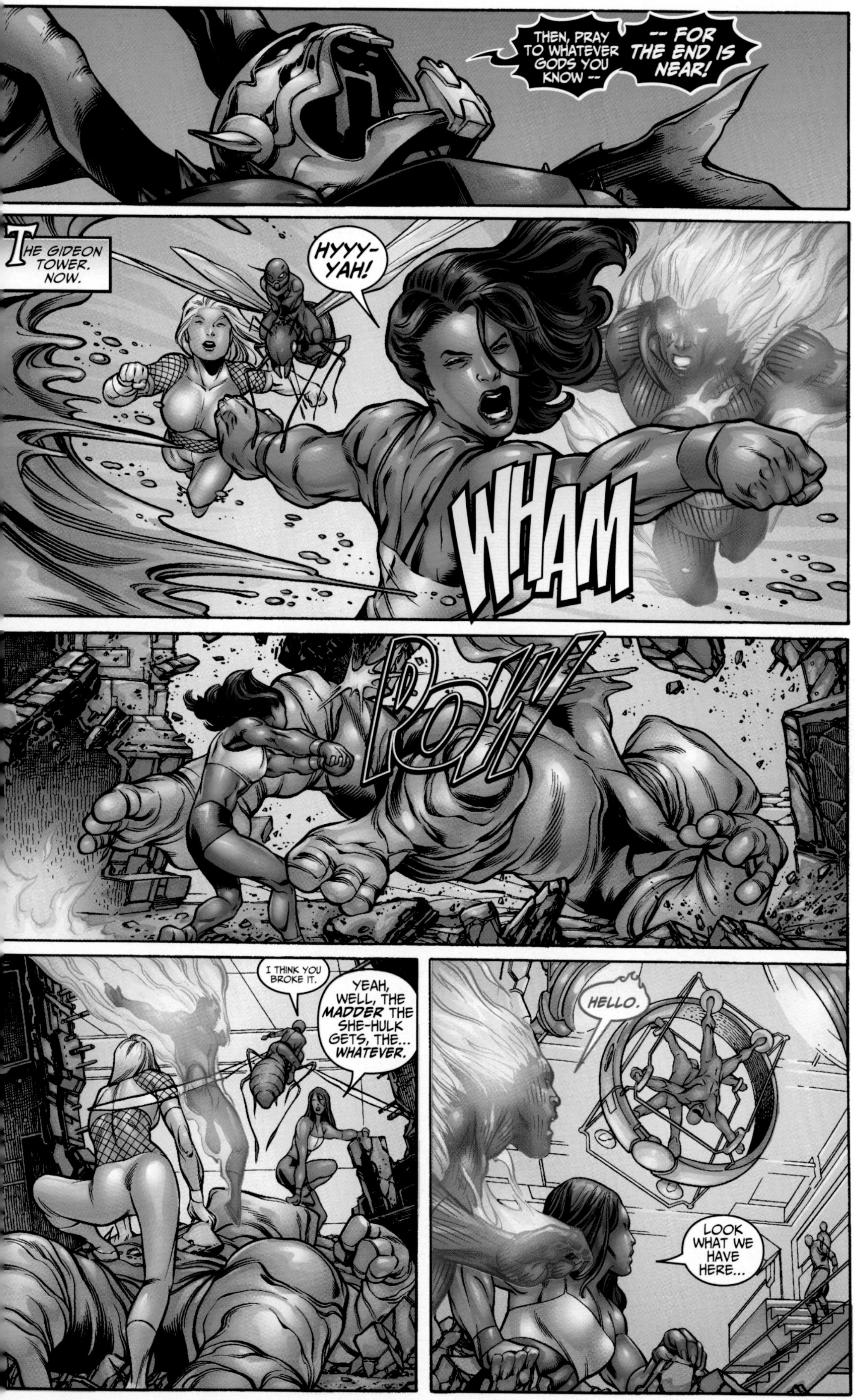
THEN, PRAY TO WHATEVER GODS YOU KNOW --
-- FOR THE END IS NEAR!
THE GIDEON TOWER. NOW.
HYYY-YAH!
WHAM
POW
I THINK YOU BROKE IT.
YEAH, WELL, THE MADDER THE SHE-HULK GETS, THE... WHATEVER.
HELLO.
LOOK WHAT WE HAVE HERE...

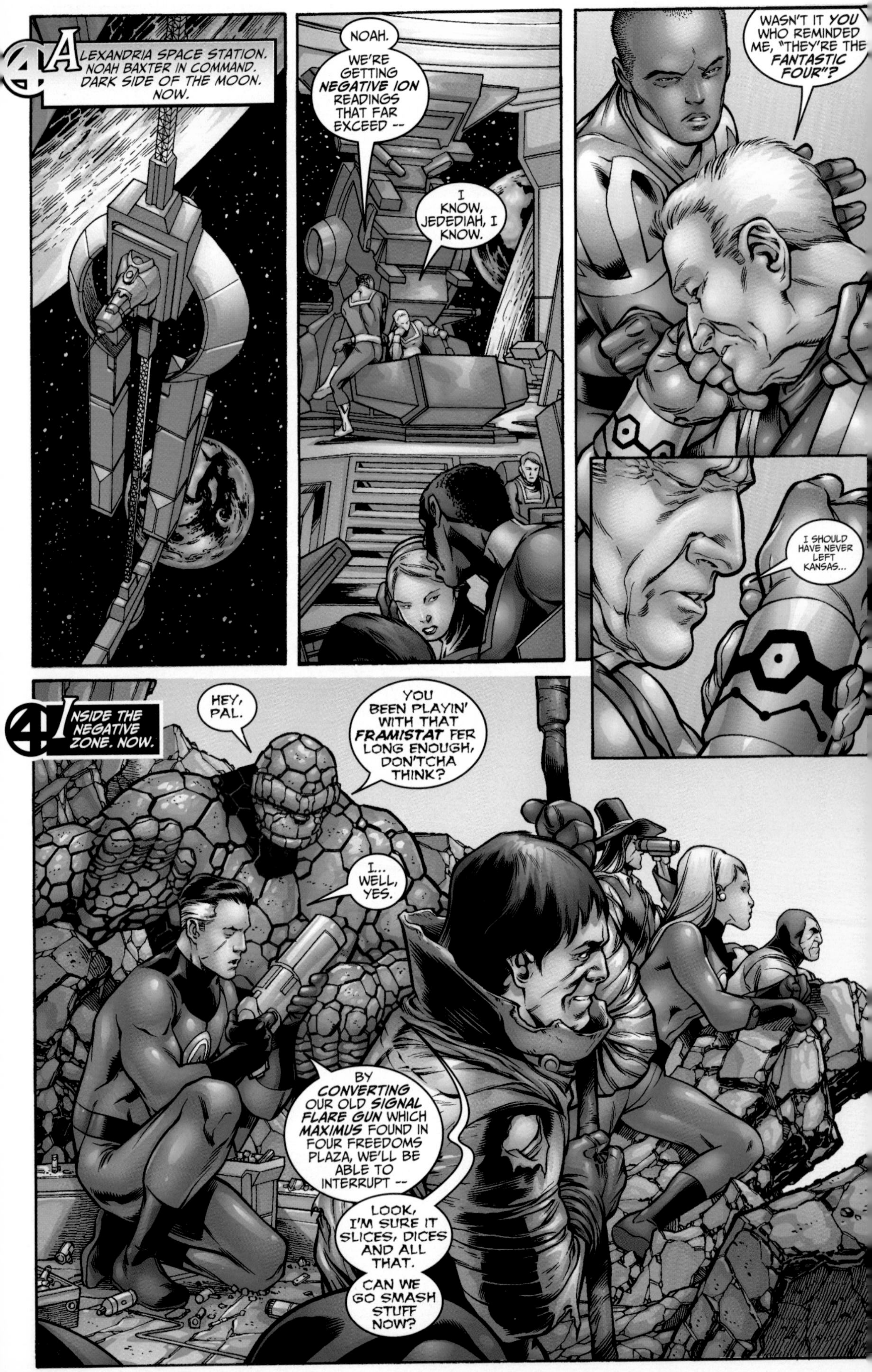
ALEXANDRIA SPACE STATION. NOAH BAXTER IN COMMAND. DARK SIDE OF THE MOON. NOW.
NOAH.
WE'RE GETTING NEGATIVE ION READINGS THAT FAR EXCEED --
I KNOW, JEDEDIAH, I KNOW.
WASN'T IT YOU WHO REMINDED ME, "THEY'RE THE FANTASTIC FOUR"?
I SHOULD HAVE NEVER LEFT KANSAS...
INSIDE THE NEGATIVE ZONE. NOW.
HEY, PAL.
YOU BEEN PLAYIN' WITH THAT FRAMISTAT FER LONG ENOUGH, DON'TCHA THINK?
I... WELL, YES.
BY CONVERTING OUR OLD SIGNAL FLARE GUN WHICH MAXIMUS FOUND IN FOUR FREEDOMS PLAZA, WE'LL BE ABLE TO INTERRUPT --
LOOK, I'M SURE IT SLICES, DICES AND ALL THAT.
CAN WE GO SMASH STUFF NOW?

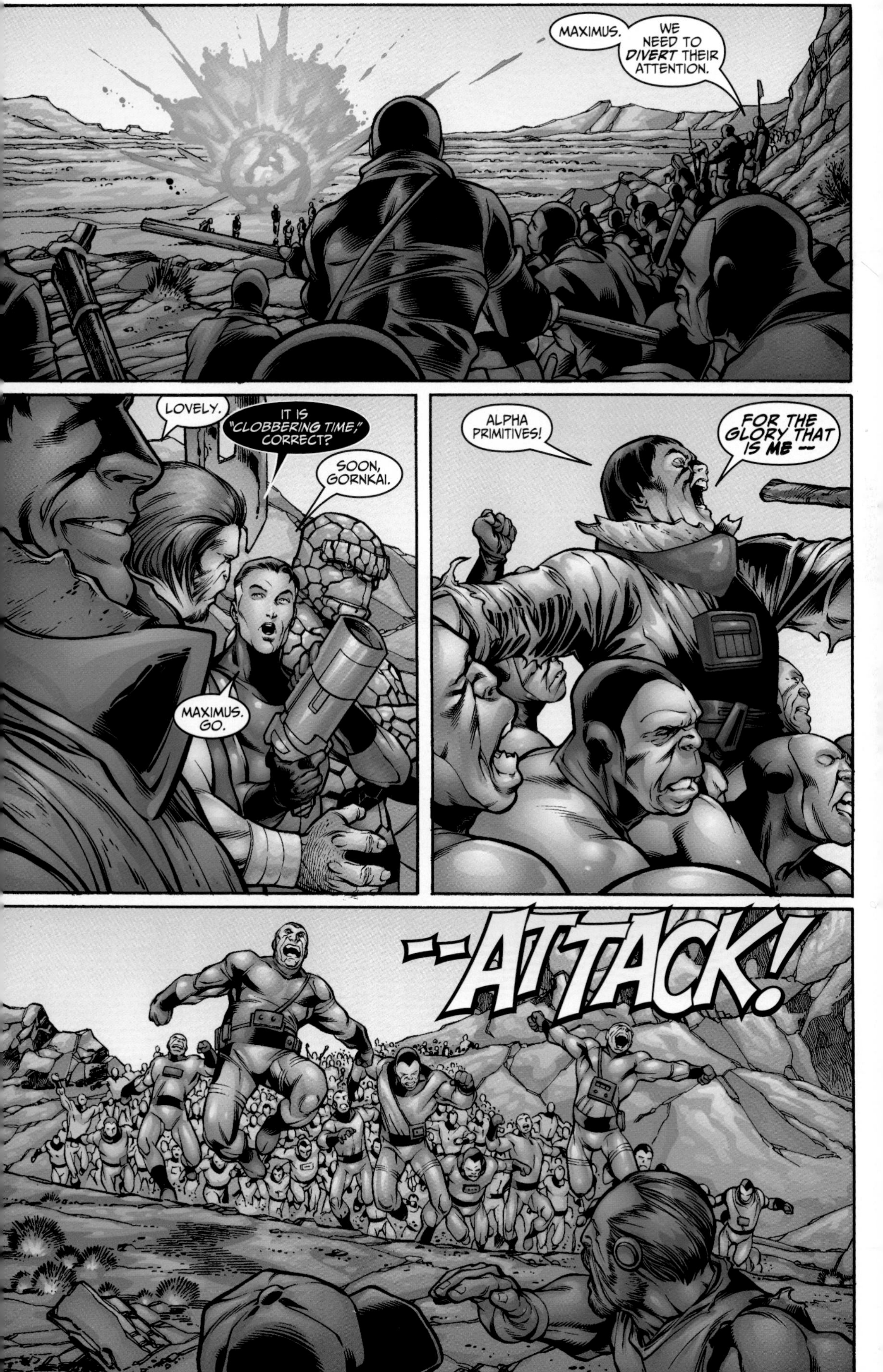
MAXIMUS.
WE NEED TO DIVERT THEIR ATTENTION.
LOVELY.
IT IS "CLOBBERING TIME," CORRECT?
SOON, GORNKAI.
MAXIMUS. GO.
ALPHA PRIMITIVES!
FOR THE GLORY THAT IS ME --
--ATTACK!

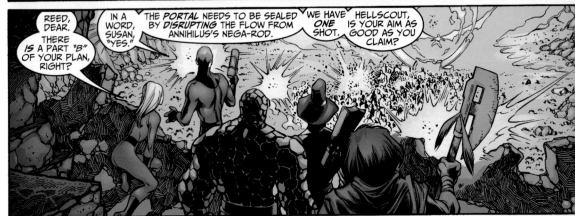

REED, DEAR. THERE *IS* A PART "*B*" OF YOUR PLAN, RIGHT?

IN A WORD, SUSAN, "*YES.*"

THE *PORTAL* NEEDS TO BE SEALED BY *DISRUPTING* THE FLOW FROM ANNIHILUS'S NEGA-ROD.

WE HAVE *ONE* SHOT.

HELLSCOUT, IS YOUR AIM AS GOOD AS YOU CLAIM?

BETTER.

TAKE THIS.

MAY THE LORD BE MY GUIDE.

INCOMING.

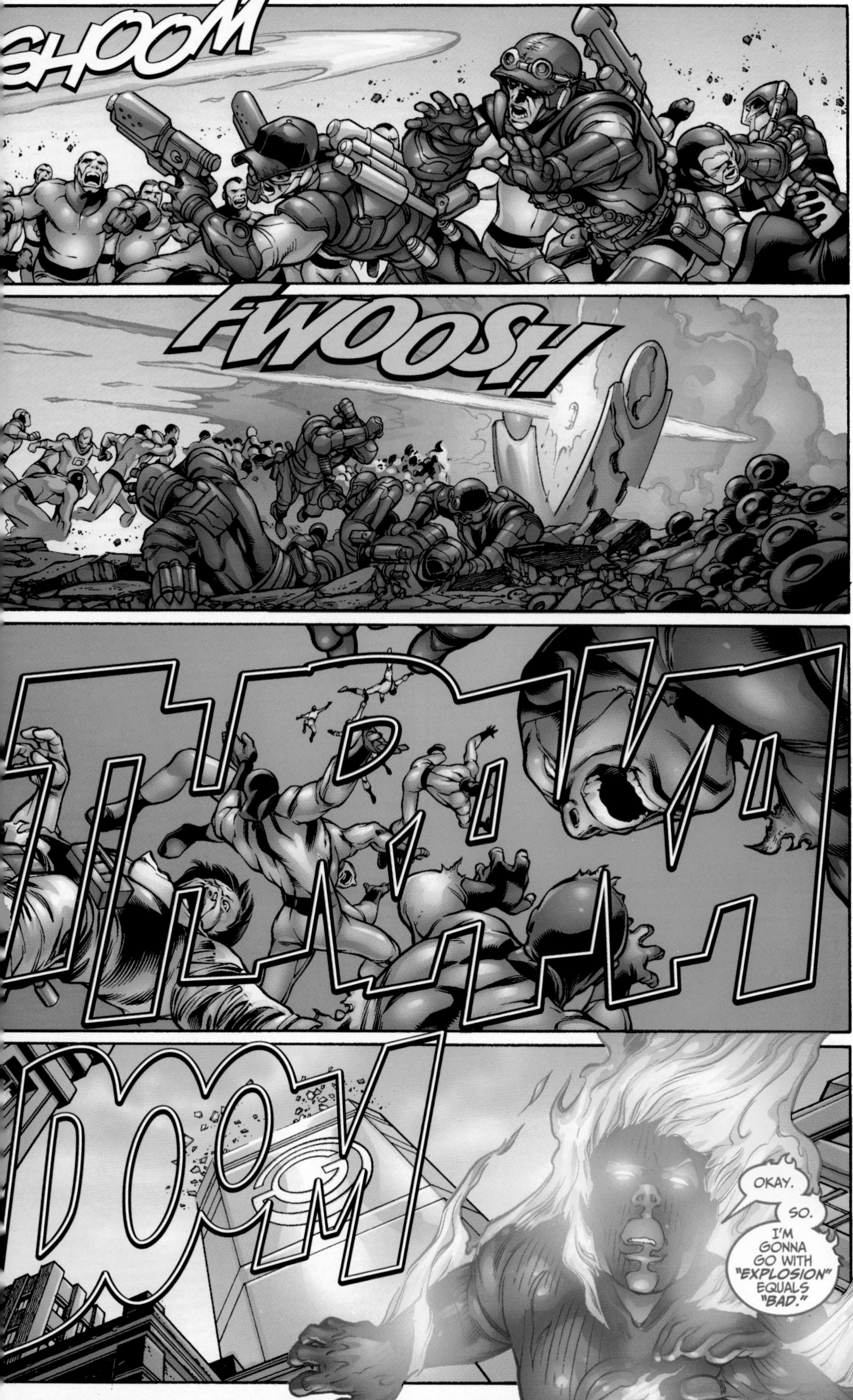
SHOOM
FWOOSH
OKAY.
SO.
I'M GONNA GO WITH "EXPLOSION" EQUALS "BAD."

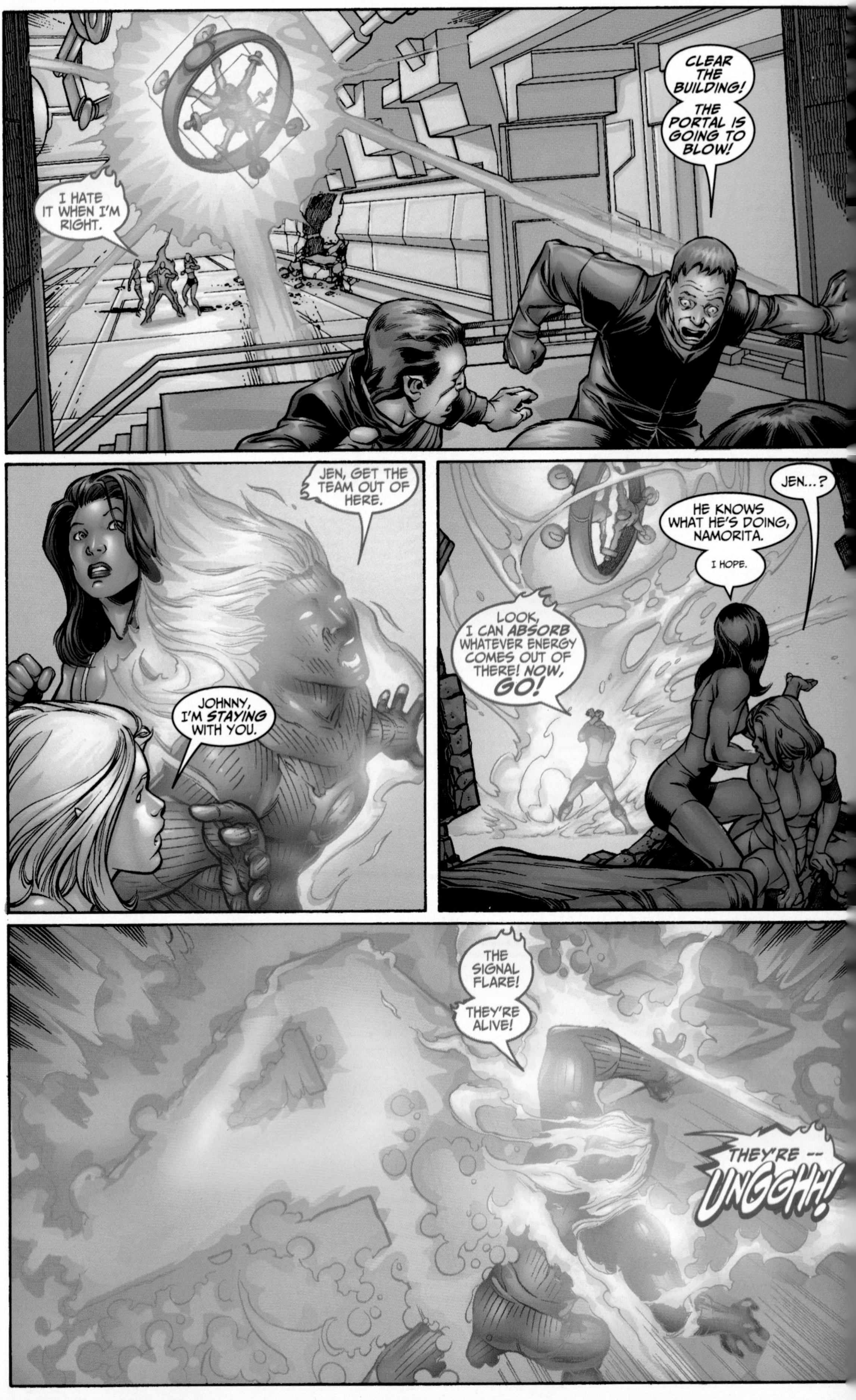
CLEAR THE BUILDING!
THE PORTAL IS GOING TO BLOW!
I HATE IT WHEN I'M RIGHT.
JEN, GET THE TEAM OUT OF HERE.
JOHNNY, I'M STAYING WITH YOU.
JEN...?
HE KNOWS WHAT HE'S DOING, NAMORITA.
I HOPE.
LOOK, I CAN ABSORB WHATEVER ENERGY COMES OUT OF THERE! NOW, GO!
THE SIGNAL FLARE!
THEY'RE ALIVE!
THEY'RE -- UNGGHH!

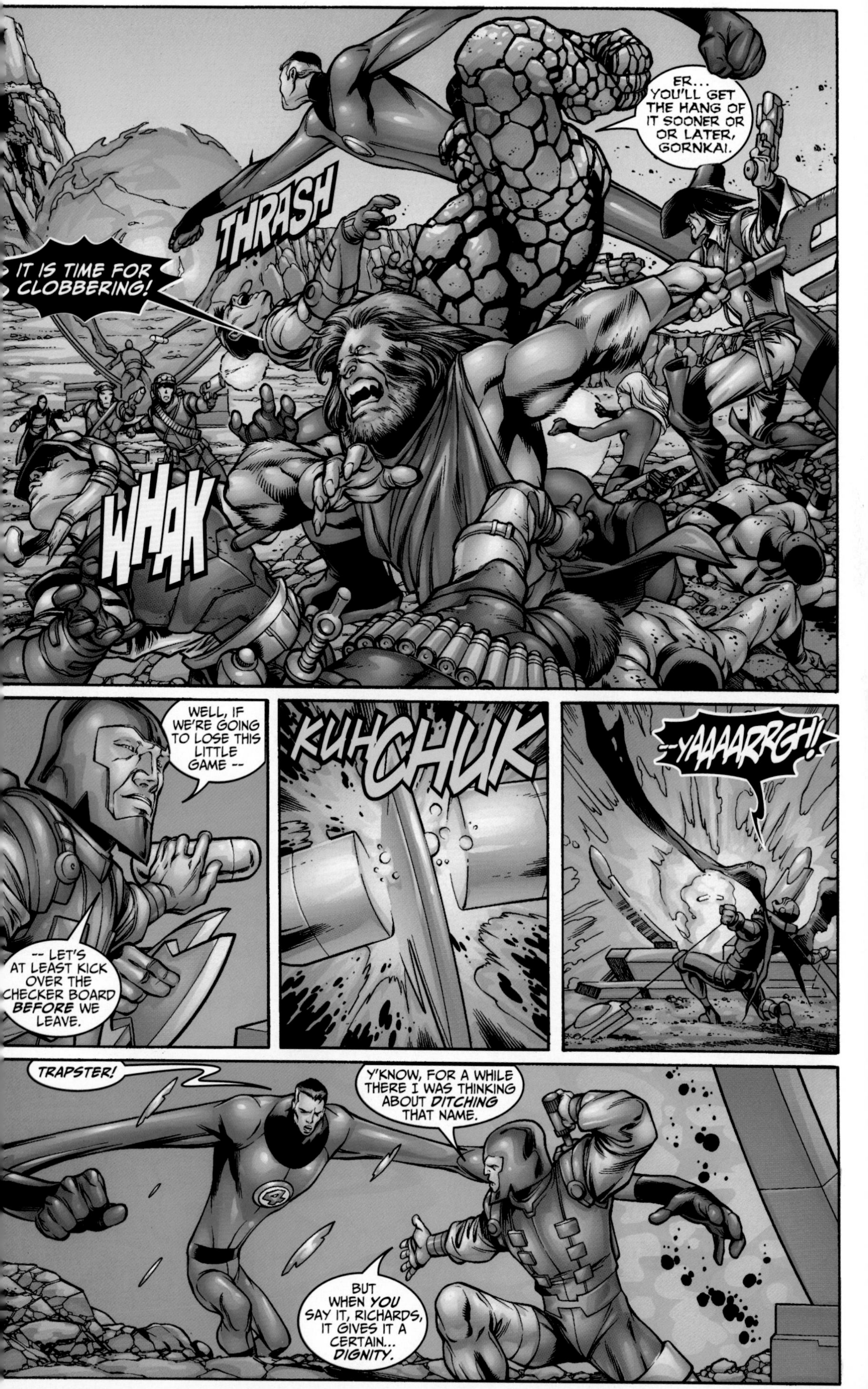
THRASH
IT IS TIME FOR CLOBBERING!
ER... YOU'LL GET THE HANG OF IT SOONER OR OR LATER, GORNKAI.
WHAK
WELL, IF WE'RE GOING TO LOSE THIS LITTLE GAME --
-- LET'S AT LEAST KICK OVER THE CHECKER BOARD *BEFORE* WE LEAVE.
KUHCHUK
--YAAAARRGH!
TRAPSTER!
Y'KNOW, FOR A WHILE THERE I WAS THINKING ABOUT *DITCHING* THAT NAME.
BUT WHEN *YOU* SAY IT, RICHARDS, IT GIVES IT A CERTAIN... *DIGNITY*.

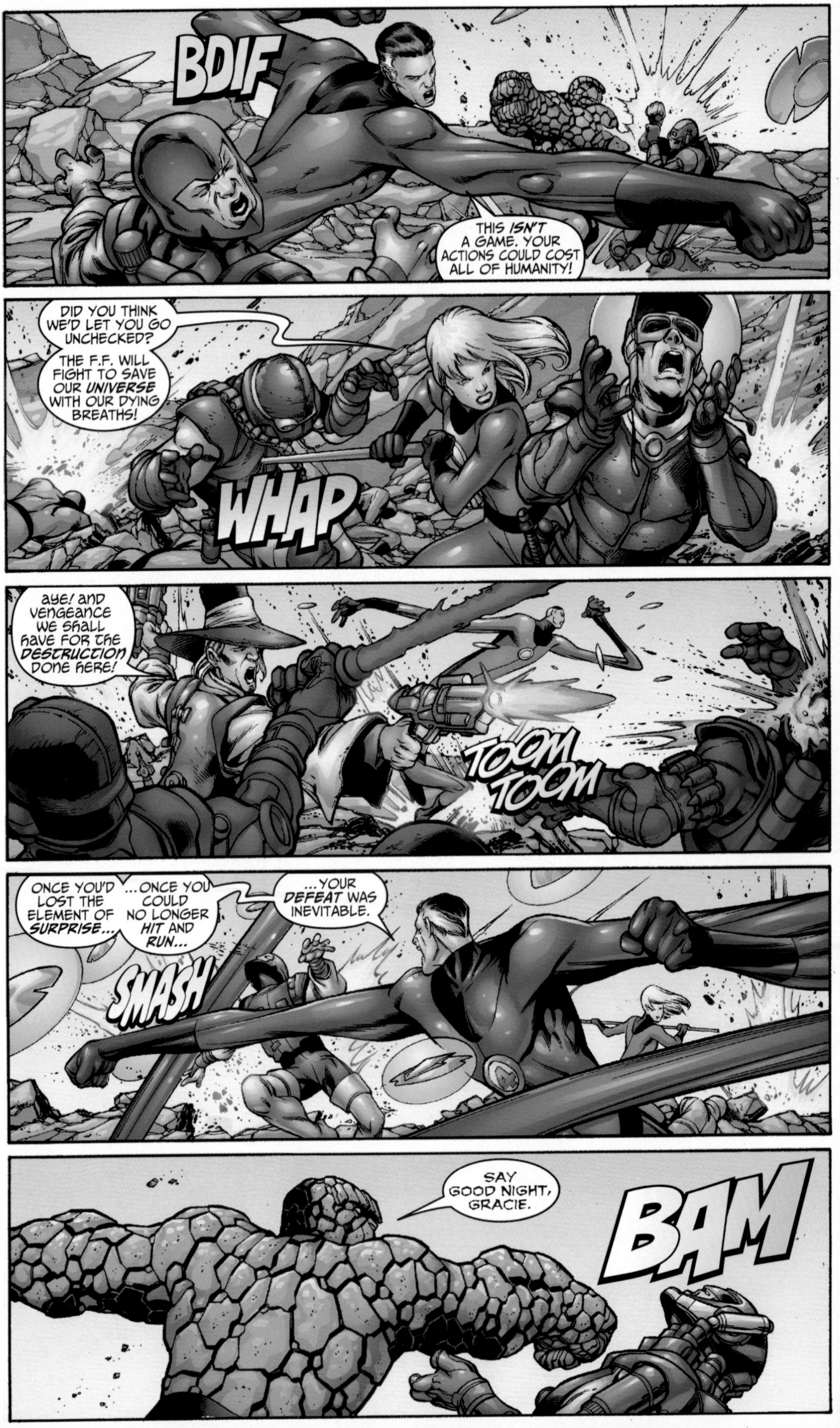
BDIF
THIS ISN'T A GAME. YOUR ACTIONS COULD COST ALL OF HUMANITY!
DID YOU THINK WE'D LET YOU GO UNCHECKED?
THE F.F. WILL FIGHT TO SAVE OUR UNIVERSE WITH OUR DYING BREATHS!
WHAP
aye! and vengeance we shall have for the destruction done here!
TOOM TOOM
ONCE YOU'D LOST THE ELEMENT OF SURPRISE...
...ONCE YOU COULD NO LONGER HIT AND RUN...
...YOUR DEFEAT WAS INEVITABLE.
SMASH
SAY GOOD NIGHT, GRACIE.
BAM

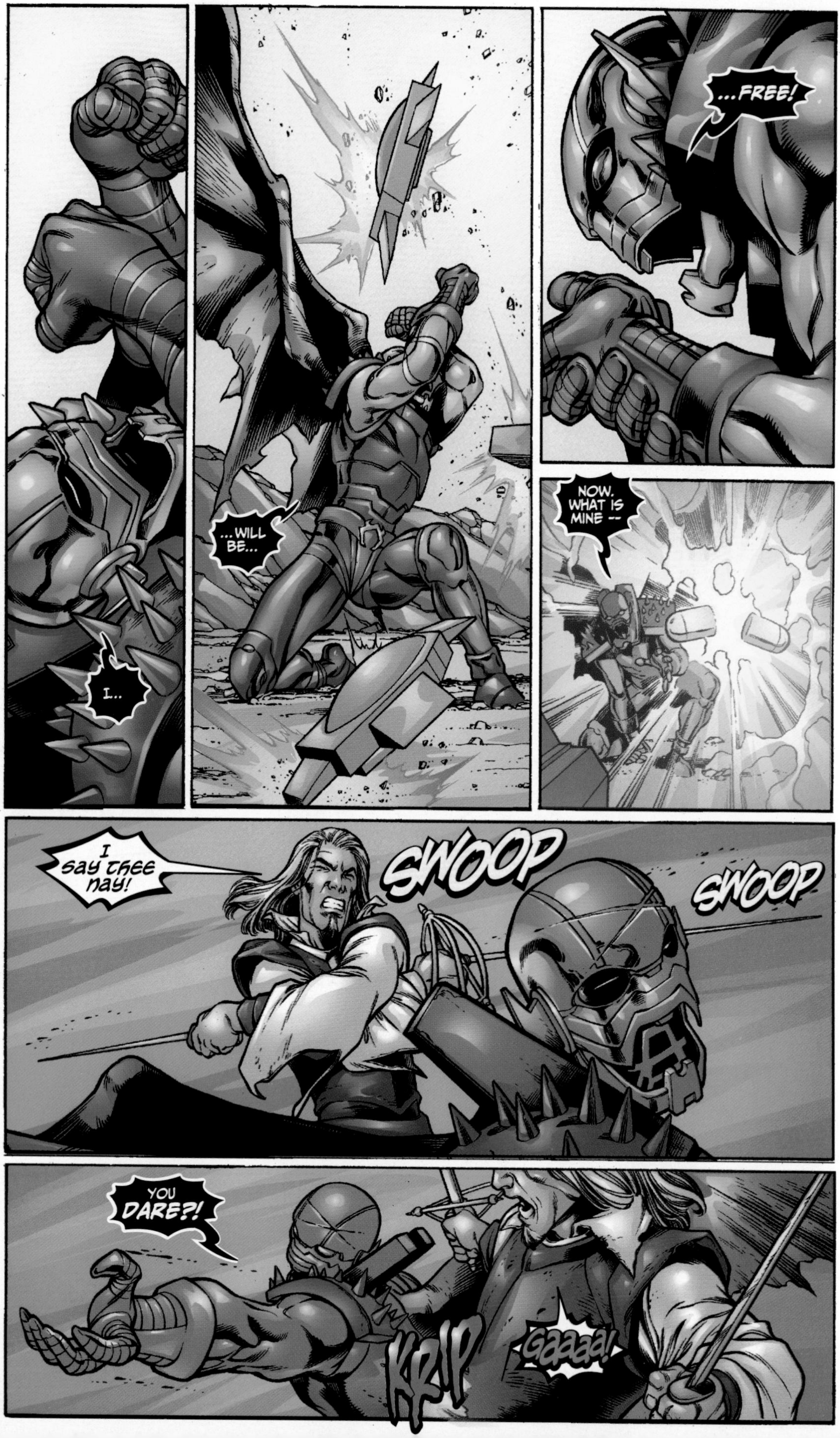
I...
...WILL BE...
...FREE!
NOW. WHAT IS MINE --
I say thee nay!
SWOOP
SWOOP
YOU DARE?!
KRIP
Gaaaa!

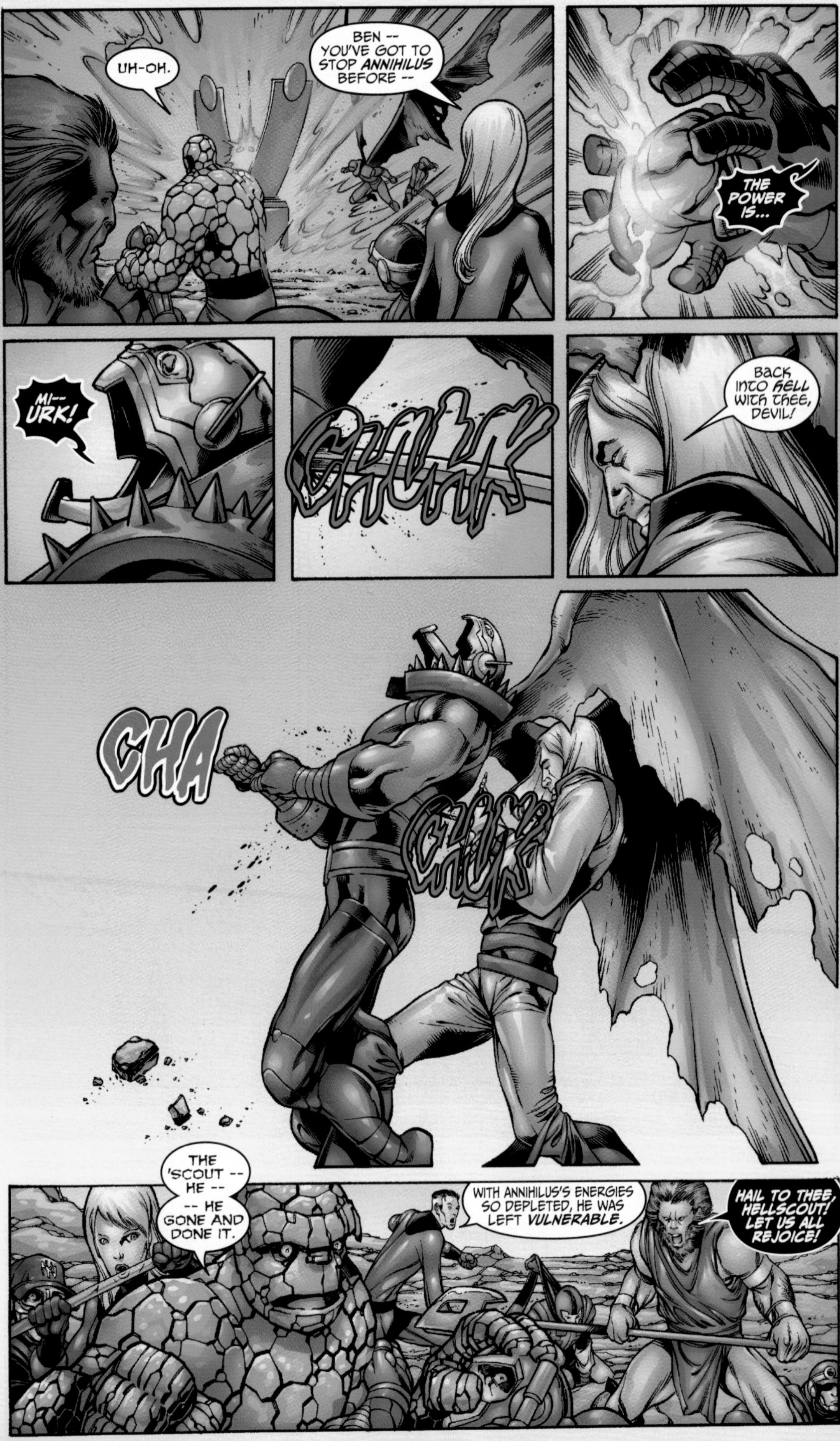
UH-OH.
BEN -- YOU'VE GOT TO STOP ANNIHILUS BEFORE --
THE POWER IS...
MI-- URK!
CHUNK
BACK INTO HELL WITH THEE, DEVIL!
CHA
CHUNK
THE 'SCOUT -- HE --
-- HE GONE AND DONE IT.
WITH ANNIHILUS'S ENERGIES SO DEPLETED, HE WAS LEFT VULNERABLE.
HAIL TO THEE, HELLSCOUT! LET US ALL REJOICE!

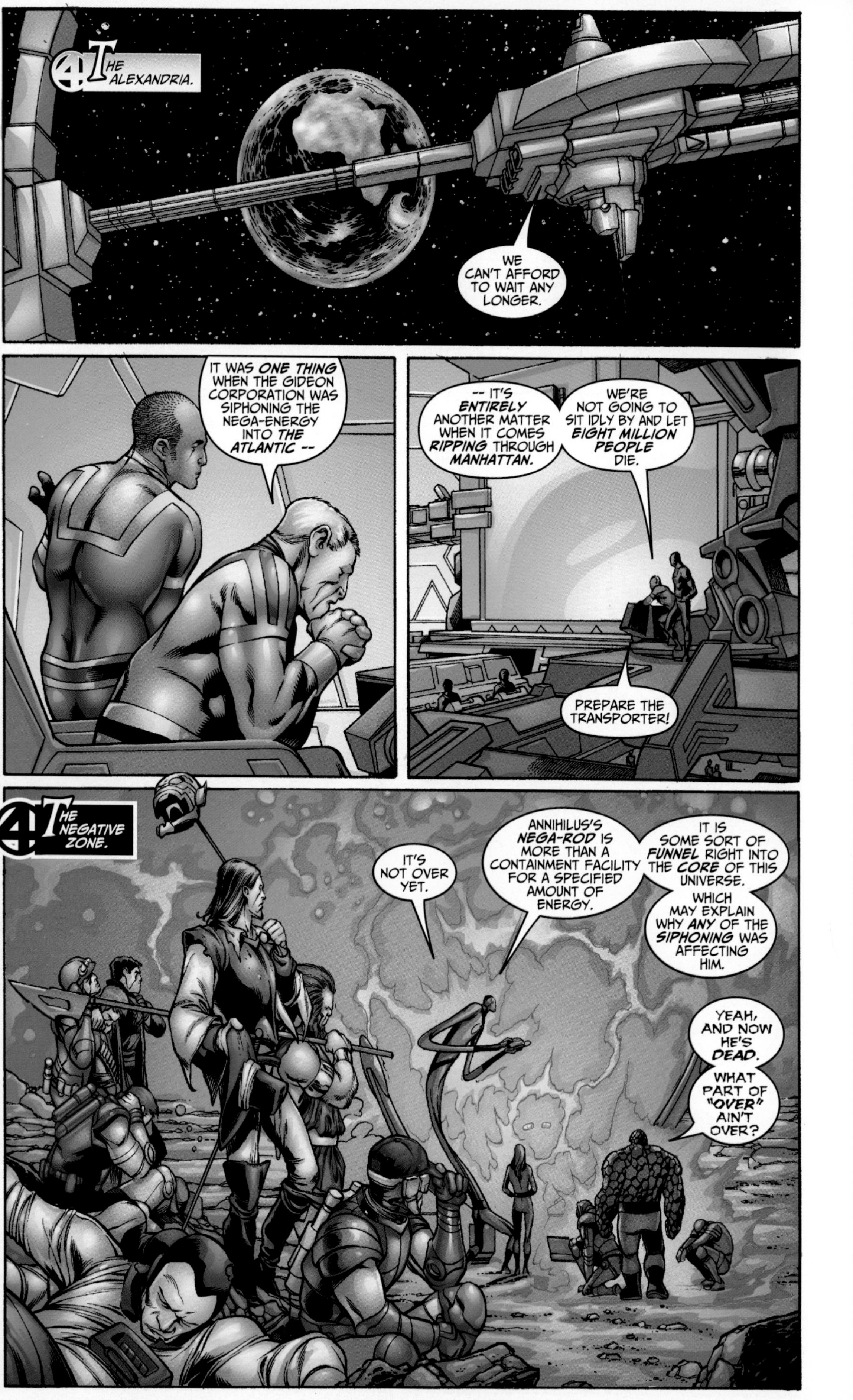
THE ALEXANDRIA.
WE CAN'T AFFORD TO WAIT ANY LONGER.
IT WAS ONE THING WHEN THE GIDEON CORPORATION WAS SIPHONING THE NEGA-ENERGY INTO THE ATLANTIC --
-- IT'S ENTIRELY ANOTHER MATTER WHEN IT COMES RIPPING THROUGH MANHATTAN.
WE'RE NOT GOING TO SIT IDLY BY AND LET EIGHT MILLION PEOPLE DIE.
PREPARE THE TRANSPORTER!
THE NEGATIVE ZONE.
IT'S NOT OVER YET.
ANNIHILUS'S NEGA-ROD IS MORE THAN A CONTAINMENT FACILITY FOR A SPECIFIED AMOUNT OF ENERGY.
IT IS SOME SORT OF FUNNEL RIGHT INTO THE CORE OF THIS UNIVERSE.
WHICH MAY EXPLAIN WHY ANY OF THE SIPHONING WAS AFFECTING HIM.
YEAH, AND NOW HE'S DEAD.
WHAT PART OF "OVER" AIN'T OVER?

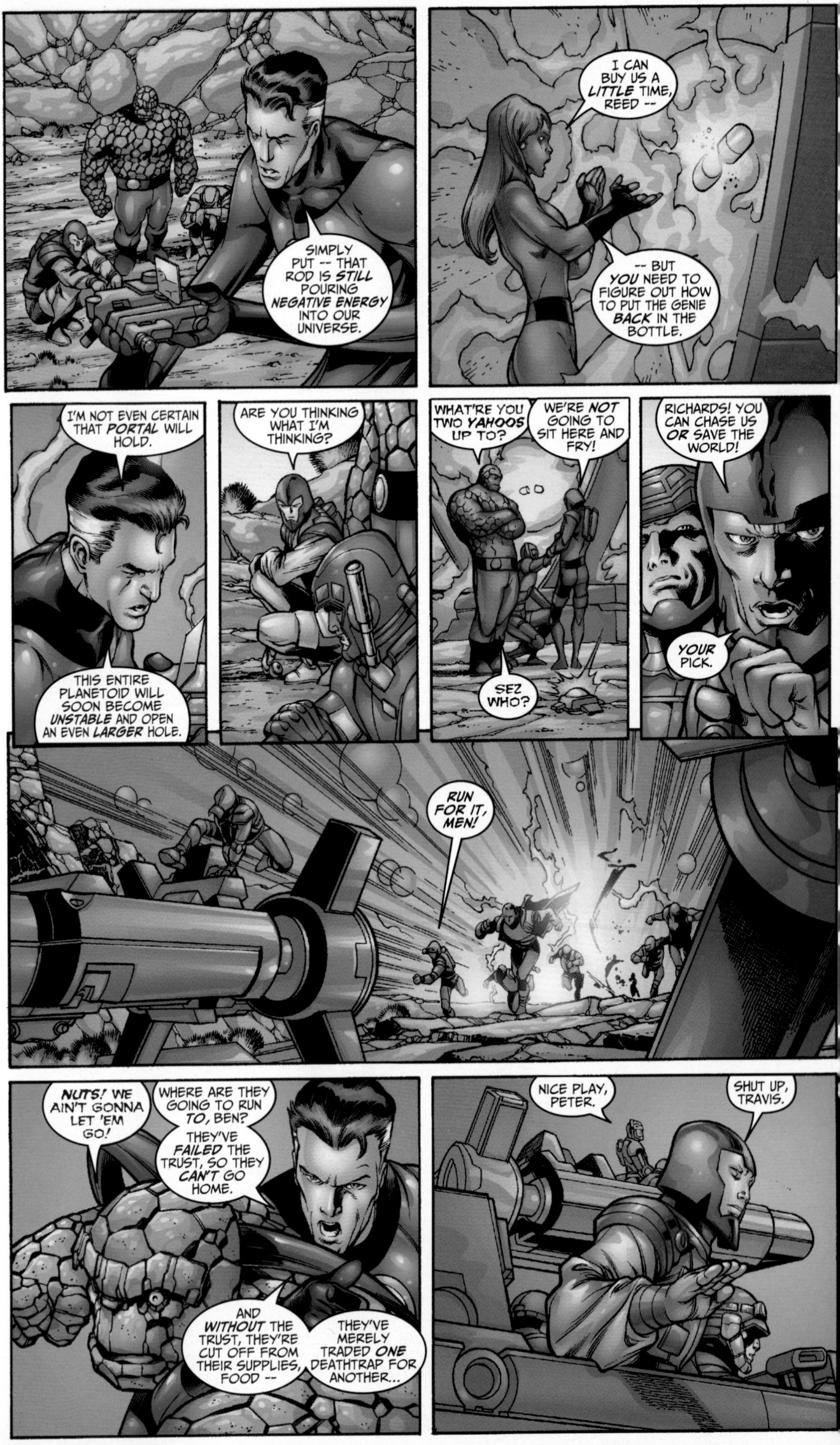
SIMPLY PUT -- THAT ROD IS STILL POURING NEGATIVE ENERGY INTO OUR UNIVERSE.
I CAN BUY US A LITTLE TIME, REED --
-- BUT YOU NEED TO FIGURE OUT HOW TO PUT THE GENIE BACK IN THE BOTTLE.
I'M NOT EVEN CERTAIN THAT PORTAL WILL HOLD.
THIS ENTIRE PLANETOID WILL SOON BECOME UNSTABLE AND OPEN AN EVEN LARGER HOLE.
ARE YOU THINKING WHAT I'M THINKING?
WHAT'RE YOU TWO YAHOOS UP TO?
WE'RE NOT GOING TO SIT HERE AND FRY!
SEZ WHO?
RICHARDS! YOU CAN CHASE US OR SAVE THE WORLD!
YOUR PICK.
RUN FOR IT, MEN!
NUTS! WE AIN'T GONNA LET 'EM GO!
WHERE ARE THEY GOING TO RUN TO, BEN?
THEY'VE FAILED THE TRUST, SO THEY CAN'T GO HOME.
AND WITHOUT THE TRUST, THEY'RE CUT OFF FROM THEIR SUPPLIES, FOOD --
THEY'VE MERELY TRADED ONE DEATHTRAP FOR ANOTHER...
NICE PLAY, PETER.
SHUT UP, TRAVIS.

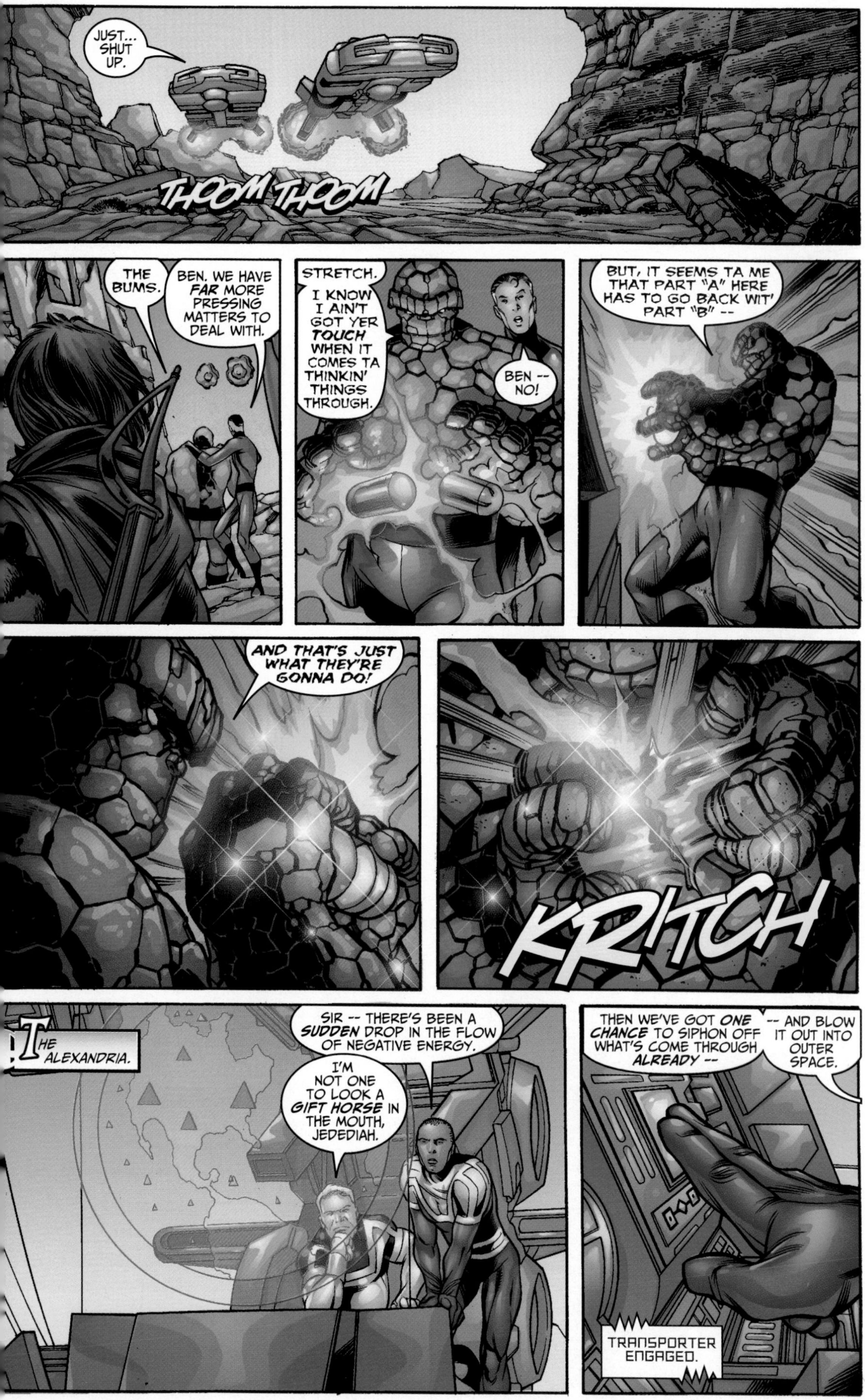
JUST... SHUT UP.
THOOM THOOM
THE BUMS.
BEN. WE HAVE FAR MORE PRESSING MATTERS TO DEAL WITH.
STRETCH.
I KNOW I AIN'T GOT YER TOUCH WHEN IT COMES TA THINKIN' THINGS THROUGH.
BEN -- NO!
BUT, IT SEEMS TA ME THAT PART "A" HERE HAS TO GO BACK WIT' PART "B" --
AND THAT'S JUST WHAT THEY'RE GONNA DO!
KRITCH
THE ALEXANDRIA.
SIR -- THERE'S BEEN A SUDDEN DROP IN THE FLOW OF NEGATIVE ENERGY.
I'M NOT ONE TO LOOK A GIFT HORSE IN THE MOUTH, JEDEDIAH.
THEN WE'VE GOT ONE CHANCE TO SIPHON OFF WHAT'S COME THROUGH ALREADY --
-- AND BLOW IT OUT INTO OUTER SPACE.
TRANSPORTER ENGAGED.

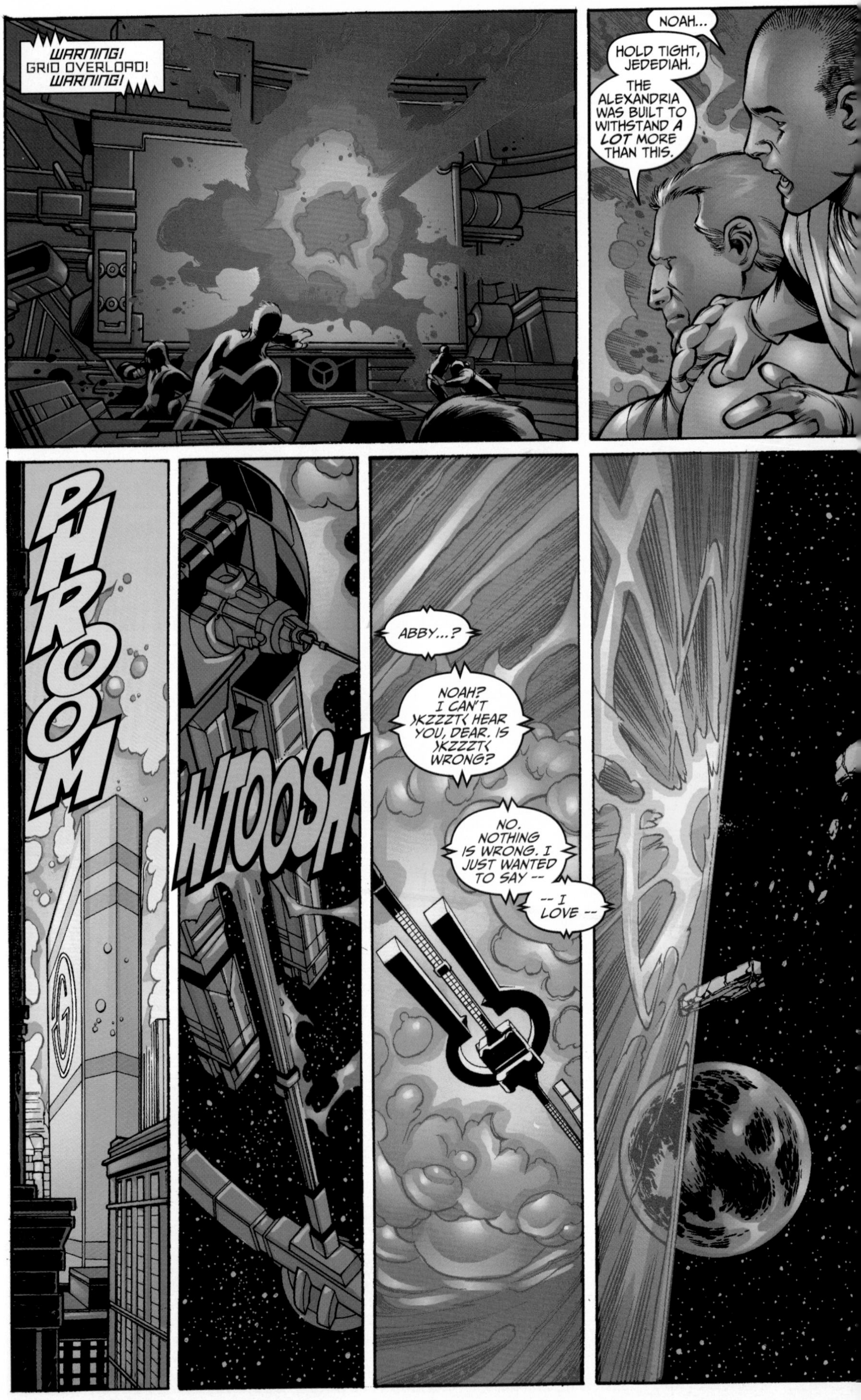

WARNING!
GRID OVERLOAD!
WARNING!
NOAH...
HOLD TIGHT, JEDEDIAH.
THE ALEXANDRIA WAS BUILT TO WITHSTAND A LOT MORE THAN THIS.
PHROOM
WTOOSH
ABBY...?
NOAH? I CAN'T >KZZZT< HEAR YOU, DEAR. IS >KZZZT< WRONG?
NO. NOTHING IS WRONG. I JUST WANTED TO SAY --
-- I LOVE --

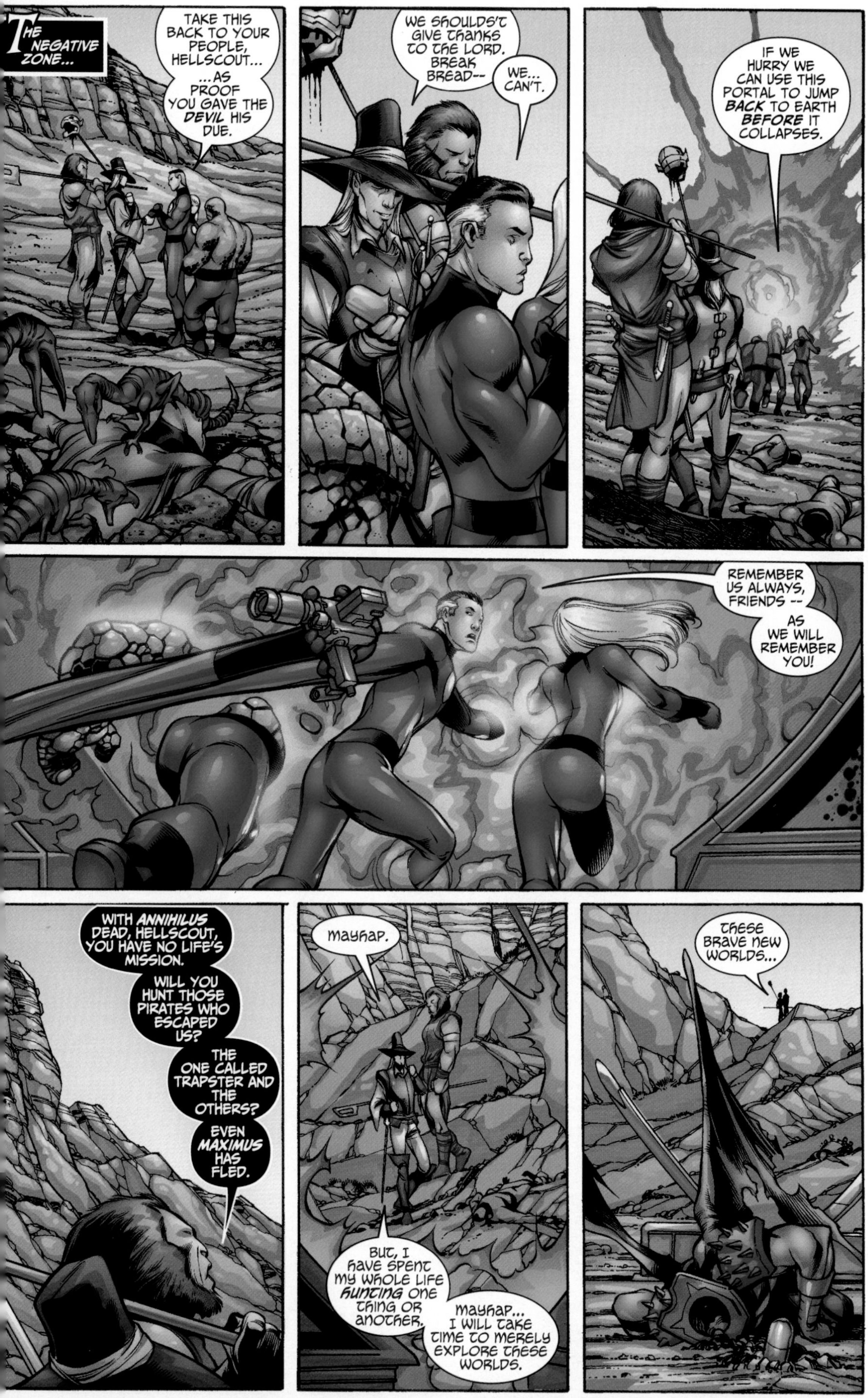
THE NEGATIVE ZONE...
TAKE THIS BACK TO YOUR PEOPLE, HELLSCOUT...
...AS PROOF YOU GAVE THE DEVIL HIS DUE.
WE SHOULDS'T GIVE THANKS TO THE LORD. BREAK BREAD--
WE... CAN'T.
IF WE HURRY WE CAN USE THIS PORTAL TO JUMP BACK TO EARTH BEFORE IT COLLAPSES.
REMEMBER US ALWAYS, FRIENDS --
AS WE WILL REMEMBER YOU!
WITH ANNIHILUS DEAD, HELLSCOUT, YOU HAVE NO LIFE'S MISSION.
WILL YOU HUNT THOSE PIRATES WHO ESCAPED US?
THE ONE CALLED TRAPSTER AND THE OTHERS?
EVEN MAXIMUS HAS FLED.
MAYHAP.
BUT, I HAVE SPENT MY WHOLE LIFE HUNTING ONE THING OR ANOTHER.
MAYHAP... I WILL TAKE TIME TO MERELY EXPLORE THESE WORLDS.
THESE BRAVE NEW WORLDS...

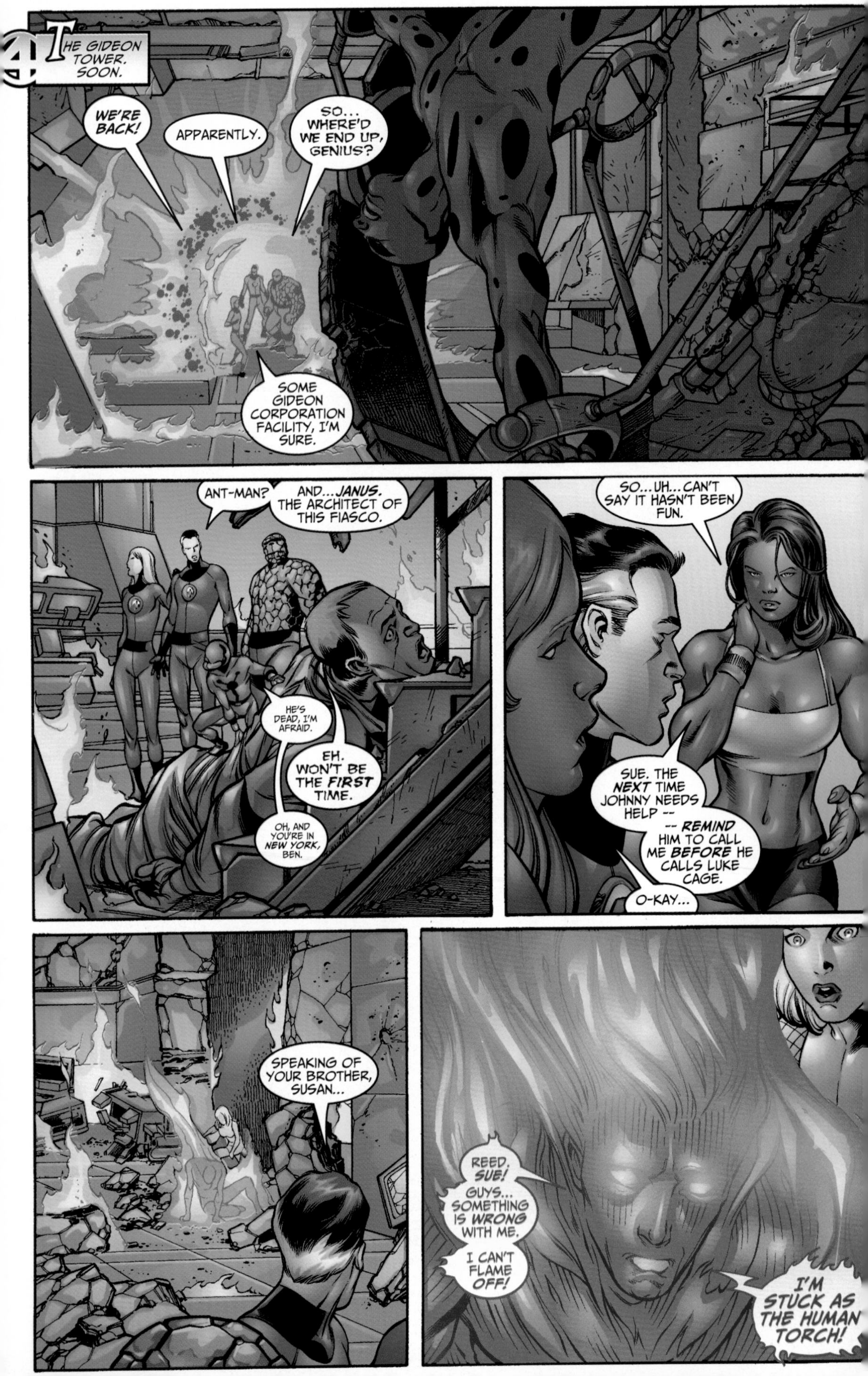
THE GIDEON TOWER. SOON.
WE'RE BACK!
APPARENTLY.
SO... WHERE'D WE END UP, GENIUS?
SOME GIDEON CORPORATION FACILITY, I'M SURE.
ANT-MAN?
AND... JANUS. THE ARCHITECT OF THIS FIASCO.
HE'S DEAD, I'M AFRAID.
EH. WON'T BE THE FIRST TIME.
OH, AND YOU'RE IN NEW YORK, BEN.
SO... UH... CAN'T SAY IT HASN'T BEEN FUN.
SUE. THE NEXT TIME JOHNNY NEEDS HELP --
-- REMIND HIM TO CALL ME BEFORE HE CALLS LUKE CAGE.
O-KAY...
SPEAKING OF YOUR BROTHER, SUSAN...
REED. SUE! GUYS... SOMETHING IS WRONG WITH ME.
I CAN'T FLAME OFF!
I'M STUCK AS THE HUMAN TORCH!

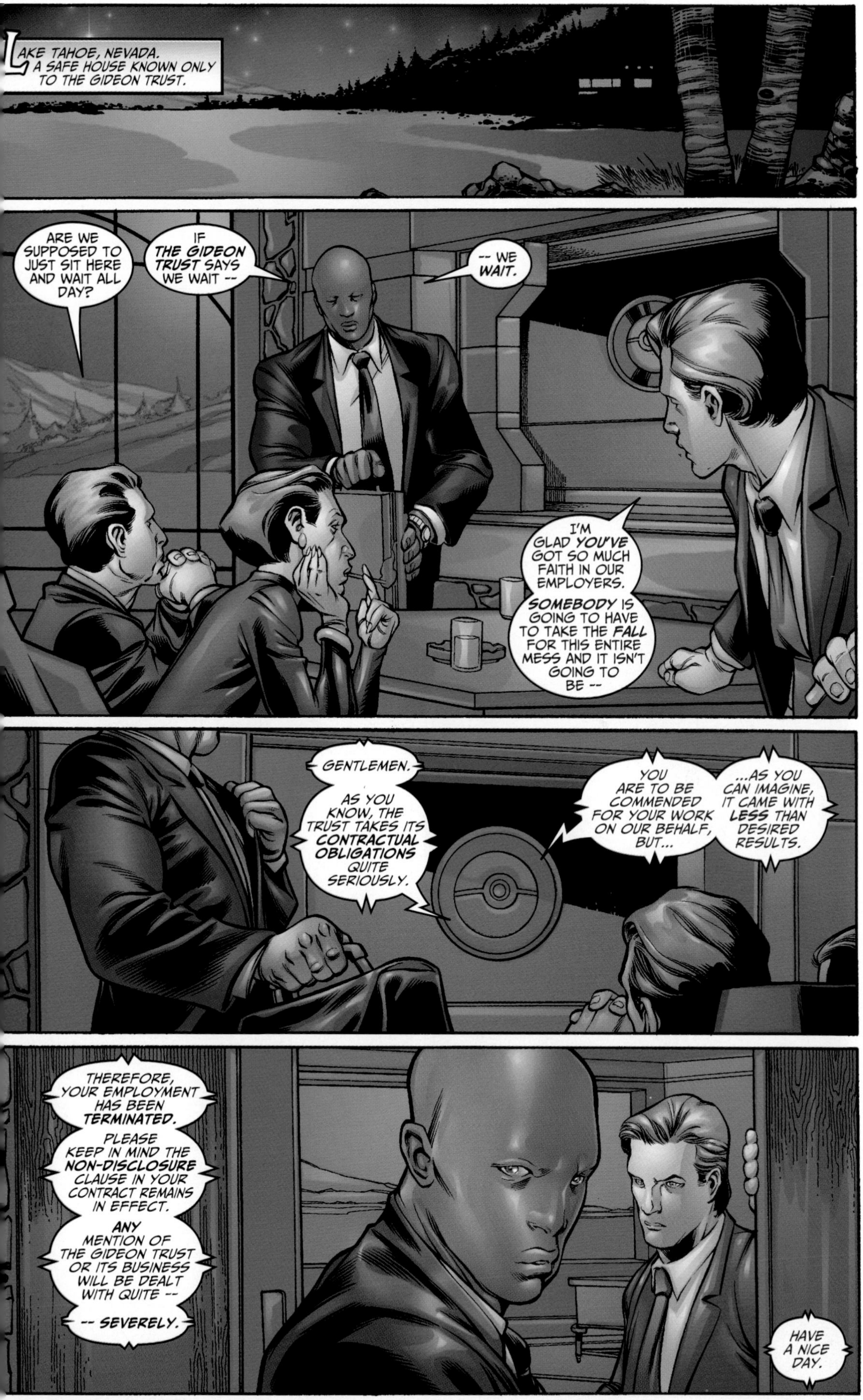

LAKE TAHOE, NEVADA. A SAFE HOUSE KNOWN ONLY TO THE GIDEON TRUST.
ARE WE SUPPOSED TO JUST SIT HERE AND WAIT ALL DAY?
IF THE GIDEON TRUST SAYS WE WAIT --
-- WE WAIT.
I'M GLAD YOU'VE GOT SO MUCH FAITH IN OUR EMPLOYERS.
SOMEBODY IS GOING TO HAVE TO TAKE THE FALL FOR THIS ENTIRE MESS AND IT ISN'T GOING TO BE --
GENTLEMEN.
AS YOU KNOW, THE TRUST TAKES ITS CONTRACTUAL OBLIGATIONS QUITE SERIOUSLY.
YOU ARE TO BE COMMENDED FOR YOUR WORK ON OUR BEHALF, BUT...
...AS YOU CAN IMAGINE, IT CAME WITH LESS THAN DESIRED RESULTS.
THEREFORE, YOUR EMPLOYMENT HAS BEEN TERMINATED.
PLEASE KEEP IN MIND THE NON-DISCLOSURE CLAUSE IN YOUR CONTRACT REMAINS IN EFFECT.
ANY MENTION OF THE GIDEON TRUST OR ITS BUSINESS WILL BE DEALT WITH QUITE --
-- SEVERELY.
HAVE A NICE DAY.

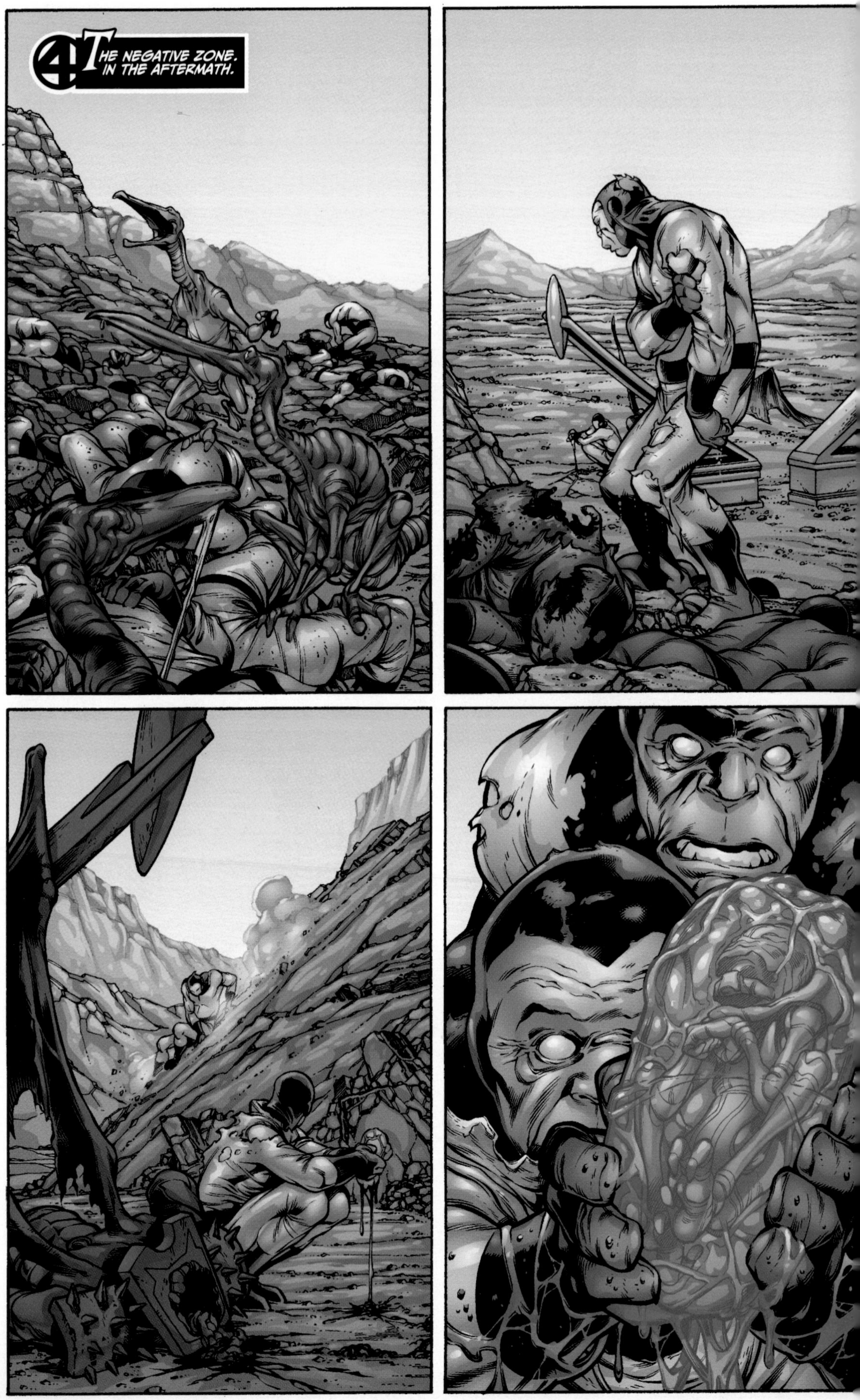
THE NEGATIVE ZONE.
IN THE AFTERMATH.

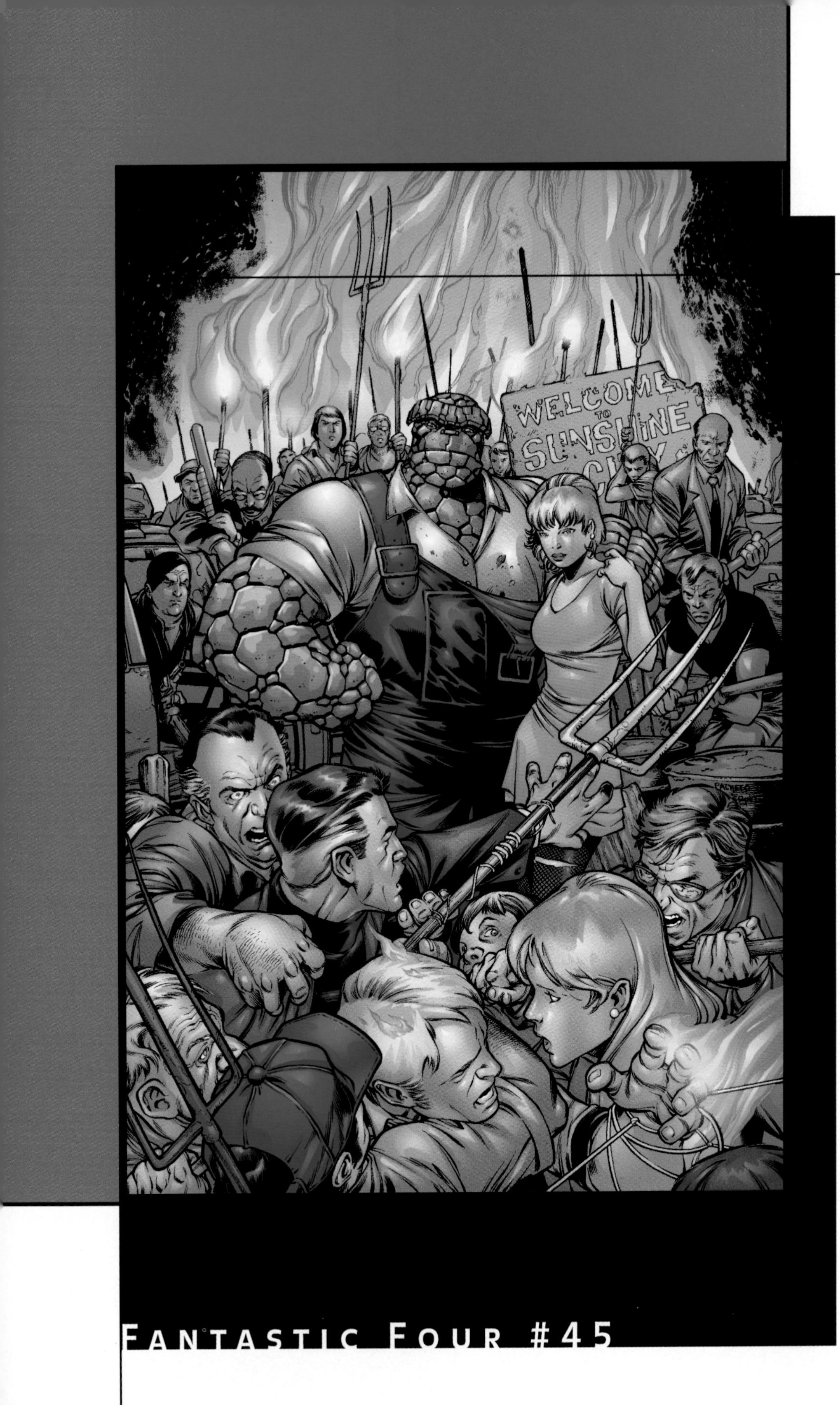
WELCOME
TO
SUNSHINE

FANTASTIC FOUR #45

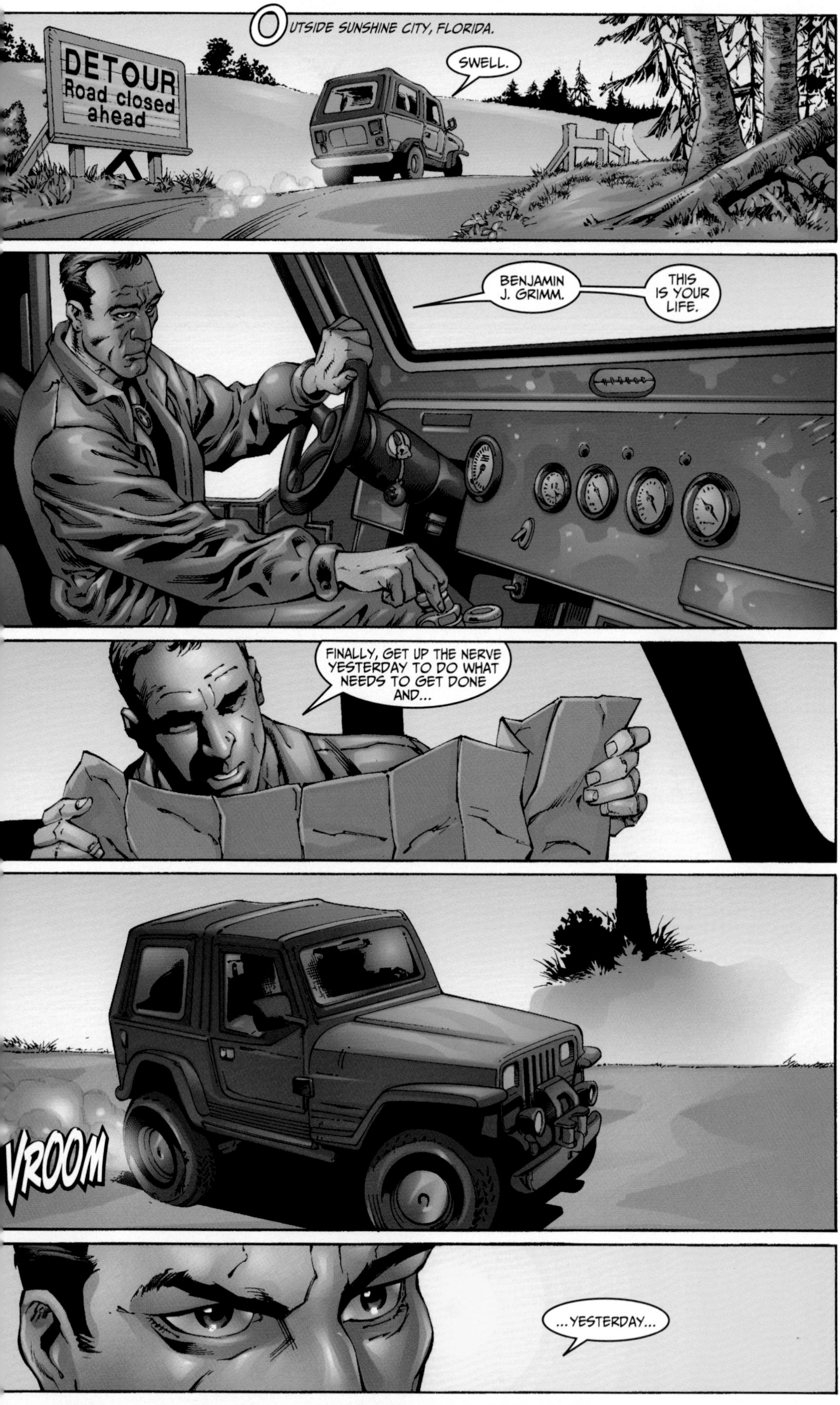
OUTSIDE SUNSHINE CITY, FLORIDA.
DETOUR Road closed ahead
SWELL.
BENJAMIN J. GRIMM.
THIS IS YOUR LIFE.
FINALLY, GET UP THE NERVE YESTERDAY TO DO WHAT NEEDS TO GET DONE AND...
VROOM
...YESTERDAY...

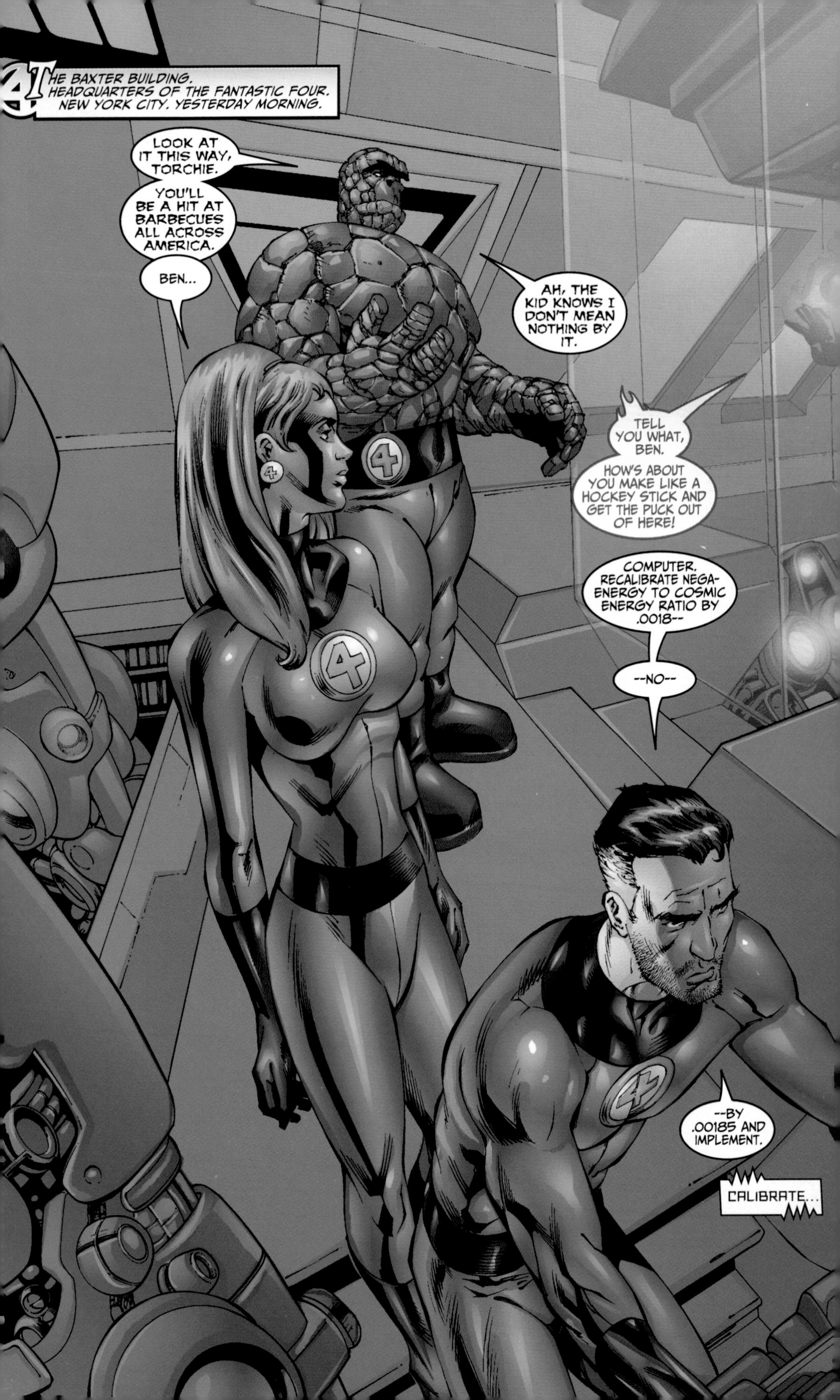
THE BAXTER BUILDING. HEADQUARTERS OF THE FANTASTIC FOUR. NEW YORK CITY. YESTERDAY MORNING.
LOOK AT IT THIS WAY, TORCHIE.
YOU'LL BE A HIT AT BARBECUES ALL ACROSS AMERICA.
BEN...
AH, THE KID KNOWS I DON'T MEAN NOTHING BY IT.
TELL YOU WHAT, BEN.
HOW'S ABOUT YOU MAKE LIKE A HOCKEY STICK AND GET THE PUCK OUT OF HERE!
COMPUTER. RECALIBRATE NEGA-ENERGY TO COSMIC ENERGY RATIO BY .0018--
--NO--
--BY .00185 AND IMPLEMENT.
CALIBRATE...

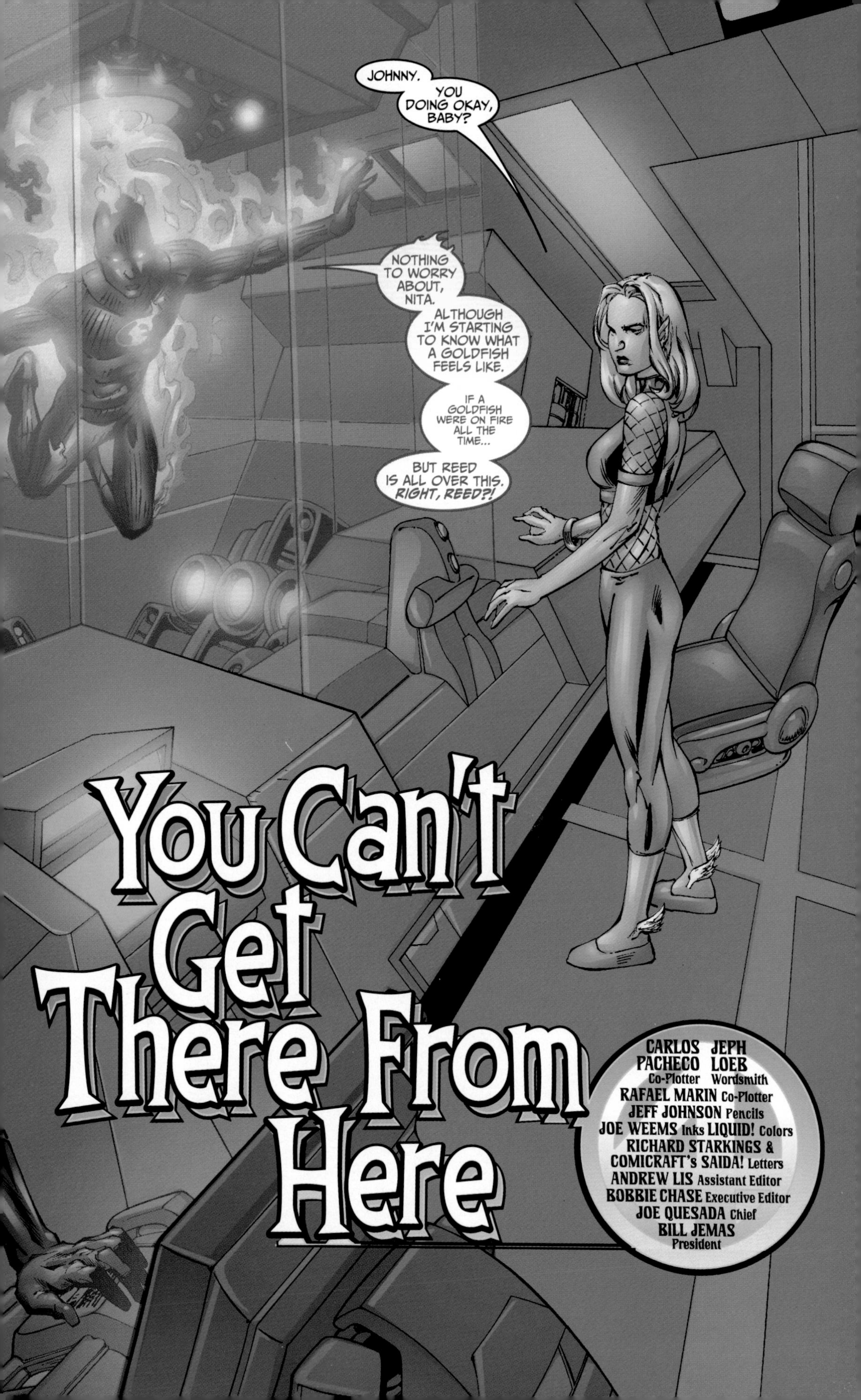
JOHNNY.
YOU DOING OKAY, BABY?
NOTHING TO WORRY ABOUT, NITA.
ALTHOUGH I'M STARTING TO KNOW WHAT A GOLDFISH FEELS LIKE.
IF A GOLDFISH WERE ON FIRE ALL THE TIME...
BUT REED IS ALL OVER THIS. RIGHT, REED?!
You Can't Get There From Here
CARLOS PACHECO Co-Plotter
JEPH LOEB Wordsmith
RAFAEL MARIN Co-Plotter
JEFF JOHNSON Pencils
JOE WEEMS Inks LIQUID! Colors
RICHARD STARKINGS & COMICRAFT's SAIDA! Letters
ANDREW LIS Assistant Editor
BOBBIE CHASE Executive Editor
JOE QUESADA Chief
BILL JEMAS President

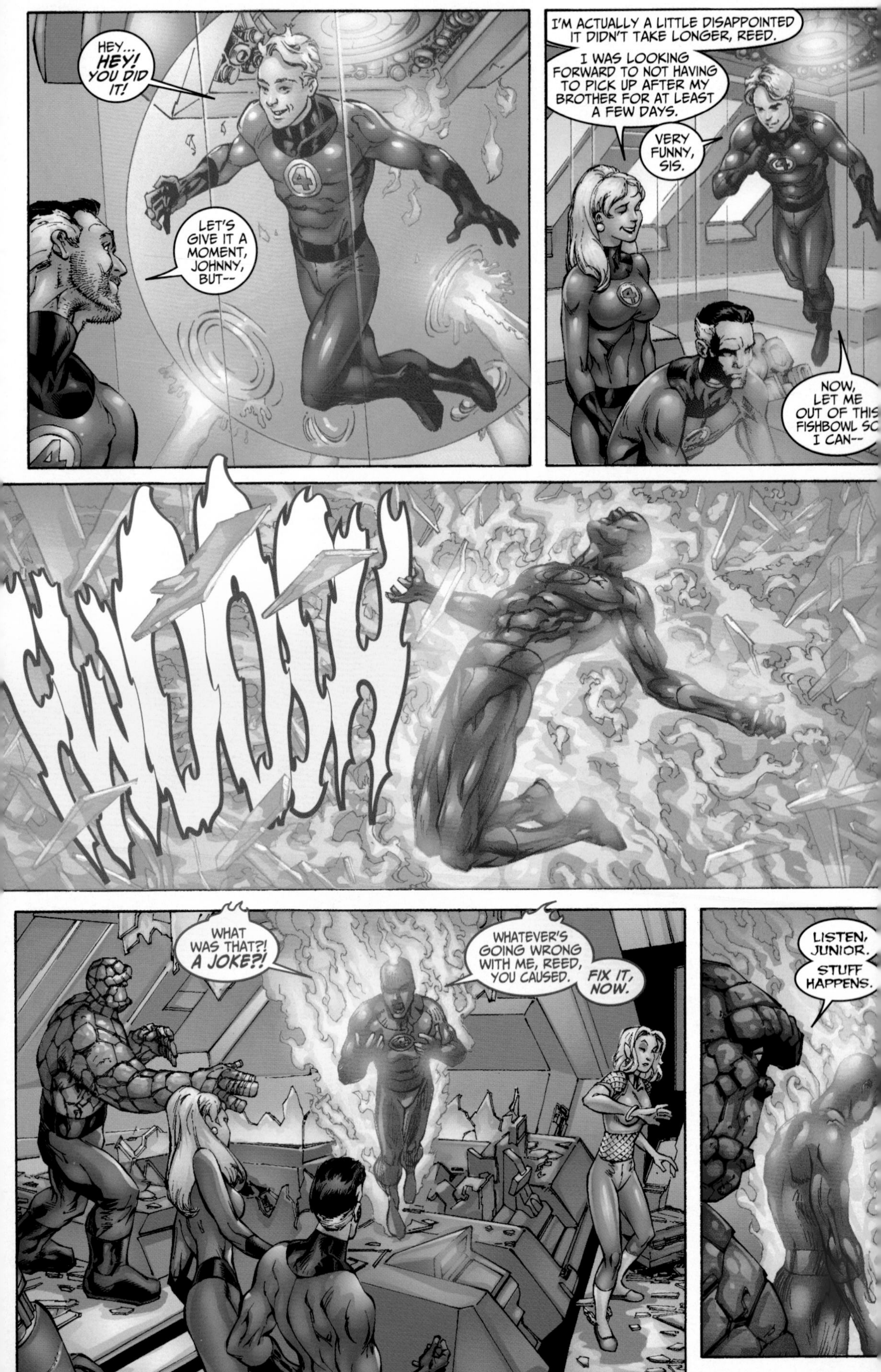
HEY... HEY! YOU DID IT!
LET'S GIVE IT A MOMENT, JOHNNY, BUT--
I'M ACTUALLY A LITTLE DISAPPOINTED IT DIDN'T TAKE LONGER, REED.
I WAS LOOKING FORWARD TO NOT HAVING TO PICK UP AFTER MY BROTHER FOR AT LEAST A FEW DAYS.
VERY FUNNY, SIS.
NOW, LET ME OUT OF THIS FISHBOWL SO I CAN--
WHAT WAS THAT?! A JOKE?!
WHATEVER'S GOING WRONG WITH ME, REED, YOU CAUSED.
FIX IT, NOW.
LISTEN, JUNIOR.
STUFF HAPPENS.

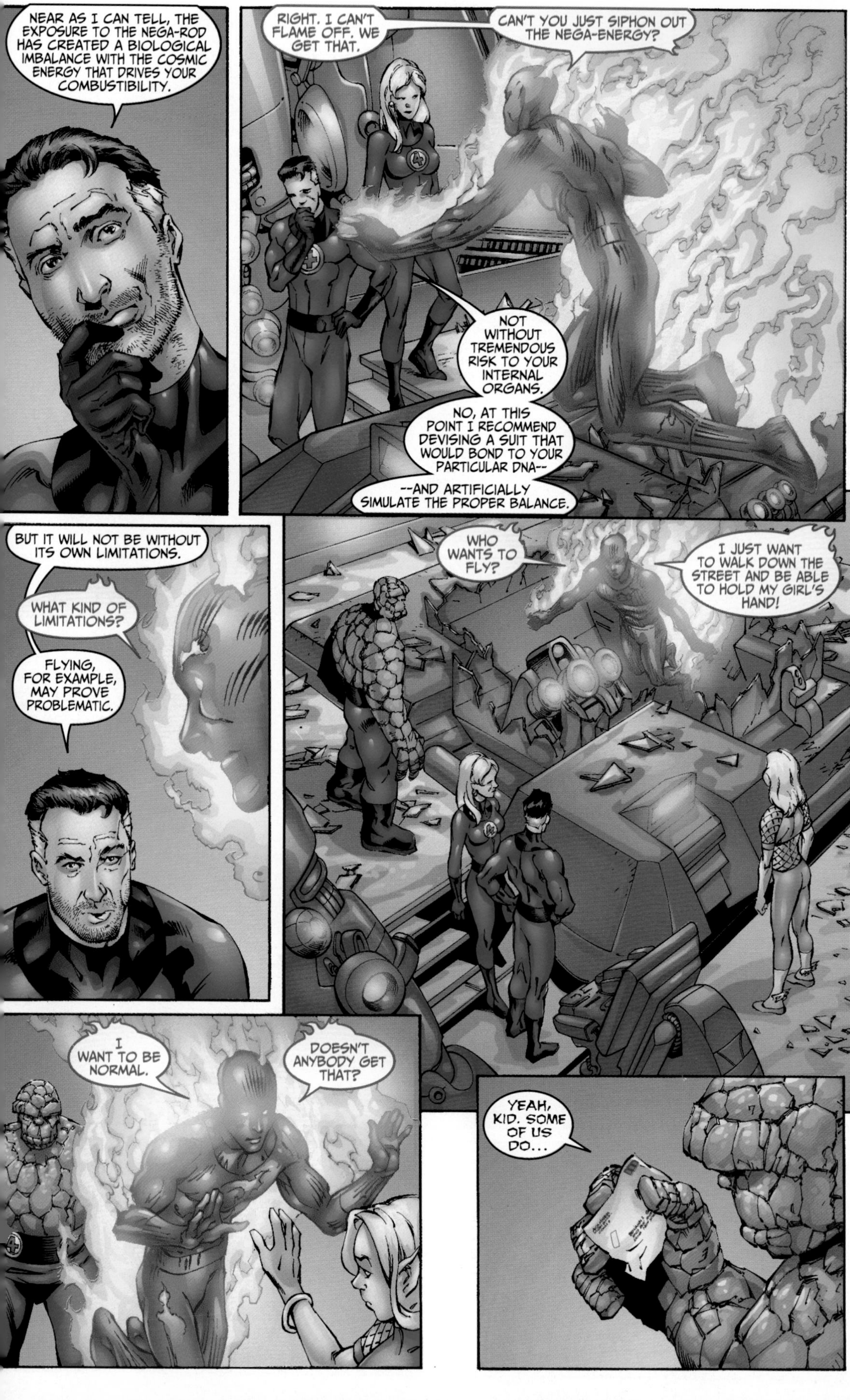
NEAR AS I CAN TELL, THE EXPOSURE TO THE NEGA-ROD HAS CREATED A BIOLOGICAL IMBALANCE WITH THE COSMIC ENERGY THAT DRIVES YOUR COMBUSTIBILITY.
RIGHT. I CAN'T FLAME OFF. WE GET THAT.
CAN'T YOU JUST SIPHON OUT THE NEGA-ENERGY?
NOT WITHOUT TREMENDOUS RISK TO YOUR INTERNAL ORGANS.
NO, AT THIS POINT I RECOMMEND DEVISING A SUIT THAT WOULD BOND TO YOUR PARTICULAR DNA--
--AND ARTIFICIALLY SIMULATE THE PROPER BALANCE.
BUT IT WILL NOT BE WITHOUT ITS OWN LIMITATIONS.
WHAT KIND OF LIMITATIONS?
FLYING, FOR EXAMPLE, MAY PROVE PROBLEMATIC.
WHO WANTS TO FLY?
I JUST WANT TO WALK DOWN THE STREET AND BE ABLE TO HOLD MY GIRL'S HAND!
I WANT TO BE NORMAL.
DOESN'T ANYBODY GET THAT?
YEAH, KID. SOME OF US DO...

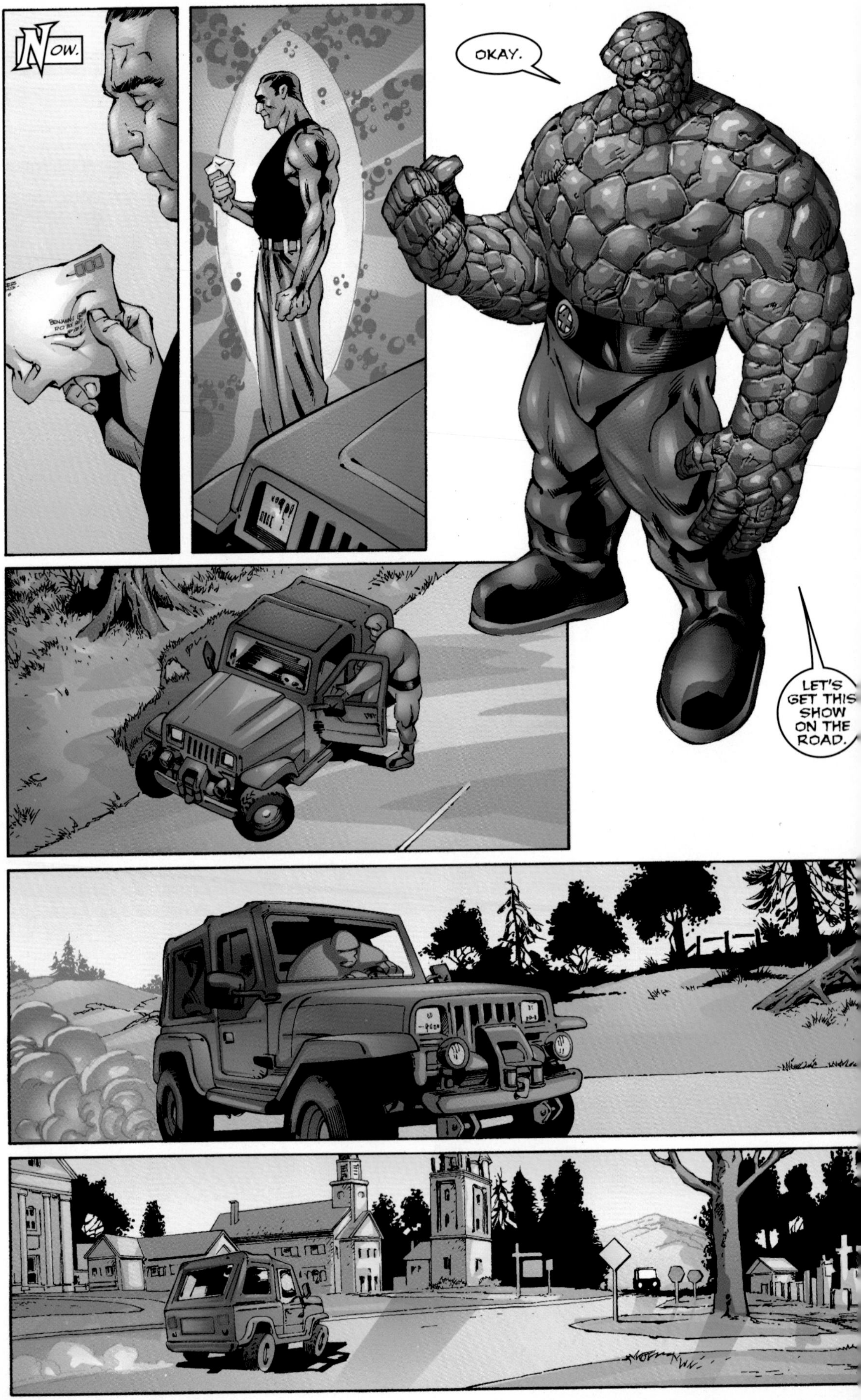
NOW.
OKAY.
LET'S GET THIS SHOW ON THE ROAD.

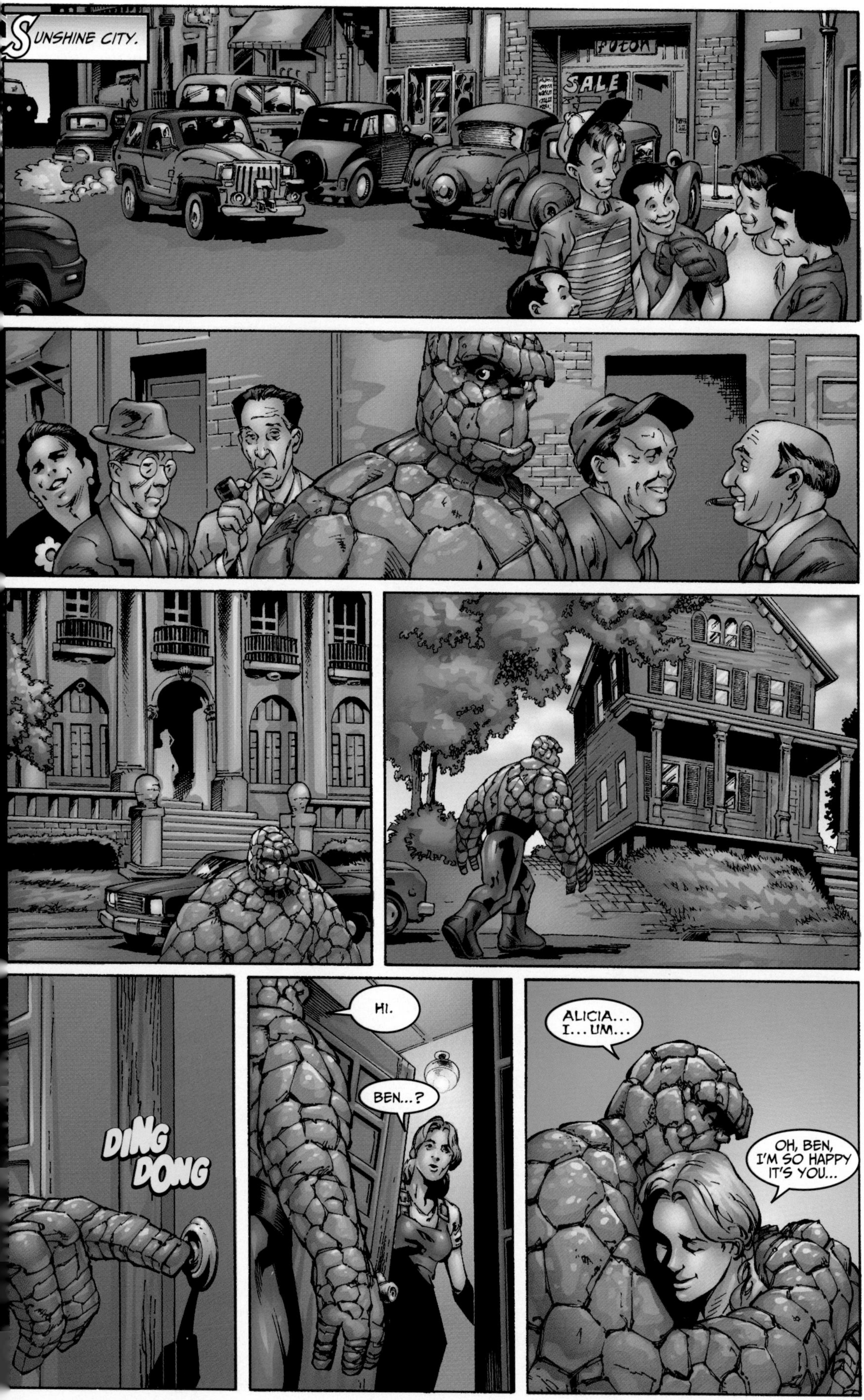
SUNSHINE CITY.
SALE
DING DONG
HI.
BEN...?
ALICIA... I... UM...
OH, BEN, I'M SO HAPPY IT'S YOU...

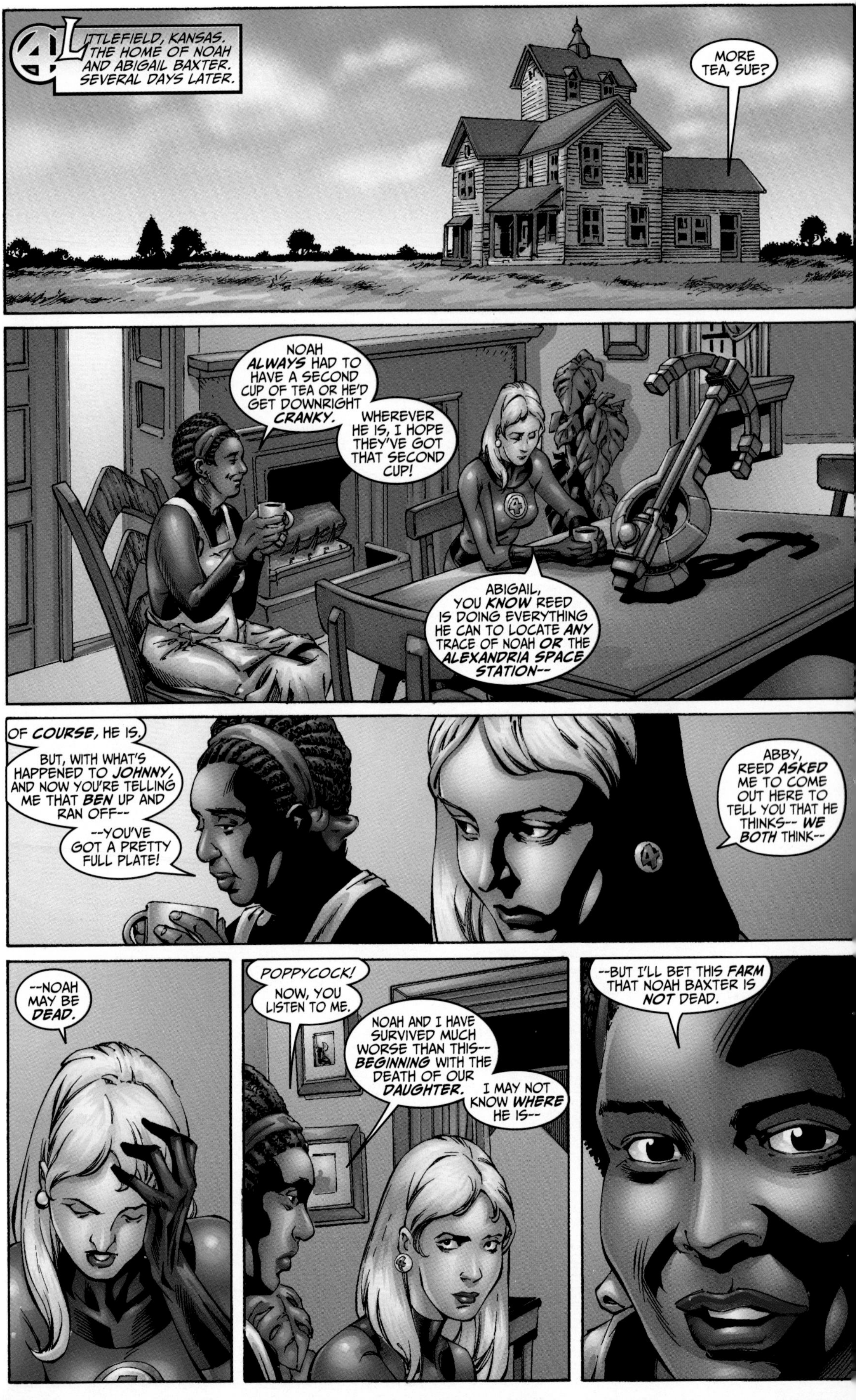
LITTLEFIELD, KANSAS. THE HOME OF NOAH AND ABIGAIL BAXTER. SEVERAL DAYS LATER.
MORE TEA, SUE?
NOAH ALWAYS HAD TO HAVE A SECOND CUP OF TEA OR HE'D GET DOWNRIGHT CRANKY.
WHEREVER HE IS, I HOPE THEY'VE GOT THAT SECOND CUP!
ABIGAIL, YOU KNOW REED IS DOING EVERYTHING HE CAN TO LOCATE ANY TRACE OF NOAH OR THE ALEXANDRIA SPACE STATION--
OF COURSE, HE IS.
BUT, WITH WHAT'S HAPPENED TO JOHNNY, AND NOW YOU'RE TELLING ME THAT BEN UP AND RAN OFF--
--YOU'VE GOT A PRETTY FULL PLATE!
ABBY, REED ASKED ME TO COME OUT HERE TO TELL YOU THAT HE THINKS-- WE BOTH THINK--
--NOAH MAY BE DEAD.
POPPYCOCK! NOW, YOU LISTEN TO ME.
NOAH AND I HAVE SURVIVED MUCH WORSE THAN THIS-- BEGINNING WITH THE DEATH OF OUR DAUGHTER.
I MAY NOT KNOW WHERE HE IS--
--BUT I'LL BET THIS FARM THAT NOAH BAXTER IS NOT DEAD.

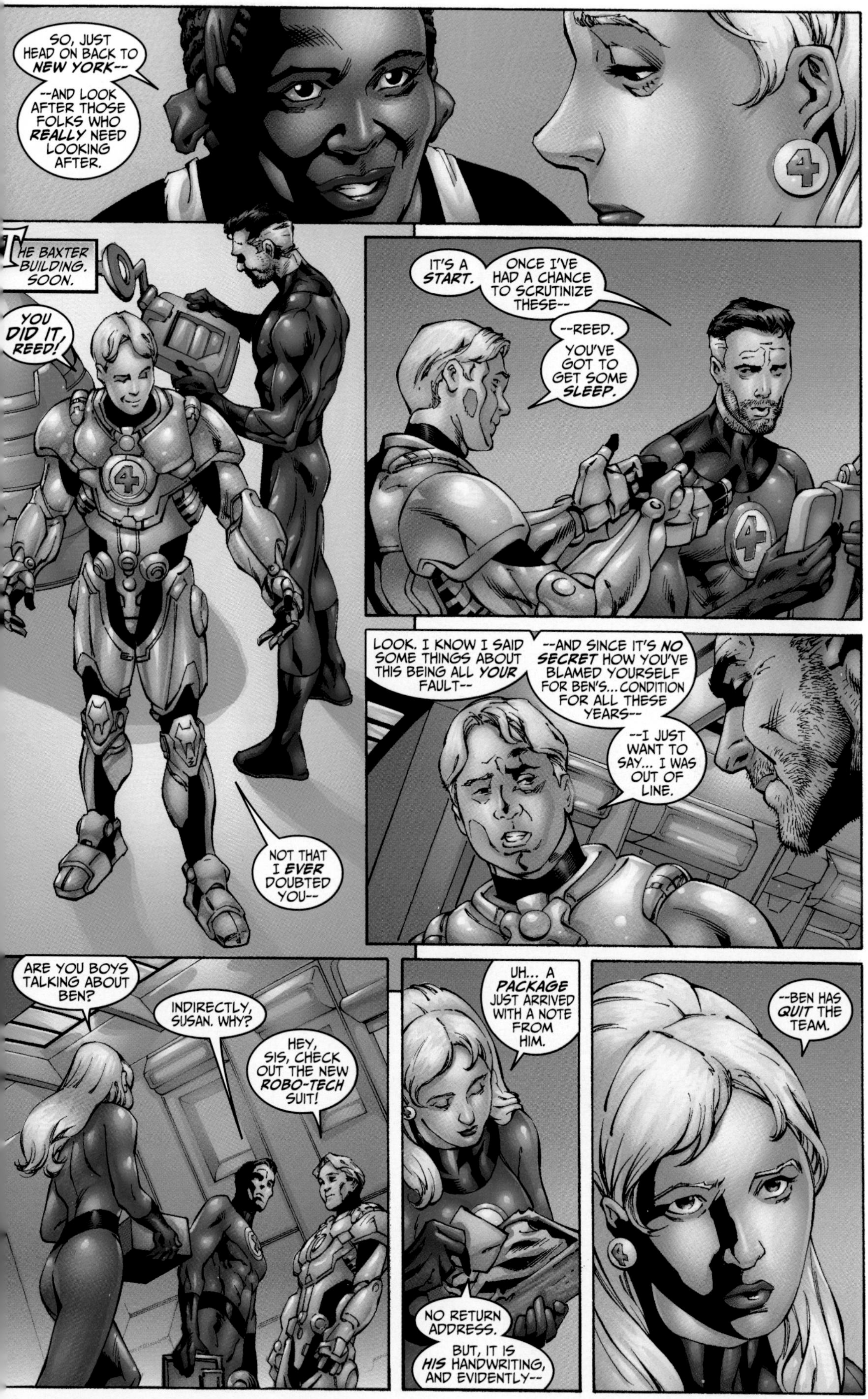
SO, JUST HEAD ON BACK TO NEW YORK--
--AND LOOK AFTER THOSE FOLKS WHO REALLY NEED LOOKING AFTER.
THE BAXTER BUILDING. SOON.
YOU DID IT, REED!
NOT THAT I EVER DOUBTED YOU--
IT'S A START.
ONCE I'VE HAD A CHANCE TO SCRUTINIZE THESE--
--REED. YOU'VE GOT TO GET SOME SLEEP.
LOOK. I KNOW I SAID SOME THINGS ABOUT THIS BEING ALL YOUR FAULT--
--AND SINCE IT'S NO SECRET HOW YOU'VE BLAMED YOURSELF FOR BEN'S...CONDITION FOR ALL THESE YEARS--
--I JUST WANT TO SAY... I WAS OUT OF LINE.
ARE YOU BOYS TALKING ABOUT BEN?
INDIRECTLY, SUSAN. WHY?
HEY, SIS, CHECK OUT THE NEW ROBO-TECH SUIT!
UH... A PACKAGE JUST ARRIVED WITH A NOTE FROM HIM.
NO RETURN ADDRESS.
BUT, IT IS HIS HANDWRITING, AND EVIDENTLY--
--BEN HAS QUIT THE TEAM.

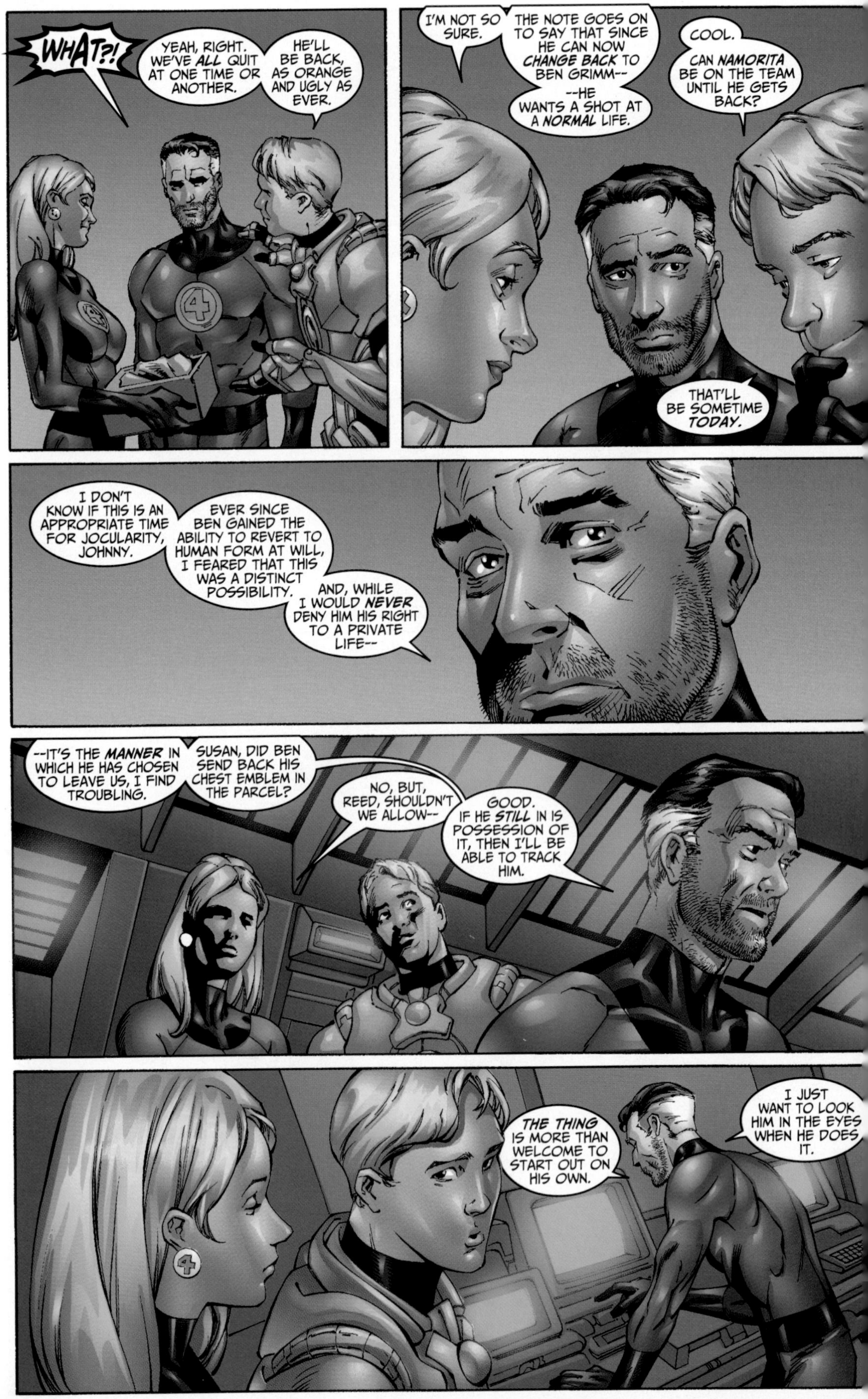
WHAT?!
YEAH, RIGHT. WE'VE ALL QUIT AT ONE TIME OR ANOTHER.
HE'LL BE BACK, AS ORANGE AND UGLY AS EVER.
I'M NOT SO SURE.
THE NOTE GOES ON TO SAY THAT SINCE HE CAN NOW CHANGE BACK TO BEN GRIMM--
--HE WANTS A SHOT AT A NORMAL LIFE.
COOL.
CAN NAMORITA BE ON THE TEAM UNTIL HE GETS BACK?
THAT'LL BE SOMETIME TODAY.
I DON'T KNOW IF THIS IS AN APPROPRIATE TIME FOR JOCULARITY, JOHNNY.
EVER SINCE BEN GAINED THE ABILITY TO REVERT TO HUMAN FORM AT WILL, I FEARED THAT THIS WAS A DISTINCT POSSIBILITY.
AND, WHILE I WOULD NEVER DENY HIM HIS RIGHT TO A PRIVATE LIFE--
--IT'S THE MANNER IN WHICH HE HAS CHOSEN TO LEAVE US, I FIND TROUBLING.
SUSAN, DID BEN SEND BACK HIS CHEST EMBLEM IN THE PARCEL?
NO, BUT, REED, SHOULDN'T WE ALLOW--
GOOD. IF HE STILL IN IS POSSESSION OF IT, THEN I'LL BE ABLE TO TRACK HIM.
THE THING IS MORE THAN WELCOME TO START OUT ON HIS OWN.
I JUST WANT TO LOOK HIM IN THE EYES WHEN HE DOES IT.

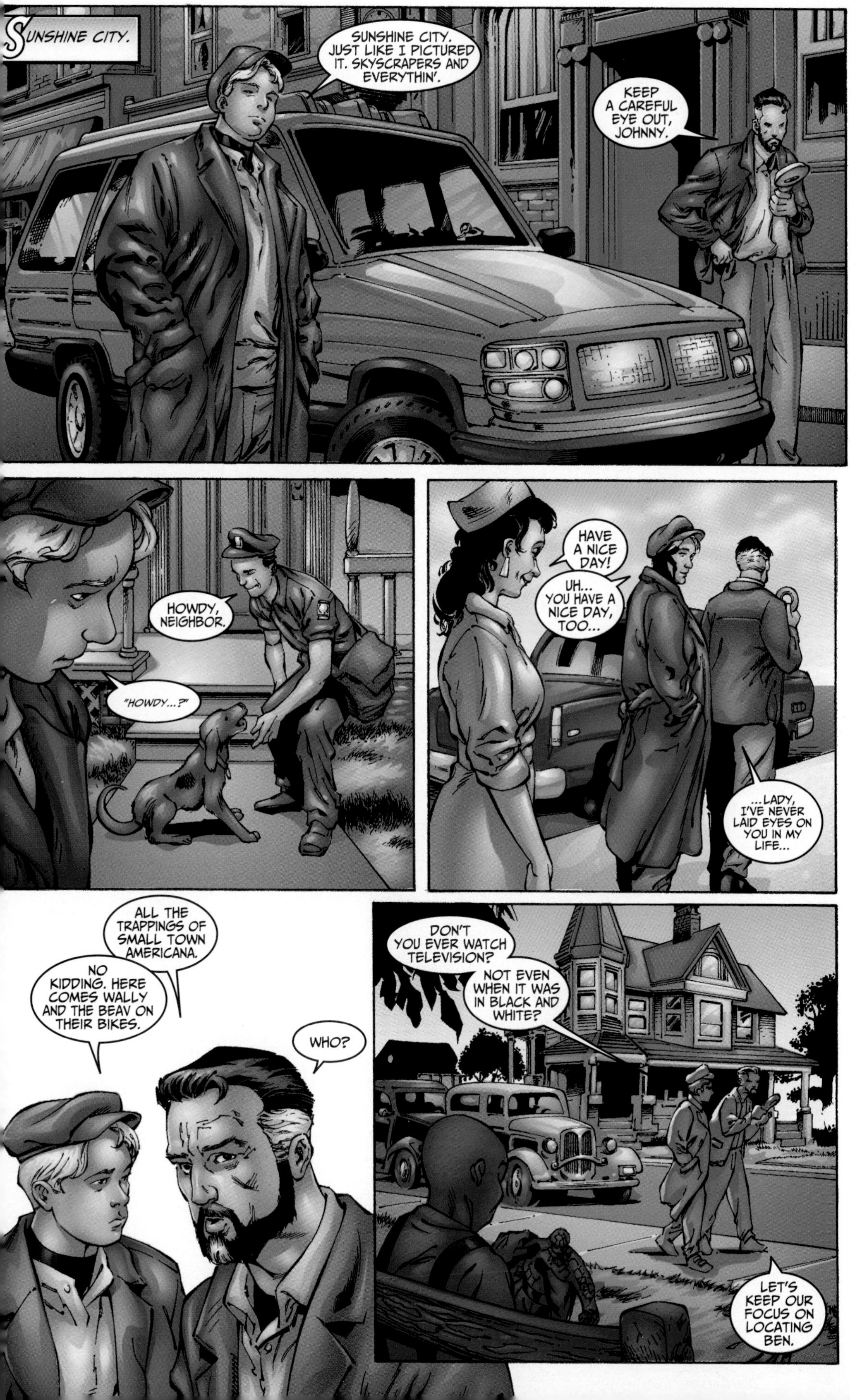
SUNSHINE CITY.
SUNSHINE CITY. JUST LIKE I PICTURED IT. SKYSCRAPERS AND EVERYTHIN'.
KEEP A CAREFUL EYE OUT, JOHNNY.
HOWDY, NEIGHBOR.
"HOWDY...?"
HAVE A NICE DAY!
UH... YOU HAVE A NICE DAY, TOO...
...LADY, I'VE NEVER LAID EYES ON YOU IN MY LIFE...
ALL THE TRAPPINGS OF SMALL TOWN AMERICANA.
NO KIDDING. HERE COMES WALLY AND THE BEAV ON THEIR BIKES.
WHO?
DON'T YOU EVER WATCH TELEVISION?
NOT EVEN WHEN IT WAS IN BLACK AND WHITE?
LET'S KEEP OUR FOCUS ON LOCATING BEN.

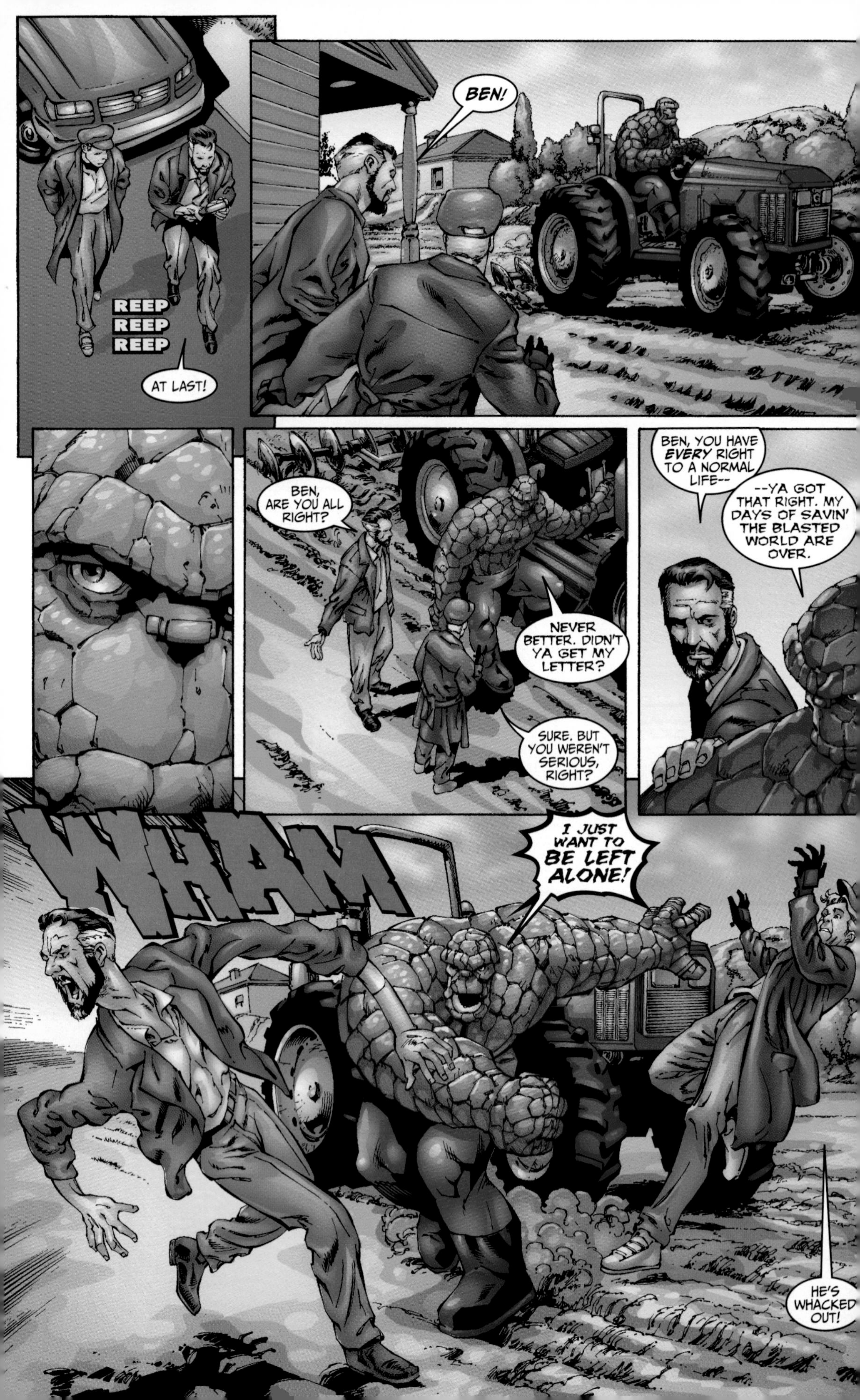
REEP
REEP
REEP
AT LAST!
BEN!
BEN, ARE YOU ALL RIGHT?
NEVER BETTER. DIDN'T YA GET MY LETTER?
SURE. BUT YOU WEREN'T SERIOUS, RIGHT?
BEN, YOU HAVE EVERY RIGHT TO A NORMAL LIFE--
--YA GOT THAT RIGHT. MY DAYS OF SAVIN' THE BLASTED WORLD ARE OVER.
WHAM
I JUST WANT TO BE LEFT ALONE!
HE'S WHACKED OUT!

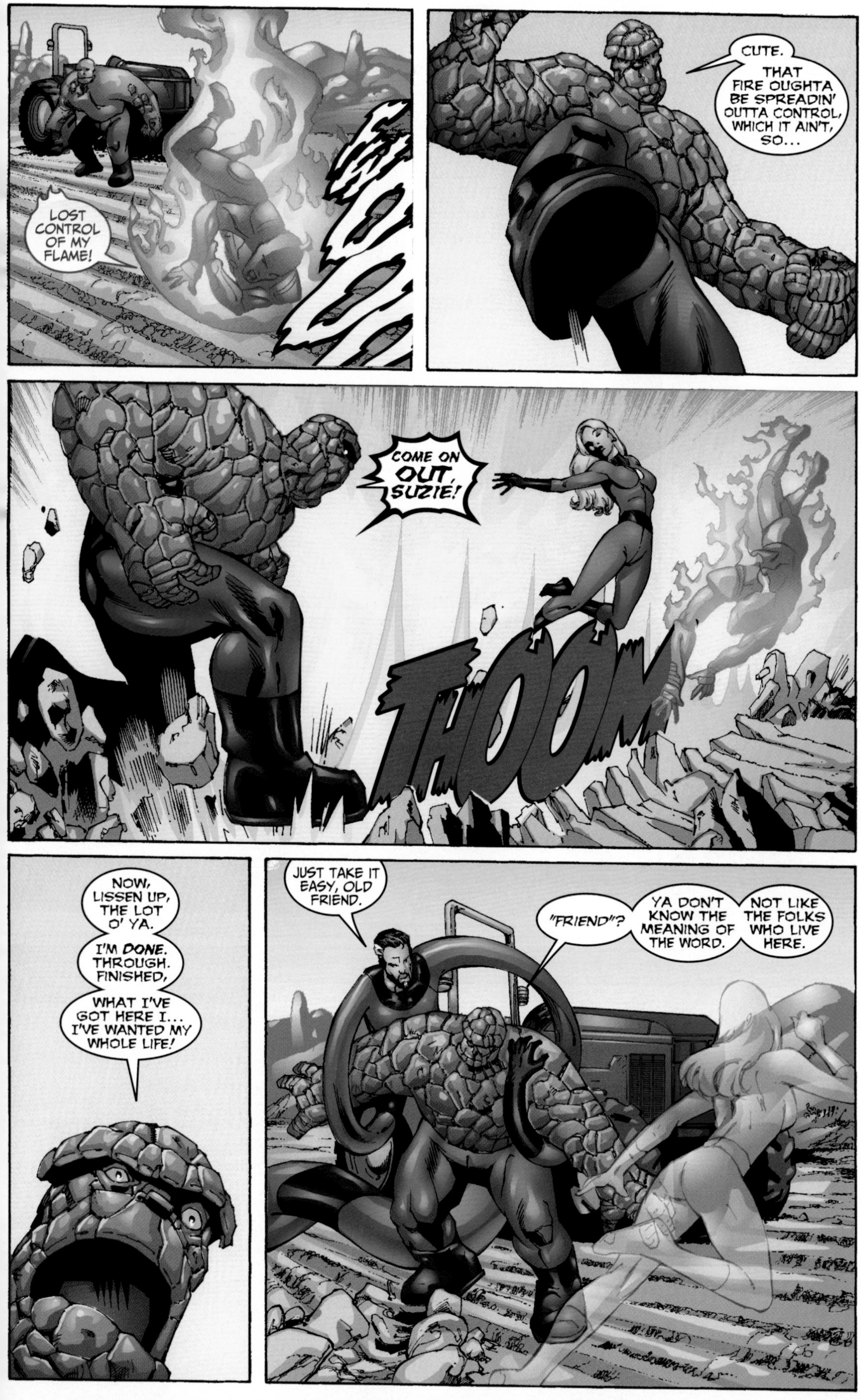
LOST CONTROL OF MY FLAME!
CUTE.
THAT FIRE OUGHTA BE SPREADIN' OUTTA CONTROL, WHICH IT AIN'T, SO...
COME ON OUT, SUZIE!
THOOM
NOW, LISSEN UP, THE LOT O' YA.
I'M DONE. THROUGH. FINISHED,
WHAT I'VE GOT HERE I... I'VE WANTED MY WHOLE LIFE!
JUST TAKE IT EASY, OLD FRIEND.
"FRIEND"?
YA DON'T KNOW THE MEANING OF THE WORD.
NOT LIKE THE FOLKS WHO LIVE HERE.

INSIDE THE HOUSE.

BEN...?

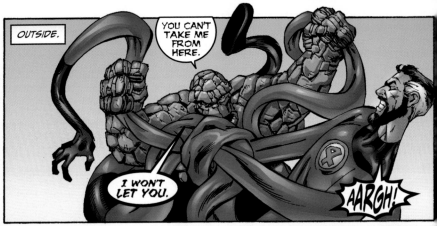

OUTSIDE.

YOU CAN'T TAKE ME FROM HERE.

I WON'T LET YOU.

AARGH!

BEN-- I DON'T WANT TO BURN YOU--

FAT CHANCE.

I GOTTA MAKE YOU GO!

WHAROM

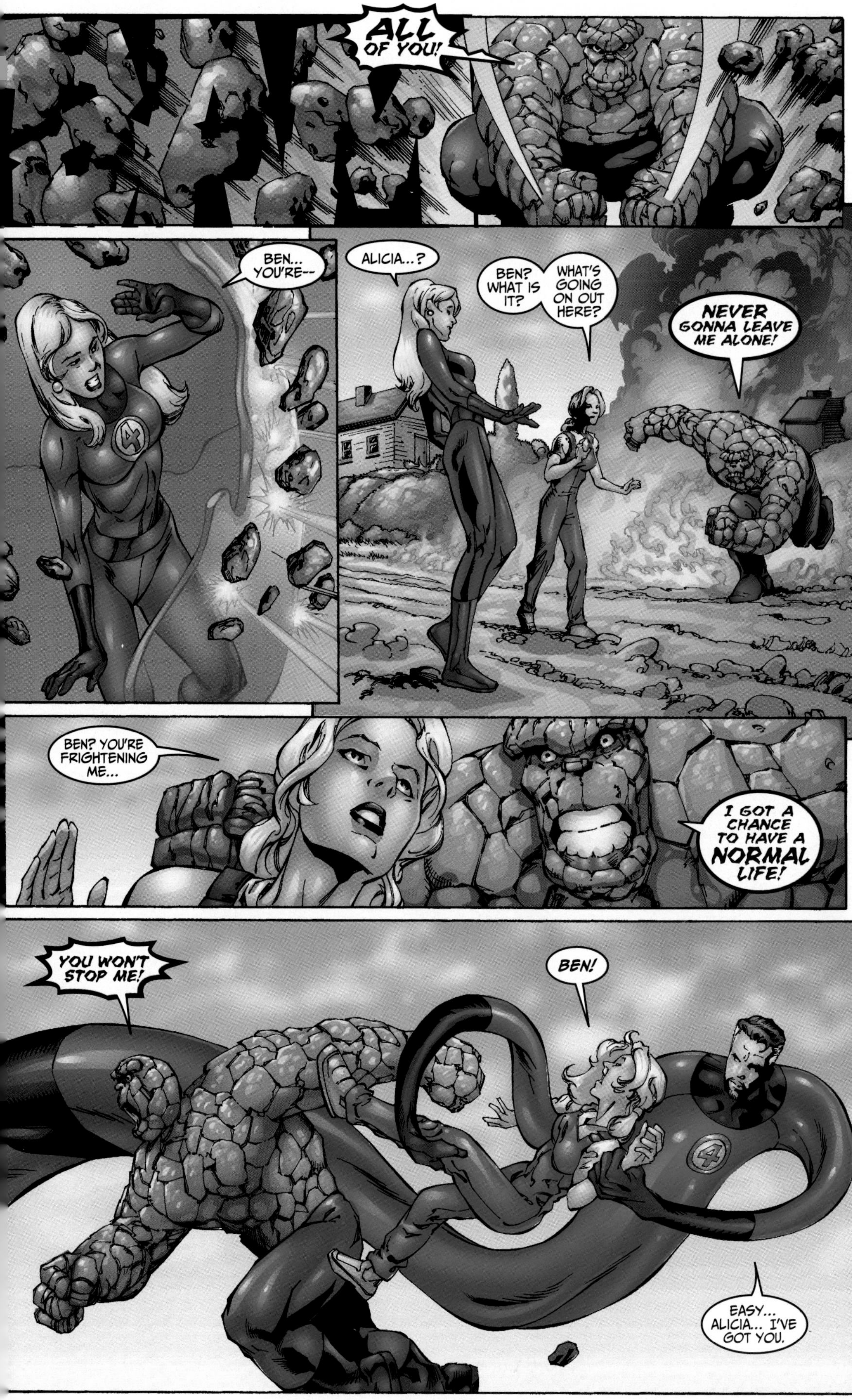
ALL OF YOU!
BEN... YOU'RE--
ALICIA...?
BEN? WHAT IS IT?
WHAT'S GOING ON OUT HERE?
NEVER GONNA LEAVE ME ALONE!
BEN? YOU'RE FRIGHTENING ME...
I GOT A CHANCE TO HAVE A NORMAL LIFE!
YOU WON'T STOP ME!
BEN!
EASY... ALICIA... I'VE GOT YOU.

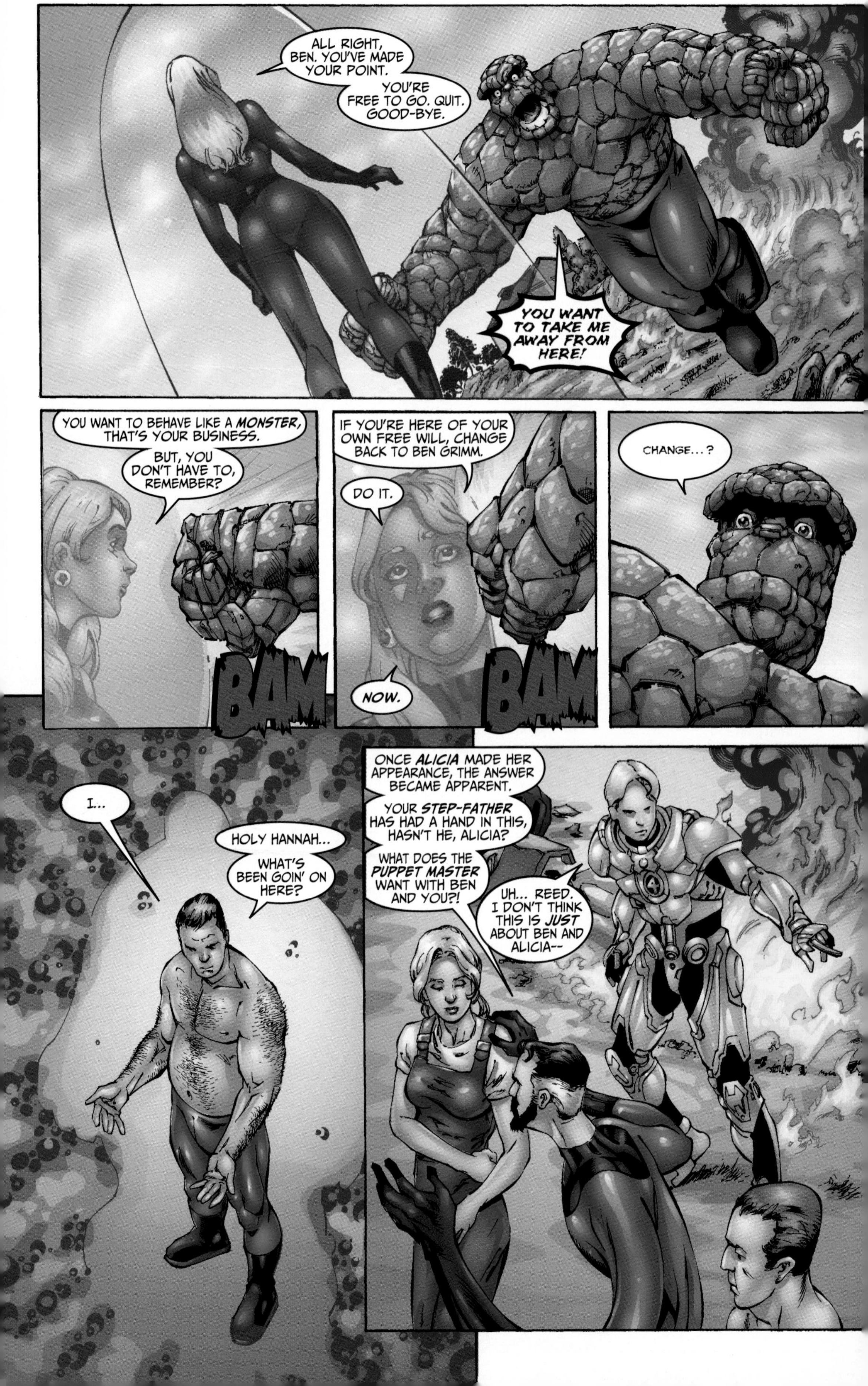
ALL RIGHT, BEN. YOU'VE MADE YOUR POINT.
YOU'RE FREE TO GO. QUIT. GOOD-BYE.
YOU WANT TO TAKE ME AWAY FROM HERE!
YOU WANT TO BEHAVE LIKE A MONSTER, THAT'S YOUR BUSINESS.
BUT, YOU DON'T HAVE TO, REMEMBER?
BAM
IF YOU'RE HERE OF YOUR OWN FREE WILL, CHANGE BACK TO BEN GRIMM.
DO IT.
NOW.
BAM
CHANGE...?
I...
HOLY HANNAH...
WHAT'S BEEN GOIN' ON HERE?
ONCE ALICIA MADE HER APPEARANCE, THE ANSWER BECAME APPARENT.
YOUR STEP-FATHER HAS HAD A HAND IN THIS, HASN'T HE, ALICIA?
WHAT DOES THE PUPPET MASTER WANT WITH BEN AND YOU?!
UH... REED. I DON'T THINK THIS IS JUST ABOUT BEN AND ALICIA--

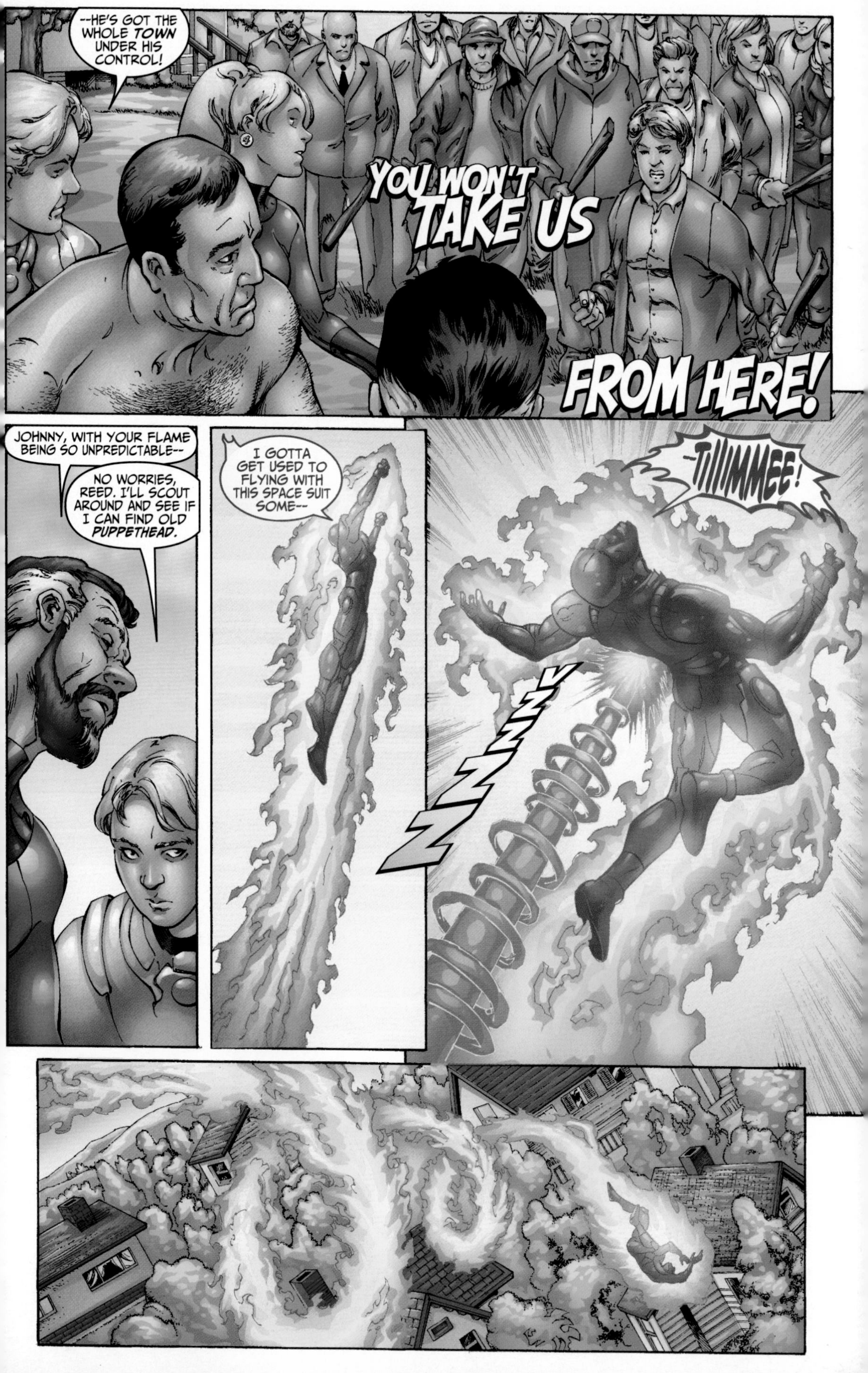
--HE'S GOT THE WHOLE *TOWN* UNDER HIS CONTROL!
YOU WON'T TAKE US FROM HERE!
JOHNNY, WITH YOUR FLAME BEING SO UNPREDICTABLE--
NO WORRIES, REED. I'LL SCOUT AROUND AND SEE IF I CAN FIND OLD *PUPPETHEAD*.
I GOTTA GET USED TO FLYING WITH THIS SPACE SUIT SOME--
--TIIIIMMEE!
VNNNNN

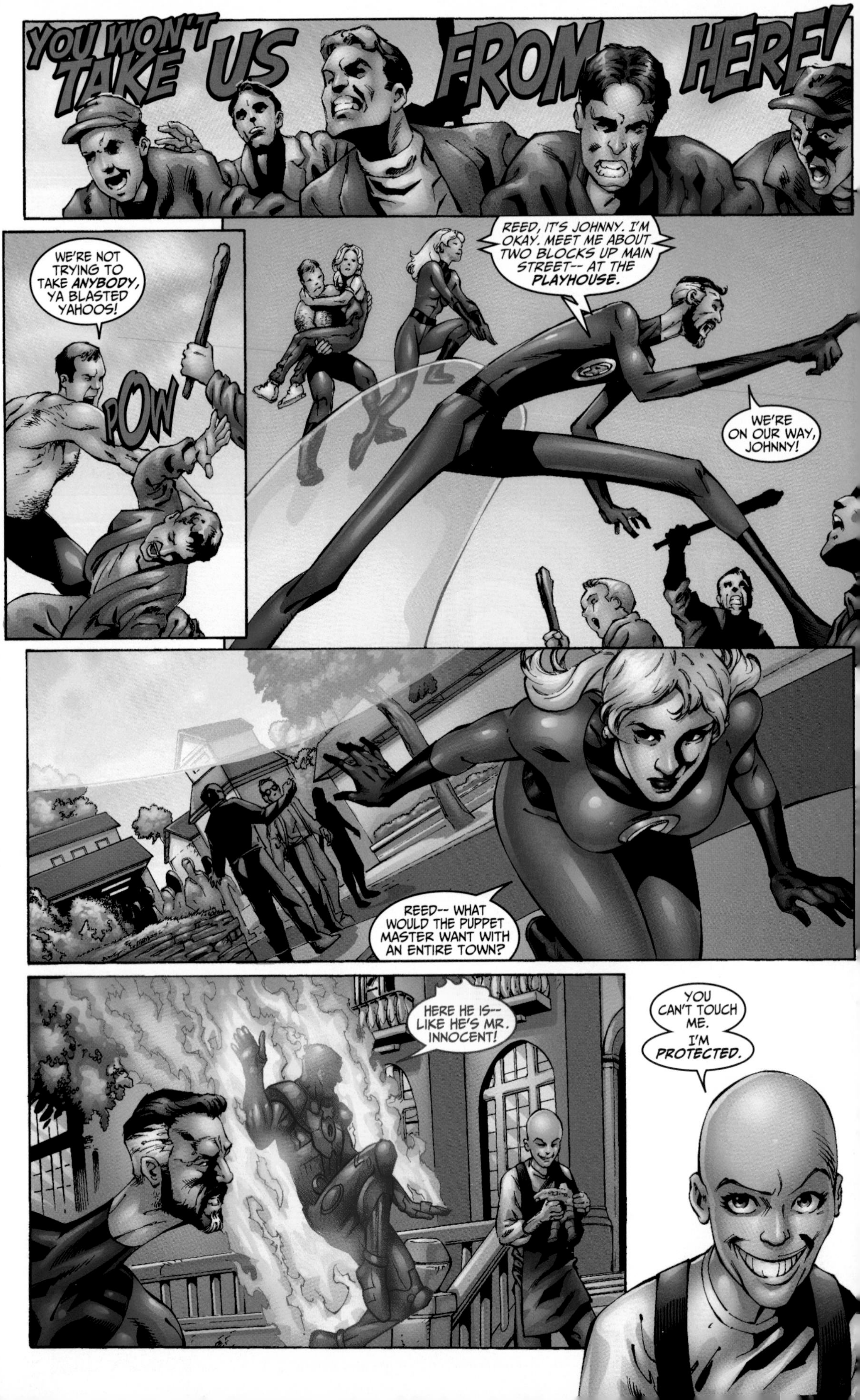
YOU WON'T TAKE US FROM HERE!
WE'RE NOT TRYING TO TAKE ANYBODY, YA BLASTED YAHOOS!
POW
REED, IT'S JOHNNY. I'M OKAY. MEET ME ABOUT TWO BLOCKS UP MAIN STREET-- AT THE PLAYHOUSE.
WE'RE ON OUR WAY, JOHNNY!
REED-- WHAT WOULD THE PUPPET MASTER WANT WITH AN ENTIRE TOWN?
HERE HE IS-- LIKE HE'S MR. INNOCENT!
YOU CAN'T TOUCH ME.
I'M PROTECTED.

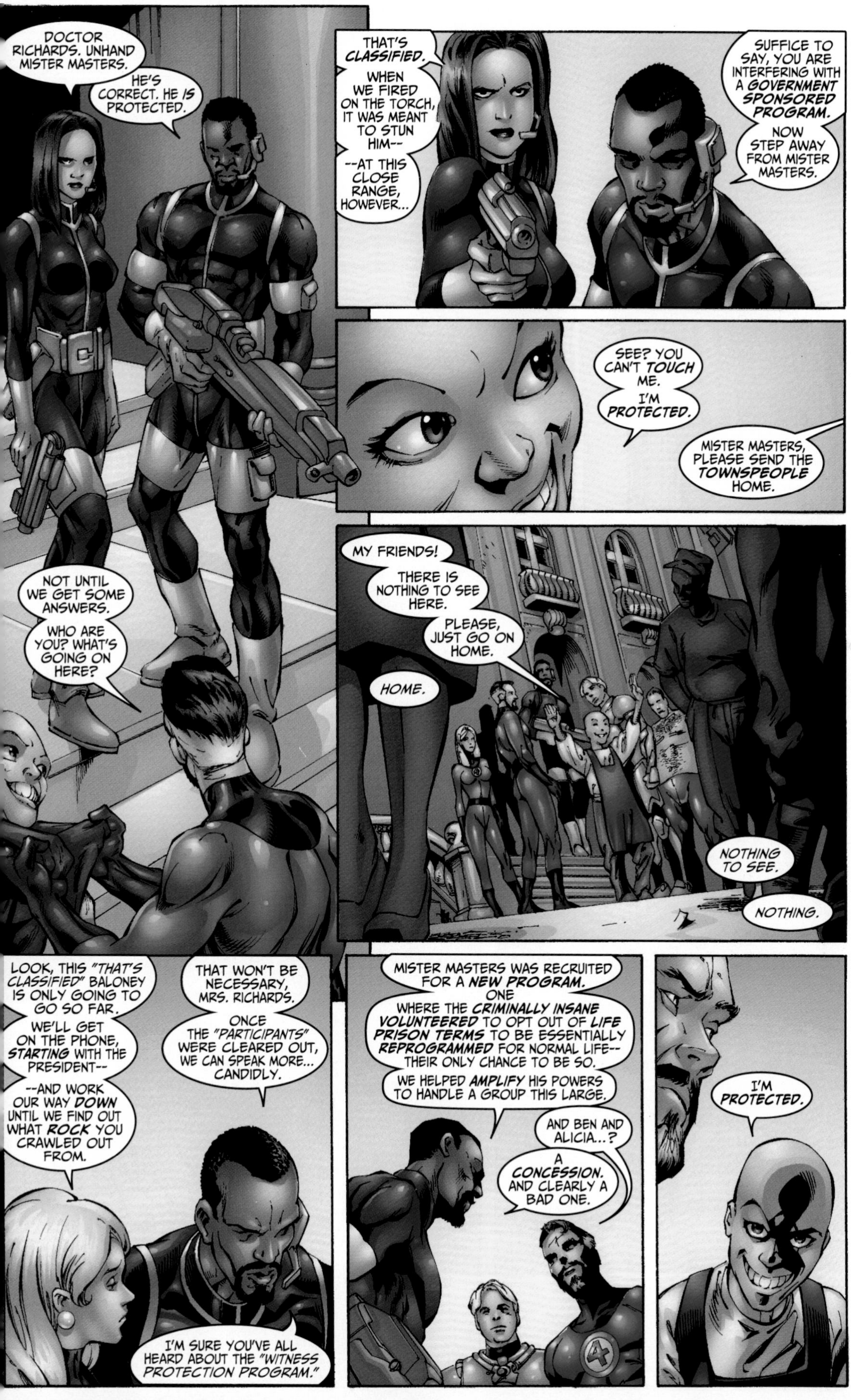

DOCTOR RICHARDS. UNHAND MISTER MASTERS.
HE'S CORRECT. HE IS PROTECTED.
THAT'S CLASSIFIED.
WHEN WE FIRED ON THE TORCH, IT WAS MEANT TO STUN HIM--
--AT THIS CLOSE RANGE, HOWEVER...
SUFFICE TO SAY, YOU ARE INTERFERING WITH A GOVERNMENT SPONSORED PROGRAM.
NOW STEP AWAY FROM MISTER MASTERS.
SEE? YOU CAN'T TOUCH ME.
I'M PROTECTED.
MISTER MASTERS, PLEASE SEND THE TOWNSPEOPLE HOME.
NOT UNTIL WE GET SOME ANSWERS.
WHO ARE YOU? WHAT'S GOING ON HERE?
MY FRIENDS!
THERE IS NOTHING TO SEE HERE.
PLEASE, JUST GO ON HOME.
HOME.
NOTHING TO SEE.
NOTHING.
LOOK, THIS "THAT'S CLASSIFIED" BALONEY IS ONLY GOING TO GO SO FAR.
WE'LL GET ON THE PHONE, STARTING WITH THE PRESIDENT--
--AND WORK OUR WAY DOWN UNTIL WE FIND OUT WHAT ROCK YOU CRAWLED OUT FROM.
THAT WON'T BE NECESSARY, MRS. RICHARDS.
ONCE THE "PARTICIPANTS" WERE CLEARED OUT, WE CAN SPEAK MORE... CANDIDLY.
I'M SURE YOU'VE ALL HEARD ABOUT THE "WITNESS PROTECTION PROGRAM."
MISTER MASTERS WAS RECRUITED FOR A NEW PROGRAM. ONE WHERE THE CRIMINALLY INSANE VOLUNTEERED TO OPT OUT OF LIFE PRISON TERMS TO BE ESSENTIALLY REPROGRAMMED FOR NORMAL LIFE-- THEIR ONLY CHANCE TO BE SO.
WE HELPED AMPLIFY HIS POWERS TO HANDLE A GROUP THIS LARGE.
AND BEN AND ALICIA...?
A CONCESSION. AND CLEARLY A BAD ONE.
I'M PROTECTED.

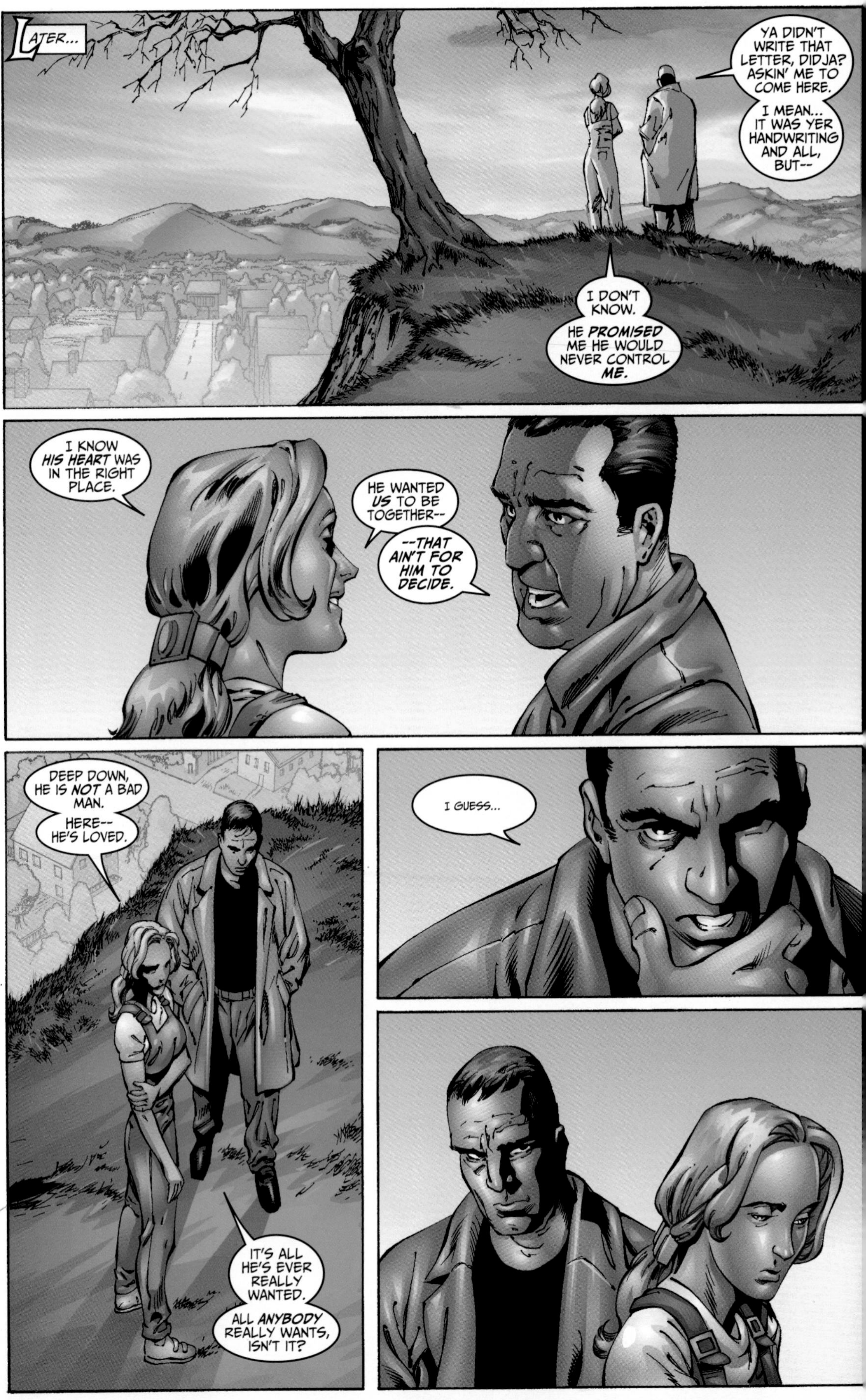
LATER...
YA DIDN'T WRITE THAT LETTER, DIDJA? ASKIN' ME TO COME HERE.
I MEAN... IT WAS YER HANDWRITING AND ALL, BUT--
I DON'T KNOW.
HE PROMISED ME HE WOULD NEVER CONTROL ME.
I KNOW HIS HEART WAS IN THE RIGHT PLACE.
HE WANTED US TO BE TOGETHER--
--THAT AIN'T FOR HIM TO DECIDE.
DEEP DOWN, HE IS NOT A BAD MAN.
HERE--HE'S LOVED.
IT'S ALL HE'S EVER REALLY WANTED.
ALL ANYBODY REALLY WANTS, ISN'T IT?
I GUESS...

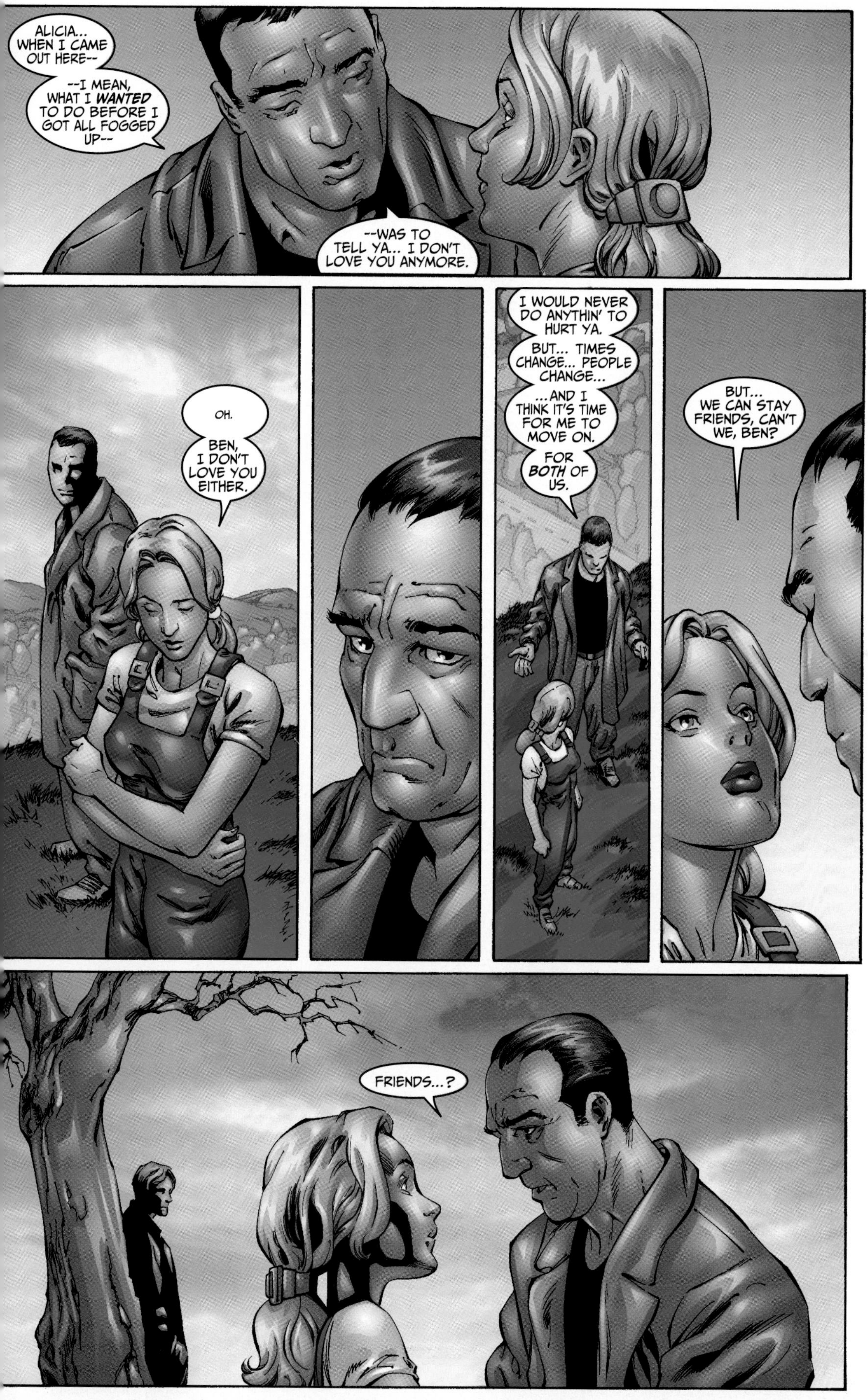
ALICIA... WHEN I CAME OUT HERE--
--I MEAN, WHAT I WANTED TO DO BEFORE I GOT ALL FOGGED UP--
--WAS TO TELL YA... I DON'T LOVE YOU ANYMORE.
OH.
BEN, I DON'T LOVE YOU EITHER.
I WOULD NEVER DO ANYTHIN' TO HURT YA.
BUT... TIMES CHANGE... PEOPLE CHANGE...
...AND I THINK IT'S TIME FOR ME TO MOVE ON.
FOR BOTH OF US.
BUT... WE CAN STAY FRIENDS, CAN'T WE, BEN?
FRIENDS...?

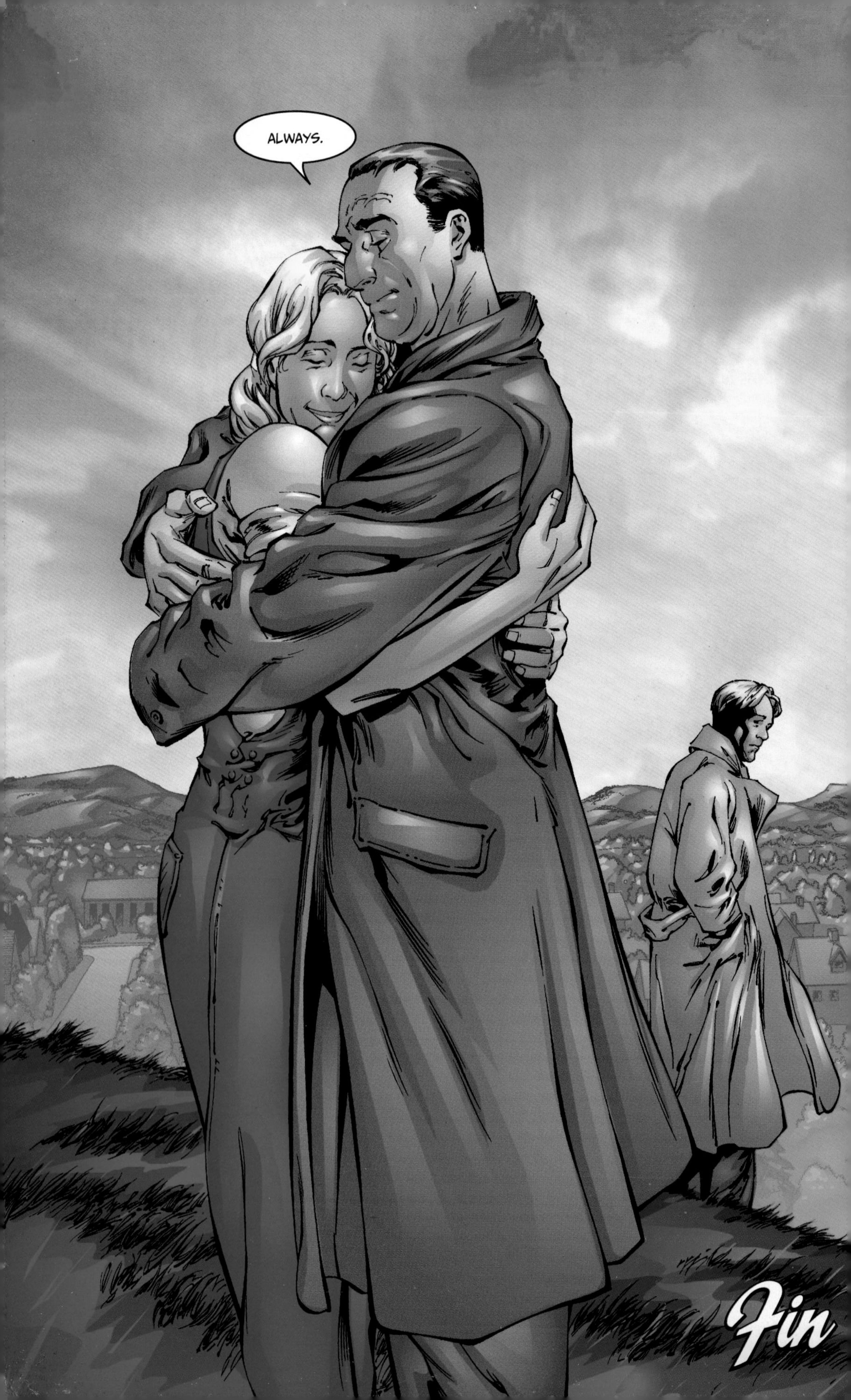
ALWAYS.
Fin